INTERNATIONAL SERIES OF MONOGRAPHS IN

LIBRARY AND INFORMATION SCIENCE

GENERAL EDITOR: G. CHANDLER

VOLUME 15

THE
ADMINISTRATION
OF ARCHIVES

FRONTISPIECE. Hall d'exposition, Archives Départementales de la Seine-Maritime, Rouen.

THE
ADMINISTRATION
OF ARCHIVES

by

J. H. HODSON

PERGAMON PRESS

Oxford · New York · Toronto
Sydney · Braunschweig

Pergamon Press Ltd., Headington Hill Hall, Oxford
Pergamon Press Inc., Maxwell House, Fairview Park, Elmsford,
New York 10523
Pergamon of Canada Ltd., 207 Queen's Quay West, Toronto 1
Pergamon Press (Aust.) Pty. Ltd., 19a Boundary Street,
Rushcutters Bay, N.S.W. 2011, Australia
Vieweg & Sohn GmbH, Burgplatz 1, Braunschweig

First edition 1972
Reprinted 1974
Library of Congress Catalog Card No. 72-163642

Printed in Great Britain by A. Wheaton & Co., Exeter

08 016676 8

In memory Nell

CONTENTS

LIST OF ILLUSTRATIONS

PREFACE

This book, which originated in a course of lectures given in the Department of Librarianship, Manchester College of Commerce, in 1967, is an attempt to sum up fifteen years' experience of archive administration in three types of record repository: county, public library, and university. My own conversion from distaste for a dusty death among the last syllables of recorded time to enthusiasm for their lively communication dates from a spring day at the Lancashire Record Office in 1948 when the post-war atmosphere sparkled with the excitement of a new, democratic, and sociable scholarship. I am grateful for that experience, and to all the other record offices I have since visited, many of them imprinted with their own brand of the pioneering fervour of those days.

With the certainty of vocation I took the course in archive administration at the London School of Librarianship and Archives, and my enthusiasm grew with diversifying academic horizons. I became aware of dichotomies in the profession—between record offices and libraries, between central archives and local archives—but they only increased my involvement. Embedded in the following pages are attitudes, techniques, facts which derive from lectures I attended at that time. I should like to pay tribute to mentors for whom record-keeping was a historic craft, but who reinforced in their hearers the sense of belonging to a new profession.

In the early days of their employment not all those engaged in the archives profession were budded on to congenial stocks. The result, maybe, was the generation of colourful and engaging characters. In the palmier climate of acceptance it is a pleasure to acknowledge the charm, hospitality, and wonderfully skilled amateurism of members of that *avant-garde*. The institutions for which one worked, also, have a large claim on one's gratitude. The milieu created by others is soothing in its sympathy or stimulating by its contrariety; either way, beneficent.

Since the war archives have received a large amount of professional comment. As well as offering a personal interpretation this book tries to digest some of that rich material. What I owe to all these commentators will be obvious; I hope that it is adequately acknowledged.

My first talk as an assistant archivist was given to an audience who came expecting to hear the county architect. That such a misunderstanding would be unlikely today is due to the campaigns of a generation of devoted, educating, proselytizing archivists. Of some of the battles which made this transition possible it is warming to be able to say "I was there".

ACKNOWLEDGEMENTS

I ACKNOWLEDGE with many thanks the suggestion of Dr. G. Chandler, City Librarian of Liverpool, that I write this book. I am grateful to several archivists and librarians who helped me along during its writing with answers to a number of inquiries—Miss J. M. Ayton, Archivist, Manchester Public Libraries, Mrs. H. D. Brewster, Records Clerk, Nottingham University Department of Manuscripts, M. François Burckard, Directeur des Services d'Archives de la Seine-Maritime, Mr. N. Carrick, Archivist, Liverpool Record Office, Mr. G. A. Chinnery, Keeper of Archives, Leicester Museums, Mrs. M. A. Welch, Keeper of the Manuscripts, Nottingham University Department of Manuscripts; and Mr. D. B. Wardle, formerly Principal Assistant Keeper (Repository and Technical) at the Public Record Office, who generously allowed me to use his unpublished diagrams and formulae of strong room storage which appear on pp. 113–15.

I am indebted to the following repositories for their ready kindness in supplying the photographs used as illustrations: Archives Départementales de la Seine-Maritime (Frontispiece), Leicester Museums (Fig. 9), Manchester Public Libraries (Figs. 10, 11) and Nottingham University Department of Manuscripts (Figs. 1–8, 12).

Finally, I thank my wife for her detailed interest in this book, and for her persistent willingness to believe that it would ever appear.

INTRODUCTION

In Rouen the *archives départementales* of Seine-Maritime rear in a concrete block, twenty-nine storeys high, above the south side of the city. In the modest town of Évreux (pop. 20,000) the departmental archives of Eure are housed in, comparatively, little more than a bungalow— a demure building, except that across its face is written, startlingly, the single word *ARCHIVES*. To find in England the physical equivalent of the Rouen repository one would have to go to the Victoria Tower of the Palace of Westminster, laundered gothic without, fairly lavishly modernized within—but, then, the archives which this repository is intended to receive are not the records of some province, they are the muniments of the legislature of the nation. Psychologically, there is no equivalent at all in England of the repository at Évreux— no building which simply proclaims, to one and all, with unstudied panache, *ARCHIVES*.

One of the most relaxed of Anglo-Saxon archivists has said that if you ask the man in the street, "what should be done with archives?", he will at first look blank; on being told what archives are he will very likely say, "why not burn the stuff?"[1]* Similarly, that other pragmatist, the business man, will say that he is not interested in what happened fifty years ago, ten years ago, or even yesterday; what he is interested in is today and tomorrow, and, like the local councillor who condemns as Victorian rubbish the Georgian houses which hold up the flow of modern traffic, sees no value in the grimy remnants of his indifferently cluttering past. At the opposite extreme is the professional archivist— his instinct, to preserve every scrap of evidence of the past, down to the laundry bills. Yet even he, confronted by the multitudinous seas of modern records, must compromise; somewhere, the compounding archivist willing to face the facts of modern administrative life and

---

* Reference figures (¹·² etc.) in text indicate Notes appearing at end of book on pp. 183–92.

accept selective destruction, meets the informed business man prepared to destroy only 96% of his records.[2]

The characteristic archivist of today is a seasoned professional with a generation of missionary enthusiasm behind him. The years immediately after the war were a golden age of collecting, discovering, pioneering, and communication. In sunny search rooms the dusty tang of freshly opened parchment tingled the nostrils of youthful acolytes of a new order, zested by a delicious pot-pourri of newly burgeoning antiquity, purposeful scholarship, educational altruism, and sensitive organization. The case for the preservation of the documentary past has largely been won. It is the jeopardy of today's records which now conditions the archivist's response. How far can the archivist ride the crest of modern records, and not submerge his scholarly identity? Or, as on a tandem, with first the archives of the past and then the records of the present up front, how convincingly can he make them drive in the same direction, and so double the power of his machine? One thing is fairly certain: his vehicle is always likely to remain relatively small—a bicycle, say, rather than a high-powered car; but that way he will see more of the scenery, and feel more at home in the landscape.

Meanwhile, whatever the future offers, archives provide a satisfying career for practical and popularizing scholars. Already they hold the community in debt. In a remarkably short time, and often with ludicrously insufficient means, they have preserved a large slice of the country's past which might otherwise have vanished. Adequate acknowledgement has been slow in coming, but now, on occasion, the tribute is generous and just:

> When the historiography of the twentieth century comes to be studied, the foundation of county and regional record offices will undoubtedly be regarded as one of the most constructive developments of our time. The revolution in the study of English provincial society which has begun in the last few years could not have occurred without the gallant work of local archivists up and down the country, often in the face of grave staff-shortages, and sometimes without adequate consideration or recognition from students and scholars.[3]

Archivally, too, England in the last generation has experienced revolution. What happened in France by political decree in 1796 has happened here a century and a half later by social process—through economic transformation, education, imitation, consent, and stealth.

Perhaps it is a little unfair to stress the unequivocal *éclat* of the French name *archives*; because of an unfortunate semantic tangle "archives" seems likely to remain, in some popular contexts, an alien word in England. But the homelier "record office" gradually permeates the country's educational consciousness at various levels—university, college, secondary, even primary; although as yet by no means a household word, eventually the name should need as little explanation as "library".

The case for the preservation of archives is usually put by the professional archivist. In times of need, however, nations become aware of their documentary heritage and use it for patriotic ends—as the French, the Americans, the Australians. Even the English, in the cruel uncertainties of a post-war age, carry a neatly repaired copy of Magna Carta in solemn procession, and, more audaciously, decide that "the making of adequate arrangements for the preservation of its records is an inescapable duty of the Government of a civilized state"[4].

I. THEORY

1. THE NATURE OF ARCHIVES

THE *Oxford English Dictionary* defines archives as "a place in which public records or historic documents are kept; a historical record or document so preserved". Although this definition includes some important incidental characteristics of archives—their historical value, their public origin in some cases, their preservation in a repository— it does not catch their essential nature and would not satisfy a modern archivist.[1] In a definition now considered classic Sir Hilary Jenkinson, doyen of English archivists of the last generation, describes an archival document as one "drawn up or used in the course of an administrative or executive transaction (whether public or private) of which itself formed a part; and subsequently preserved in their own custody for their own information by the person or persons responsible for that transaction and their legitimate successors".[2]

From his definition Jenkinson derived four essential qualities of archives.[3] Firstly, impartiality: since archives are "an actual part of the Administration which produced them",[4] "provided . . . that the student understands their administrative significance they cannot tell him anything but the truth".[5] Secondly, authenticity: archives are characterized by "unbroken custody, a reasonable presumption of which is the *differentia* between a Document that is and one that is not an Archive".[6] Thirdly, naturalness: "Archives are not Documents collected artificially, like the objects in a Museum . . . but accumulating naturally in Offices for the practical purposes of Administration". And finally, interrelationship: "any Archive is potentially related closely to others both inside and outside the group in which it is preserved and . . . its significance depends on these relations".[7]

Perhaps the most important of these four qualities of archives, and one which distinguishes them from other kinds of manuscripts, is their impartiality. Because archives and literary manuscripts enjoy a common characteristic of uniqueness they have frequently been confused

3

in the past, particularly by librarians.[8] Yet the essential difference is clear: archives "record not merely achievements but also the processes by which they were accomplished",[9] they are "the product of activity";[10] and so they are impersonal, unself-conscious. Literary manuscripts, on the other hand, "represent conscious strivings . . . towards literary . . . excellence",[11] they are the product of individual imagination, the whole of the thing aimed at; and so they are personal, subjective.

These peculiar qualities of archives have practical implications which are important for custodians and students alike. Firstly, because archives are unself-conscious by-products of human activity, they have the objective formlessness of raw material, compared with the subjective roundedness of literary artefacts like books, whether printed or manuscript. Secondly, the significance of archives lies not only in the matter of each document, but also in the interrelationship of documents within a group: the student needs to appreciate this in his researches, but, even more important, the custodian must understand and carefully preserve the original interdependence of documents if their evidence is not to be confused or falsified. Lastly, in order to safeguard this objectivity and this original order in his documents, the custodian must protect them against unauthorized access: he must protect them "morally"[12] as well as physically.[13]

Jenkinson's magisterial definition of archives has not gone unchallenged. At variance, for instance, with his contention that documents become archives while still in the hands of those who created them is the distinction made by the American archivist, T. R. Schellenberg, between "records for current use" and "records for research use": "records" becoming "archives" only when they are handed over to "custodians of research material—archivists, manuscript curators, and librarians".[14] In fact, and in despite of Jenkinson, it is Schellenberg's view which has been adopted by English archivists: for them, the documents of a business, a school, a local authority, are "records", however unused they may be, so long as they remain in the custody of their creators; they become "archives" only when deposited with an archives repository. Owing, no doubt, to the influence of the Public Record Office, such a repository is usually known in England as a "record office", but it is significant that its head is normally an "archivist", while the assistant who supervises the transfer of the authority's modern documents from current use to repository preservation is called a "records clerk".

Jenkinson's own attempt to distinguish the moment at which documents become archives appears a little uncertain: "probably . . . the point at which, having ceased to be in current use, they are definitely set aside for preservation, tacitly adjudged worthy of being kept."[15] In a gloss he adds, "not necessarily ceased to be in use altogether. There are plenty of cases where documents have been drawn into the administrative circle again after a century or more of idleness." Jenkinson instances a few such cases,[16] but they seem little candles in a naughty world: most precedent-hunting in ancient records is laboriously hopeful, and only fortuitously successful. All records that are not useless are current records. Administrators are not interested in the preservation of archives in the Jenkinsonian sense—"documents set aside for preservation in official custody" — and Jenkinson, explicitly, agrees: "If they are left long enough all documents become useless for the purposes of current business and [the Administrator] might therefore destroy all or nearly all",[17] and, again, "there might be danger of keeping documents so long in suspense that eventually all, or nearly all, might come to be regarded as unimportant and be destroyed".[18] Between the life, however tenuous, of imagined usefulness, and the death of contemptuous neglect or determined destruction, there is no spoilt archival limbo.

The sudden truth of this is known to every archivist who, on the briefest of intelligence, arrives, or fails to arrive, in time to stay the committal of a complete corpus of records to total oblivion. Theoretically, Jenkinson must condone such destruction: "for an Administrative body to destroy what it no longer needs is a matter entirely within its competence and an action which future ages (even though they may find reason to deplore it) cannot possibly criticise as illegitimate".[19] Indeed, by conferring on the administrator the honour of destroying documents before they become archives, Jenkinson neatly rescues his archivist from an unethical responsibility. In practice, however, although this "reversion to old procedure"[20] is welcome, "we must see that our Administrator does not revert too completely to primitive habits and destroy unreasonably".[21] How is this indiscriminate

destruction to be avoided? By making sure, says Jenkinson, that the
administrator leaves a "memorial"[22] in the shape of his papers "in
such a state of completeness and order that, supposing himself and his
staff to be by some accident obliterated, a successor totally ignorant
of the work of the office would be able to take it up and carry it on with
the least possible inconvenience and delay simply on the strength of
a study of the Office Files".[23]

As striking as its psychological unlikeliness is the logical incompati-
bility of this proposal. Jenkinson has already said that the administrator
is master of his own documents and the only person qualified to destroy
them. Now, however, he says that, if left entirely to himself, the administrator is capable of destroying all, or nearly all, his documents
when they cease to be of use to him. He therefore suggests grafting on
to the administrator's consciousness (and conscience) awareness of
the need to preserve a complete documentary record of his activities.
From this it is clear that, if the administrator has no intrinsic need for
such preservation, then the need must be an extrinsic one, stemming
from historical purposes—"potential value for Research is no doubt
the reason why we continue to spend time and money on preserving
Archives and making them available."[24] But Jenkinson has also already
made the proviso that, in destruction, the administrator must proceed
"only upon those grounds upon which alone it is competent to make a
decision—the needs of its own practical business; provided, that is,
that it can refrain from thinking of itself as a body producing historical
evidences."[25]

The full significance of Jenkinson's refusal to acknowledge a change
in the status of documents transferred to an archive repository is now
clear. In effect, they have been accorded archival quality while still
in official custody, not by the administrator but by the archivist who
intervenes to insist that the administrator preserve adequate record
of his office business. Schellenberg, on the other hand, prefers to make
the influence of the archivist (and hence the historian) explicit by
retaining the word "records" for the documents "preserved or appropriate for preservation" by the administration "as evidence of its
functions, policies, decisions, procedures, operations, or other activities
or because of the informational value of the data contained therein";
and reserving the word "archives" for "those records . . . which are

adjudged worthy of permanent preservation for reference and research purposes and which have been deposited or have been selected for deposit in an archival institution".[26]

A simple but graphic instance of the relentless transition from precisely used business documents to amorphously surviving historical archives is provided by such a casually noticed entry in the *Guide to the Contents of the Public Record Office*, 1963, as "Chancery Files or Brevia Regia. Henry II to 1921. Some 1,300 files, bundles and sacks, most of them still unsorted and unlisted . . . the Chancery preserved a great variety of these single documents for purposes of reference and as warrants to justify its own actions."[27] A much more elaborate illustration of the same process is given by Jenkinson in an appendix to his *Manual*, 1965, in which he brilliantly analyses the complex history of the records of the Exchequer of Receipt, and the "extraordinary chapter of mistakes", some of them "inexcusable", in the treatment accorded them by successive custodians, as a result of which "these Archives had to remain for about fifty years, practically useless for any serious work, before time could be found to reconstruct their correct arrangement".[28] As the chief culprits in this example of "nearly all the Archive mistakes that have ever been made, not only in ancient but in modern times", Jenkinson identifies "the authors of the 1859 arrangement" (i.e. after the transfer of the records to the Public Record Office): "by destruction of lists and references they obliterated almost all traces of what their predecessors had done and of the provenance of their Archives, making it impossible ever to re-establish with certainty the original state of the documents. In doing this they committed the worst, because the most elementary, crime of which an Archivist can be guilty". But, says Jenkinson,

it is not suggested that the authors of the 1859 arrangement are responsible for all the confusion we see in it. . . . There was, in fact, a remarkable consensus of ignorance in the opening part of the nineteenth century among the officials of the Receipt (who were still supposed to carry on "the ancient course of the Exchequer" as laid down in the *Dialogus*) about the early history of their own Office and Archives. Thus in 1800 . . . the Deputy Clerk of the Pells . . . admits having records from 1715 onwards, but remarks that "the want of space in the Office wherein the principal duties of the Clerk of the Pells are performed has necessarily compelled our predecessors and ourselves when encumbered by the increase of books and the engrossed copies [i.e. the Rolls] hereinbefore described to remove the most antient and useless into the two upper rooms of the tower occupied by the Clerk of the Pells: they are deposited therein, for the most part, without order or method and covered by the lapse of time with dust and dirt. The collections of more than a century, perhaps of two, are in general confusion";

"and this", comments Jenkinson, "with a large proportion of the medieval Archives of the Exchequer of Receipt, from the thirteenth century downwards, lying somewhere on their premises and in their care!" More, he continues, "general ignorance of the early history of the Receipt and its archives did not begin in the nineteenth century. The 1731 Report, the 1718 Report, and (most striking of all) Madox in his *History of the Exchequer*, all . . . shew a like ignorance". In fact, he concludes,

> it is not till we get back to the period of Agarde, Fanshawe, Skinner, and Wardour, in the end of the sixteenth and beginning of the seventeenth centuries, that we find a generation of officials familiar with the ancient triplicate arrangement, and the part borne by the Chamberlains of the Receipt in that department's functions: from which it would seem that Devon may have been right in his conjecture that confusion began under the Commonwealth.

Jenkinson's illuminating excursus points the moral that an administrator's interest in his documents does not long outlive their usefulness to him. On a grander scale the same axiom emerges from the whole history of the medieval records. Occasionally, "provision was made for the proper care of the Documents and valuable work in listing and arranging them was done by the Custodians", but, in general, disorders

> grew in frequency and in destructiveness as the centuries went by . . . loss and destruction due to accident or to the casual adjustments required by convenience or personal considerations [persisted] for five centuries . . . the difficulty of finding space for the ever growing mass was then, as now, a continually recurring problem . . . the tendency was strong to bestow the older Documents in places which could not be used for any other purpose and then to forget them . . . the priceless *Ancient Miscellanea* of the King's Remembrancer's Department [became] "a mass of putrid filth, stench, dirt and decomposition". . . . The Records of the "Receipt" itself were some of them rescued ultimately from cellars below tide level under Somerset House . . . and yet another section was sold as waste in the early nineteenth century and appears still at intervals in fragments in Auctioneers' Catalogues.[29]

The whole sorry story is a far cry from Jenkinson's own idyllic evocation of documents "definitely set aside for preservation, tacitly adjudged worthy of being kept". A more realistic valediction might appear to be, "regarded as useless lumber".[30] Even were it possible for an operation to be simultaneously "definite" and "tacit", would such a dispensation as Jenkinson recounts merit the name of "preservation"? More apt altogether would seem his own sardonic assessment of the attitude of these soi-disant custodians: "Thou may'st not kill but need'st not strive Officiously to keep alive."[31]

The close association which Jenkinson feels to be necessary between archive-receiving repository and document-creating institution (and which does in fact, as we have seen, intimately influence the extent and the nature of the records that survive) stems from his doctrine of custody. Anxious to preserve the authenticity which he sees as a principal quality of archives, Jenkinson stipulates elaborate conditions for a chain of responsibility when archives are handed on. Official custody must not cease without express transfer of the function of archives keeper to "some other responsible person". What is a responsible person? Can "any public body ... constitute itself an Archivist *ad hoc*?" Yes, answers Jenkinson, but only "under conditions which leave the documents so taken over with their full archive value". These conditions are: "reasonable probability of the Authority's own continued existence"; the archives to be "taken over direct from the original owner or his official heir or representative"; the authority to "subscribe to the ordinary rules of Archive management directed to the preservation of Archive character"; and the archives to be taken over "*en bloc*: there must be no selecting of 'pretty' specimens".[32]

Jenkinson thus pictures a measured handing on of archives as the natural, normal, official process. Yet surely the truth is very much the reverse. Left to themselves the great majority of documents either disappear or survive accidentally; that is the natural process. The artificial, self-conscious way is to preserve them for historical research. The influence of accident is shown in the haphazard survival of medieval documents, until decay and destruction were halted by the historically minded reformers of the nineteenth century. The fact of disappearance is evident in attitudes to modern business records: an efficient firm will today destroy 96% of its documents as a matter of course; less efficient businesses keep everything, destroy everything, then start again. That it is possible to start again was shown in the ability of institutions to survive the complete destruction of their records in wartime, and is also suggested by the extreme infrequency with which documents, once deposited in a repository, are referred to by their makers.

The same point is made by V. H. Galbraith when, having trenchantly defined archives as "dead papers put by for future reference", he concedes that, in fact, they have mostly been of no use at all to their makers: "for centuries the national archives were mainly left to rot in damp cellars or attics, in 'safe custody' in no other sense than that they were regarded as useless lumber". He argues that Jenkinson's concept of authenticity is illusory: the legal doctrine that public records which have never been out of custody have a weight of evidence denied to other documents which are not "of record" and have to be "proved" by the testimony of experts "has not much historical basis in fact". The doctrine of safe custody may have saved English archives from the quality of a museum, but it has also been partly responsible for enormous gaps which "beyond all question it is the duty of the State" to fill "by purchase or otherwise".[33]

In the field of local records, too, Jenkinson's doctrine of custody has been challenged. Even if archives are taken over direct from their owner or his representative there is no guarantee that their archive value has been preserved: friends, relatives, historical inquirers, the owner himself, may have dabbled amongst them, extracting, adding, sorting, upsetting the original order; who can say how this large accumulation of documents got scattered over the floors of a deserted mill, or that wicker-basket full of deeds got under the cook's bed? As for Jenkinson's directive that archivists "should not take any stray papers—they had better go to a museum"—it is virtually impossible to discover how intact an accumulation is: "it is not unusual for a local archivist to receive parts of the same original accumulation from several sources, or to be offered odd items which he knows will fill gaps if and when the main accumulation is received".[35]

The most convincing critique, however, of Jenkinson's definition of archives has come from T. R. Schellenberg in his *Modern Archives: Principles and Techniques* (1956). Having analysed definitions of archives from England, Germany, Holland, and Italy, Schellenberg decides that, in fact, only two factors are essential: firstly, to be archives, documents must have been created or accumulated in the accomplishment of some purpose; and secondly, the documents must have been preserved for reasons other than those for which they were created or accumulated. Schellenberg's first factor corresponds exactly with Jenkinson's stipulation, "drawn up or used in the course of an administrative or executive transaction"; but his second directly contravenes Jenkinson's further requirement, "subsequently preserved in their own custody for their own information by the person or persons responsible for that transaction". Jenkinson's third requisite—unbroken custody— Schellenberg considers inessential and impracticable, quoting a Dutch definition which merely requires that archives should have been intended to remain in the originating office, and maintaining, that in modern conditions of large, complex, and haphazardly developing accumulations of records, proof of unbroken custody of individual documents is not possible.[35]

Not very satisfactorily, Jenkinson replied to Schellenberg in a review of *Modern Archives*.[36] His attachment to the notion of impartiality, "one of the most valuable Archive Characteristics", which arises automatically from unself-conscious administration, made it impossible for him to accept a definition of archives involving some "external" assessment of archive quality: up to now, definitions "have generally come, as it were, from within—been based simply on an analysis of the nature of documents used in administration; which is why there is no difficulty in applying them to Archives of all categories". Jenkinson was reluctant to acknowledge that, if left to their own devices, administrators will in the end fine away their need of records practically to nothing, and that it is accident plus the wishes of researchers, not the needs of administration, which, ultimately, have preserved medieval and modern records. An external assessment of the value of archives has thus in fact been made. Hitherto this extrinsic assessment has been disguised; now the great masses of modern records impose on custodians a fundamental reassessment of archive preservation. An efficient administration can dispense with most of its records within a relatively short time. Historians, however, cannot allow this to happen. Selective preservation is therefore necessary: the modern archivist's "major problem . . . is to select archives for permanent preservation . . . it is quite obvious that modern archives are kept for the use of others than those that created them, and that conscious decisions must be made as to their value for such use". Hence "the element of selection should be implicit in the definition" (although, for the pragmatic Schellenberg, there is no ultimate definition of archives: each country may wish to introduce its own modifications).[37] Jenkinson, however, remained impenitent: to define archives by the research use made of them is like producing a rabbit from a hat and then saying that that is what hats are intended for; and "to make the fact that Archives have been subject to selection of this kind an essential part of Archive quality is to mask the sad conclusion that our generation is bringing Archives a long step nearer to the status of those artificial 'Collections' to which Dr. Schellenberg . . . assigns, in agreement with me, an inferior quality as evidence".[38]

Nevertheless, however one may reject the letter of Jenkinson's mystique of custody, it remains true that archivists owe a great deal to the rigorous spirit of his theory and practice of archive administration: the treatment which an archivist gives his archives—by his care in accessioning, sorting, and cataloguing—is coloured by much of what Jenkinson said.[39] The most important of his conditions for the preservation of archive value is unaffected: "the authority taking over must be prepared to subscribe to the ordinary rules of Archive management directed to the preservation of Archive character."[40] Respect for the great qualities of archives—their uniqueness, impartiality, naturalness, and interdependence—is now general in this country thanks to the advocacy of Jenkinson, the authority of the Public Record Office, the teaching of the archives schools, and the practice of local archivists.

2. ARCHIVES IN ENGLAND

If we accept the second element in Jenkinson's definition of archives— ". . . and subsequently preserved in their own custody for their own information by the person or persons responsible for that transaction" —it is difficult to decide when preservation of archives began in England; but if we adopt Schellenberg's definition—"preserved for reasons other than those for which they were created or accumulated" —the occasion is explicit: the moment of realization of the historical value of archives. The intervention of some extrinsic motive is now seen as essential. Records in official custody pass through successive stages of diminishing significance: immediate use, declining use, occasional use, inertia, haphazard destruction or accidental survival. Finally comes a conscious decision to preserve them for cultural purposes: "the making of adequate arrangements for the preservation of its records is an inescapable duty of the Government of a civilized state". The history of archive preservation is thus the story of the determination of individuals or small groups of people to save such records, house them in suitable archive repositories, and preserve them for the historical interests of posterity.

The preservation of archives has always been intimately associated with an appreciation of their value as "historical evidences". "We began", says Jenkinson, "to awake to the profit of exploiting old Documents for the correction or enlargement of our ideas upon points of history and antiquities so early as the sixteenth and seventeenth centuries";[1] but so scattered were the public records—"roughly speaking, there were as many keepers as there were courts or departments, and there were as many record offices as there were keepers"[2] —that it was impossible for any one individual to make a comprehensive survey of them, and men like Fanshawe, Powell, and Prynne were confined to the particular sections with which they were professionally familiar. But then the publications of historical scholars during the

13

seventeenth and eighteenth centuries—Dugdale, Madox, Rymer—slowly awakened a general consciousness of the mass of information which lay buried in the public records, and a number of eighteenth-century parliamentary inquiries followed, beginning with one in 1703 to "consider the Method of keeping Records in Offices, and how they are kept, and to consider of Ways to remedy what shall be found to be amiss". It was not, however, until the nineteenth century that a full-dress inquiry into the state of the public records produced, between 1800 and 1831, a series of six commissions (collectively known as "The Record Commission"), the first of which was asked to report "what they shall judge fit to be done for the better Arrangement, Preservation and more convenient Use of the [Public Records]".[3]

The Commission ran into a good deal of criticism: out of a vote of £400,000 it spent £1500 on the arrangement of records; the rest went on publication and general expenses. A select committee of the House of Commons felt it had got its priorities wrong, and one witness feared the substitution of a sea of print for a sea of manuscript. The main proposal of the select committee was that the public records should be collected in one place under one authority. In 1838 "an Act for keeping safely the Public Records" was passed, and so, from a disastrous dénouement of 800 years of record keeping—300–400 repositories, rolls reduced to nearly solid blocks, state papers "methodized" "under headings interesting to the later Historian"[4]—emerged the Public Record Office and "the most concentrated and centralized archive system in the world".[5] The "external assessment" of their "potential value for Research" which had determined the very survival of these national records was spelt out by the first Deputy Keeper of the Records, Sir Francis Palgrave, in his report of June 1852:

> The Public Records, accompanied by the State Papers and Government Archives . . . constitute the backbone of our civil, ecclesiastical and political history; but their value is equally great . . . for the investigation of those special and collateral subjects without which the mere knowledge of public or political affairs affords but a small portion of the information needed for elucidating the mutations and progress of society.[6]

The keeper of all the public records chosen in 1838 was the Master of the Rolls. Jenkinson says[7] that he was the authority proposed by the select committee of 1836 but, in fact, the committee recommended giving it to a reconstituted Record Commission, while the Master of the Rolls himself, Lord Langdale, proposed the Home Office or the Treasury. The (Grigg) Committee on Departmental Records, investigating the historical position of the Master of the Rolls in 1954, decided that the reasons for settling on him in 1838 "are not entirely clear . . . the [relevant] papers . . . cannot be found. It seems likely that the original decision to ask Lord Langdale to supervise the Record Commission's financial business owed more to the qualities of Lord Langdale himself than to anything inherent in the nature of the office he held."[8] Galbraith's comment is that, if anything, the King's Treasury had been the central record office of the Middle Ages; for the Master of the Rolls, originally simply the record keeper of the Chancery, to become in 1838 the keeper of all the public records, was merely an arrangement of convenience, showing that "the modern archive system is no logical, unbroken development of the medieval, but something of an historical accident".[9]

From 1838 to 1958 the Public Record Office was governed by the so-called Public Record Office Acts, actually three Acts and an order in council. The founding Act of 1838 provided for the authority of the Master of the Rolls, the appointment of a Deputy Keeper of the Records and assistant keepers, and the construction of a suitable building; a curious feature was that it created a new department of government (though one without a minister) whereas in other European countries the national archives are usually part of a ministry such as Internal Affairs or Public Instruction.[10] The second measure— an order in council issued on 5 March 1852—enlarged the field of the public records to which the Act of 1838 applied. The remaining two measures, an Act of 1877 and one of 1898, provided for the elimination of such documents as were not "of sufficient Public Value to justify their Preservation in the Public Record Office".[11] The practical success or failure of these four measures was the chief subject of the inquiries in 1910 of a Royal Commission on Public Records which issued reports in 1912, 1914, and 1919. The reports did not lead to any statutory action, but their appendices are claimed as "an authority of the first rank for the whole history of the Public Records in modern times".[12]

Although the Act of 1838 gave a comprehensive interpretation to the word "record", including "all rolls, records, writs, books, proceedings, decrees, bills, warrants, accounts, papers and documents whatsoever of a public nature", it seems clear[13] that the framers of the Act had in mind the traditional, much more limited, meaning of the word—"the embodiment of a legal memory in the form of written words",[14] or a "memorial or remembrance in rolls of parchment or the proceedings or acts of a Court of Justice".[15] The second Record Office measure, however—the order in council of 5 March 1852— momentarily unveiled the taxing world of modern records by extend- ing the scope of the Act of 1838 to include not only the "curial" or legal records, but also all records of government departments in the widest sense—what Palgrave referred to as "Government Archives" as distinct from the medieval "Public Records" and the early modern "State Papers". The order gave the Master of the Rolls power to assume custody of departmental records without the approval of heads of departments, and even without consulting them: power, in effect, suggests Jenkinson, to dislocate the whole executive machinery of the state at the stroke of a pen. But, in fact, the power was never exercised. Why, then, was the order in council of 1852 made at all? The answer provides an entertaining example of English administrative manoeuvre; Jenkinson's word for the whole non-event is "curious",[16] but, in general, he seems rather to have relished an operation whose aim was "to arrange for the desired result rather than to enjoin it".[17] Briefly, in 1849 the Deputy Keeper of the Records had heard of a plan by certain "able and influential promoters" to interfere with the intended transfer of the State Paper Office to the Public Record Office, and to draw "into the British Museum all the State Papers and other Docu- ments of an analogous description", including all non-legal documents already housed at the Public Record Office. Since the Public Record Office was a new department, the Deputy Keeper felt that something dramatic was required to prevent the records of government depart- ments falling into other hands, and so on 5 March 1852 an order in council was issued as a show of strength. Strictly speaking, from 1852 the Master of the Rolls was required to order that all departmental records be delivered into his custody. In fact he never did so: informal arrangements for the transfer of departmental records had been made between the Treasury and the Public Record Office in 1845 and 1846 when certain "principles and rules" had been agreed to, according to which the Public Record Office was explicitly recognized as "merely auxiliary or subservient to the respective offices to which the documents and papers respectively belong". These informal arrangements persisted.[18]

Even on the practical basis of the arrangements of 1845–6 great quantities of modern departmental records were received by the Public Record Office. In 1877 an Act was passed laying down the procedure for the elimination of documents "not considered of sufficient Public Value to justify their Preservation in the Public Record Office". In spite of this provision, and its extension in 1898, a questionnaire sent out by the Treasury in 1951 revealed that departments were then holding material destined for permanent preservation which would require 120 miles of shelving and a building three times the size of the existing Public Record Office; and the estimated annual accumulation showed that a new building the size of the Public Record Office would be needed every eleven years. In June 1952 (the Grigg) Committee on Departmental Records was set up. The recommendations of its report of July 1954 formed the basis of the Public Records Act, 1958, "designed to complete and extend the work of the earlier Acts, by bringing all the public records within the responsibility of a single head, who should be a minister of the Crown".[19] This minister, the Lord Chancellor, was to appoint a newly styled Keeper of Public Records. The Master of the Rolls was to become chairman of a council intended to advise the Chancellor on the administration of the Act for the benefit of the user. The other main provision of the Act was for the systematic selection of records for preservation and for their regular transfer to the Public Record Office thirty years after their creation, a Records Administration Division being set up to co-ordinate the work of selection and transfer. Public access to the records would be given, with necessary reservations, when they were fifty years old. Provision was to be made for certain public records accruing in local courts and offices to be kept in local record offices approved by the Lord Chancellor.

The burden imposed by the modern world on a great and venerable scholarly institution, housed in a building whose layout "prevents the installation of mechanical conveyance" and whose structure "makes conversion an expensive and laborious task", has been generously limned by one of its senior administrators.[20] Serving today 120 departments and other organizations which together annually create about 100 miles of records, and selecting from these an estimated 6000 feet for preservation, the Public Record Office has been compelled to lower its sights from the unrealistic destruction procedures of 1877–1959 —"though theoretically offering every safeguard against the destruction of valuable material" they "in fact provide no safeguards at all because they cannot be operated properly"—to a more modest target: "the emphasis is now on what must be preserved rather than on what may be destroyed". Even so, two intractable, interrelated problems continue to plague the Office: accommodation for records and accommodation for searchers. In 1950 "two enormous buildings" (a former R.O. factory) were acquired at Hayes in Middlesex in which to store departmental records awaiting sorting, but nine-tenths of its 1 million feet of shelving are now occupied. In 1951 a branch repository was opened in a former wartime hospital at Ashridge Park in Hertfordshire, but this is likely to be full in 1971. The accommodation for searchers at the Public Record Office was 100 seats in 1945 and was adequate. By 1967 the average daily attendance was more than 200, and during the week 8–12 July 1968 attendance exceeded 300 on some days: an explosion caused by a world-wide increase in university population (and especially in post-graduate students), a broadening public interest in records, the abolition of fees in 1962, and the introduction, first of the fifty-year rule in 1960, then of the thirty-year rule in 1968: "for the first time in the history of the Office . . . would-be readers had to be asked to wait for seats to be vacated in the search rooms and an unknown number were inhibited from coming to work there".

Palliative measures were taken: the conversion in 1961 of the Rolls Room from repository to search room use, giving an increase of 20 seats; the opening of small search rooms at Ashridge and Hayes; and (most important) the acquisition of accommodation in the Land Registry in Lincoln's Inn Fields, with the prospect by the end of 1969 of 150 seats there in addition to the 160 at Chancery Lane: "in this way we believe the short-term needs of users of the records will be met during the next few years". The long-term problems, however, remained: "if present rates are maintained by 2000 A.D. accommodation for 900 searchers a day occupying 500 seats and inspecting 4,000 documents will be required". In 1954 the Grigg Committee recommended development of the Chancery Lane site, and the Lord Chancellor's Council on Public Records agreed; so until 1969 various plans, chiefly with the object of providing more search-room facilities, were prepared, and successively abandoned because of the ultimate "realization of the inadequacy of the site to meet all requirements that can be foreseen". In Mr. Johnson's opinion "this fifteen-year exploration" probably deserved to fail: concentration on "convenience of venue for the average reader" was ill-conceived when an ever-increasing bulk of records stored away from Chancery Lane had to be brought in daily, involving heavy transport costs, uneconomic use of staff, risks to records, and delays in production.

In 1969, therefore, the decision was made to divide the Public Record Office between two sites—Chancery Lane and another site, within easy reach of London, on which could be built a purpose-designed repository "fully mechanized to facilitate the handling of records and their speedy conveyance to the search rooms": Chancery Lane probably housing mainly the older, closed classes of records, and the new repository taking the growing accumulations of modern departmental records. "Urgent discussions with interested departments are well advanced, and it is hoped that an end is in sight to the recurrent accommodation crises which have, in the words of the Grigg Committee, been a feature of the administration of the public records since 1838." On 5 November 1969 the Lord Chancellor announced in the House of Lords that the second Public Record Office was to be built in Ruskin Avenue, Kew; by February 1970 plans were being discussed. Expected to be ready by 1975, the new building will have a staff of 200 and accommodate 750 readers a day; it will probably house modern departmental records, medieval and legal documents remaining at Chancery Lane.

It would be interesting if we could trace the development of concern about private archives as clearly as this well-documented growth of care for the public records. As regards the use of private archives, Jenkinson suggests that it was only when "scholars such as Maitland, Tout and the Webbs introduced us to research upon Legal, Administrative, Social and Economic History . . . that we arrived finally at a full appreciation of modern as well as ancient Documents and a realization of the fact that the Current Files of to-day are the Archives of tomorrow".[21] As far as their preservation, however, is concerned,

Mr. R. H. Ellis can only suspect that "the prehistory of the Historical MSS. Commission dates in fact from 1838, when the Public Record Office Act made the first statutory provision for the care of the Public Records, and thoughtful people must have realized that some provision should be made for privately-owned records too".[22]

In 1859 an influential memorial to the Prime Minister urged action "to rescue from oblivion and in many cases from decay valuable collections of papers the contents of which are now unknown even to the possessors which are . . . of the highest value on account of the information which they afford in matters of history, law, legislation, biography, and several other important subjects".[23] But the Government, mindful perhaps of the trouble and expense of the Public Record Office, did nothing until April 1869 when a Royal Commission on Historical Manuscripts was appointed. The Commission invited probable owners of manuscripts—peers, landed gentry, senior clergy, universities, the older municipal corporations—to allow an examination of their manuscripts. The response was overwhelming. In the first year nearly a hundred owners asked for an inspection or even sent their manuscripts to the Public Record Office, and the Commissioners "deemed it desirable, in the first instance, merely to undertake a preliminary examination of the collections, and to abstain from calendaring any of the papers".[24] By the time the eighth Report was printed in 1886 over 500 collections had been inspected. However, by 1883, when the first of a long series of full-scale calendars of the Salisbury (Cecil) papers at Hatfield appeared, it looks as though the Commission had decided, perhaps through lack of money, perhaps because of declining response by owners, to concentrate on the calendaring of a small number of important collections rather than on summary reports on a great many; and so, "the Inspectors ceased to travel and became Editors; the documents were brought to them, and were deposited for long periods in the Commission's care".[25]

The objectives of the Historical Manuscripts Commission were thus subject to considerable vacillation. R. H. Ellis suggests that this latest change showed that "the Commissioners had not lost sight of their earlier objective, namely not merely to discover and to record but to calendar the important MS. collections".[26] On the other hand, when the flow of these calendars becomes a trickle after the First, and particularly after the Second World War, he excuses it by saying that "publication however was only one of the Commission's tasks, and not the first; the primary duty was to discover historical MSS. and to record their existence and content".[27] In other quarters the latter-day publishing record of the Commission (and of the Public Record Office) has been the subject of pungent criticism; particularly "the meagre output of the [nineteen] forties and fifties that cannot fail to provoke apprehension among those who believe that the continuous publication of texts, calendaıs, lists and indexes is an essential nutriment for the writing of history and the maintenance of academic studies".[28]

The calendaring and editorial work of the Historical Manuscripts Commission was an extension of the more limited and private investigations of family papers by the sixteenth- and seventeenth-century antiquaries. But at the end of the nineteenth century, in "the later stages of our awakening to the value of Archives", a new point of view was gradually emerging: "that of the person interested not so much in the contents of Archives and their exploitation as in the earlier and more instant problem of their preservation and in the technical processes of arrangement, care and conservation which follow . . . the character who now comes upon the scene is the Archivist".[29] Jenkinson sees a number of strands involved in this evolution. "More than fifty years ago a small body of enthusiasts was sufficiently alive to the dangers of dispersal and destruction to which Local and Private Archives were exposed in this Country to be drafting already proposals for protective legislation". Though these proposals came to nothing they "all implied the creation of a class of persons specially trained to look after the Local Repositories which they wished to set up". Local archaeological and record societies, previously mainly devoted to publication, became concerned with the threat to local records (especially family muniments no longer required to prove title) and in one or two cases actually set up muniment rooms of their own. Libraries did even better: "Historians and Archivists alike owe them a lasting debt" because they "provided storage and custody in numerous instances . . . when no other Authorities were willing to come forward". In 1924, by an amendment to the Law of Property Act of 1922, manorial records were placed in the charge and superintendence of the Master of the Rolls who proceeded to recognize as places suitable for their deposit existing muniment rooms and libraries in almost every county. In 1929 the British Records Society began the rescue of unwanted documents, particularly deeds, and their deposit in suitable repositories. The idea of a local muniment room was thus firmly established, but by creating the first county record office in Bedfordshire in 1923, G. H. Fowler gave it the support of local authority subsidy. The foundation of further record offices, with "some reasonable prospect of a succession of posts", made possible the formation of an archives profession, and in 1948 a diploma course in archive administration instituted at University College London marked its inauguration.[30]

The history of private and local archives preservation in this country in the past forty years has been one of integration of diverse elements into a unified archives climate and profession. In November 1932 the British Records Association was formed to co-ordinate all archive interests. It was afraid of "the dangers that could arise if the newly aroused archival activities undertaken by numerous local societies, libraries and other institutions were to take place in a haphazard manner, unrelated to each other and lacking a common policy or guidance from a central authority".[31] Its aims were co-operation "between all authorities, institutions or individuals concerned in the preservation, custody, study and publication of records"; the preservation of records of historical importance; the collection of technical information about archives; and the utilization of "records as historical material, particularly as regards their publication".[32] In its first year the Association had a membership of 255; in 1969 this was 1312, of whom nearly half (592) were institutional members.

Until the formation of the Society of Local Archivists in 1947 the annual conference of the British Records Association was the only central meeting-place for those concerned with archives, unless they happened to belong to other national associations with archaeological or historical interests. Although the British Records Association was by nature a diffuse body, it had contact, through its president, the Master of the Rolls, with the national archives and with Public Record Office policy on manorial records (which had come under the control of the Master of the Rolls). Indeed, from the beginning, the Association's professional flavour was determined by its Public Record Office members. With the rise of county record offices after the war, however, local archivists found themselves somewhat out of sympathy with the constitution and spirit of the Association and so formed the specialized Society of Local Archivists. In December 1954 the constitution of the Society was revised, the word "Local" was dropped from its title, and the present Society of Archivists was created whose membership (in 1969 numbering 486) is open to all those who are "primarily occupied in the practical care of archives in the British Isles and Commonwealth".[33] The Society of Archivists is now the professional body of archivists in this country; the British Records Association remains the larger, more miscellaneous, more amateur body. However, the preoccupations of the two groups cover much the same ground. Most members of the Society are also members of the Association, and the annual conferences of the two bodies are held consecutively in London. The Society has selected some of its presidents from distinguished members of the Association (and of the staff of the Public Record Office). With the agreement of the Society, the Association has been recognized by the International Council on Archives as the national representative body for Great Britain. In 1956 a standing joint committee of three members from each body was formed to discuss questions of common interest. The same year, with the agreement of the Association, the Society took over responsibility for technical and scientific problems relating to the care of archives by forming a technical committee in place of the Association's technical section.

The British Records Association shed another of its sections, that dealing with record publications, in 1950. Its Records Preservation Section, however, has continued to flourish. The work of this section —the location and preservation of records and their distribution to appropriate repositories—was inherited from the Association's predecessor, the British Records Society. A large proportion of such records has consisted of deeds from the offices of London solicitors (of whom there are about 1600), a tendency stimulated by a five-year grant for the purpose received from the Pilgrim Trust. However, as a result of an agreement made in 1963 with the Business Archives Council to collaborate in an approach to business firms, beginning with brewers' records, the Section made its first major excursion out of the London area. Such a policy raises difficulties. It had already been recognized that the continued development of local record offices made the function of the British Records Association "a matter for careful reflection": while the Association "must continue to be the national organisation where problems can be discussed and policy formulated", the actual seeking out of records and their preservation were best left to local effort.[34] And so, in announcing this novel venture, the Records Preservation Section hastened to make it clear that "its policy throughout has been to keep local archivists closely in touch with any approaches it has made to local firms and, of course, to inform them immediately where any prospects exist of records becoming available for study or deposit."[35]

In his catalogue of the factors which have led during the last two generations to the flowering of local archives repositories Jenkinson omitted social revolution. Although Fowler had established the first county record office in 1923, by 1939 only a dozen offices had been opened; the largest number of staff in any of them was six, and some had only one. Progress would, no doubt, have continued at this gentle pace, had not war changed the whole archives scene by putting masses of private records in jeopardy. The post-war archivist tasted the full flavour of this social transformation in the rear quarters of many a large country house: enormous kitchens once scurrying with servants now deserted except for one or two part-time helps; rows of stables occupied by an occasional horse; undermanned estate offices with superfluous rooms cold, damp, and decaying, and records festooned in mould. Quite apart from financial reasons, the post-war estate owner might well open his house to the public simply for the company.

These conditions have persisted. One afternoon in the late 1950s an archivist was looking for a palladian mansion deep in ducal country. He passed through surprisingly rusty gates and along a decidedly unkempt drive. At the end he turned a corner between lowering rhododendrons to find, in the centre of a largely empty arena, a solitary bulldozer removing the last bricks of the house in a cloud of dust. The owner was tracked to a large vicarage (the vicar having moved into a cottage). He was deep in a chintzey armchair, with a fat novel in his hand and a well-filled glass of whisky by his side. On the walls was the pick of the paintings from his former gallery. From a loft over the garage he helped load a large trunk of family papers into the archivist's car, and as he saw him off from the front door called after him, "Be sure to let me know if you find any stamps".

Jenkinson was, perhaps, speaking a little before the full effects of this revolution were apparent. Nevertheless, in 1943 the British Records Association, alarmed by the lack of any plan to preserve local records other than manorial documents, submitted to the Master of the Rolls a proposal for the establishment of a National Register of Archives.[36] Already, as long ago as 1926, the Historical Manuscripts Commission had suggested the desirability of a "general conspectus of the historical materials in private hands in the country",[37] and it had played a part in some interesting but unsuccessful early attempts at such a census on a county basis, for instance in Staffordshire in 1920 and in Northamptonshire in 1931.[38] However, the register of archives which eventually materialized was primarily an outcome of wartime conditions: an attempt at a national census in 1938 was interrupted by the onset of war, and even less ambitious efforts to collect information about war damage to manuscripts were impeded by the absence of details about their location. On 20 October 1943, therefore, the Master of the Rolls' Archives Committee resolved that steps should be taken as soon as possible for the construction of a National Register of Archives.

The ultimate aim of the British Records Association's proposal of 1943 was a National Archives Council, with an inspectorate investigating the whole range of English archives other than those of central government, and even as late as 1952 the National Register of Archives was still seen in some quarters as "the preliminary to legislation imposing some form of official protection and supervision on archives of all kinds".[39] "To the relief of many people",[40] the Council and the inspectorate were non-starters: "the Register had [by 1952] long outgrown its temporary beginnings", and imperceptibly was "changing in response to what were realised to be the needs of owners, custodians and users of manuscripts"—"the provision of information to scholars", "a general guide for historical workers".[41] The very name and reputation of the National Register of Archives thus curiously rest on the achievement of a secondary purpose—the register was which to have formed the basis of the scheme of preservation. Nevertheless, in the compilation of this elaborate index of locations and contents, destined ultimately to form "a vast Guide to Manuscript Sources, covering the needs not only of professional Historians but of enquirers seeking information in every field",[42] the National Register of Archives has proved triumphantly successful: there is nothing comparable with it in any other country.[43]

At its inception in 1945 the National Register of Archives had a staff of two; by 1951 it had ten. Work was divided between investigation of records in the field and the compilation of indexes at headquarters. The organization was clearly dependent on local information about records and on local help in making reports and lists. Large and enthusiastic county meetings were held, to which all owners, custodians, and helpers were invited. As a result, committees were set up in most counties and a large number of voluntary workers were enrolled (for instance, over a hundred in Worcestershire). Not many local record offices existed in the early days of the National Register of Archives. Those that did were a little suspicious of its activities and the activities of its local helpers, fearing they might intrude on their own. An early commentator claimed that the work of the Register and of the local record office was "largely complementary and that, working together, both can achieve results that might otherwise be unobtainable".[44] In fact, however, the two organizations have not proved fully compatible. When fully fledged, the local record office has taken over and professionalized the work previously done by voluntary helpers. The archivist has usually become the local Register representative, but the committee of which he is technically secretary, having fulfilled its valuable original role, has usually melted away. Relations between secretary and Register are mainly confined to his reports on records, and these he compiles on behalf of his record office, rather than as an agent of the Register.

"The Register functions, and has always functioned, largely on goodwill and reciprocal services."[45] Certainly, many archivists and many historical research workers hold the National Register of Archives in high regard. An outstanding example of a reciprocal service is the reproduction by the Register of archives lists supplied by record repositories. A specially designed photo-dyeline machine was installed when the service began in 1954, but now that "lists of ever-increasing sophistication accumulate at the rate of almost one thousand in a year",[46] it has become necessary to introduce a Multilith offset litho machine; "this, together with a Bruning Electrostatic Photocopier 1200 for making plates, a Xerox 914, and a Recordak MRD2E microfilm camera, gives the Commission a wide range of equipment for photo-copying and reproduction".[47] Research workers and libraries some-times ask record offices if they can buy copies of archives lists repro-duced by the National Register of Archives. So far the Register has been unable to comply with these requests, but now it is actively investigating "the sale of certain lists, which has long been desired by American historians and libraries . . . if the scheme fails it will be over administrative and copyright difficulties rather than from any obstruc-tionist attitude on the part of the Commission".[48] In the meantime, and as a preliminary, the Register proposes to publish by photolitho-graphy a title-page of every report, i.e. list, in its possession, giving details of ownership, location, etc., and a summary of its contents.[49]

The quirks of the Victorian archives scene which caught the quizzi-cal eye of Jenkinson have had their modern counterparts. Although the details of the relationship between the Historical Manuscripts Commission and the National Register of Archives have been clearly set out by Mr. Ellis and Miss Ranger, the influences tending to arrange them in particular patterns at different moments remain difficult to determine. When, on 20 October 1943, the Master of the Rolls' Archives Committee proposed the compilation of a National Register of Archives, it suggested that, while the work should be undertaken by the Historical Manuscripts Commission, it should be "kept quite distinct from the work at present performed by the Commission" and should be "entrusted to a Secretary specially appointed for the purpose".[50] When it was established, therefore, the Register, though described as a "special branch" of the Commission, was made respon-sible to "a small Directorate" appointed by the Master of the Rolls in which the Commission was represented along with the Public Record Office and the British Records Association.[51]

Of course, as originally envisaged, the National Register of Archives was expected to have only a temporary existence—the $2\frac{1}{2}$ years from March 1945 to October 1947 for which it received a Treasury grant. It might be thought, therefore, that the curiously careful emphasis on the differentiation of the work of the Register would last only so long as this expectation was confirmed. However, it seems clear that the change of heart must have come much later because it was only at the Historical Manuscript Commissioners' meeting of July 1957 that "Sir Hilary Jenkinson stated that he had thought until then that the National Register could function best as a separate body, but that he no longer held that view".[52] In the interim the National Register of Archives had developed into "a cuckoo in the H.M.C. nest",[53] or a lusty infant threatening to overshadow its nonagenarian parent. But now, in 1957, a course of rejuvenation of the Commission began which included reassertion of authority over the Register. The separate directorate controlling the Register had disappeared from view earlier in the 1950s and, following Jenkinson's pronouncement of July 1957, "the Secretary of the HMC applied himself to ensuring . . . that all the Commission's staff (including the Registrar and Assistant Registrars) were comprised in one unified and comprehensible establishment and command"[54] —a policy which matured in 1965 when the work of the Registrar, who had previously been responsible for the Register in all its aspects, was shared with a new Assistant Secretary of the Historical Manuscripts Commission, and the Secretary of the Commission established overall charge.

Whatever the reasons for the NRA's solicitously fostered infancy, and despite its magnificently virile adolescence, this family reunion in maturity had a formal logic and a financial inevitability: "the Register's administration and finance had always been handled by the Commission as part of its vote, and identity of organisation eventually followed identity of function and interest".[55] It was even dispassionately possible to view a complete merger as bringing "nothing but gain to both Commission and Register . . . their further development and extended usefulness depend on their unity".[56] For a whole generation of archivists, however, the National Register will remain the embodiment of a renascence, "with all the excitement of detection, discovery, and manuscripts rescued by moments only from destruction".[57] Now its heroic days were over.

The ingestion of the National Register of Archives was only one aspect of "a general reappraisal of the whole field of the Commission's activity"[58] which followed the Public Records Act of 1958. Because this Act put the Public Record Office under the Lord Chancellor while the Historical Manuscripts Commission remained under the Master of the Rolls, some new thinking was necessary about relations between the Public Record Office and the Commission, especially as regards manorial and tithe records. In the event, the Master of the Rolls decided to exercise his powers through the Commission instead of through the Public Record Office, and the registers of manorial and tithe records were transferred to the Commission's offices where they were "overhauled, simplified, and diminished in bulk, and brought into close relation with the National Register of Archives".[59]

At the same time the opportunity was taken to review and extend the Commission's terms of reference by means of a new royal warrant signed on 5 December 1959. This was intended "both to cover actual operations which, though implicit in the previous Warrant, were not specified there, and also to provide for extended activity in the future".[60] In addition to the duties of inspecting, reporting, and registering all non-public records, the warrant authorized the Commission to "promote and assist the proper preservation and storage of such manuscripts and records; assist those wishing to use such manuscripts or records for study or research; consider and advise upon general questions relating to the location, preservation and use of such manuscripts and records".[61] "Thus", says the Secretary, "by the beginning of 1960 the Commission stood upon a new and independent footing, its potential activities within its special field limited only by the number and energy of its members and staff, and by the size of the Vote which the Treasury would sanction."[62]

The generalized terms of the new warrant certainly gave the Commission the possibility of large, though ill-defined responsibilities in the future. A firm basis in fact was provided by the only two precise elements in the warrant: compilation of the National Register, and the transfer to the Commission of responsibility for manorial and tithe records. In reasserting control over the National Register of Archives the Historical Manuscripts Commission was harnessing to its own purposes an engine of considerable power, reputation, and performance. The experience and expertise of the Register now gave the Commission direct access to archivists, owners, local historians, and local authorities; through them it could hope to diffuse advice and influence, encouragement or restraint. Sometimes, however, it would be necessary to acknowledge, gracefully, a *fait accompli*: the original "aim of the National Register of Archives was to establish local representatives and local committees in every part of the country. . . . The subsequent institution of local record offices, and the appointment of local archivists, have however provided a more securely based organisation which the Commissioners view with entire approval."[63]

Elsewhere, the generalities of the warrant invited generous interpretation. Thus "promote and assist the proper preservation and storage of such manuscripts and records" could mean that sometimes "it may be necessary to mediate between a cautious owner, impatient historians, and competing repositories, and the negotiations may be long and require skill and sound judgment".[64] But the implications of the warrant might be even more far-reaching. Where, for instance, the warrant enjoins the Commission to "consider and advise upon general questions" or to "promote the co-ordinated action of all professional and other bodies" might not this be interpreted as "Surveillance" or "General Oversight" by an "impartial, enduring and authoritative body" which can "survey the whole field without partisan interest, and can guide, assist, cooperate, arbitrate, or even restrain as the case may suggest"?[65]

Some of the difficulties in the way of such a wide-ranging brief did not go undetected: "In 1869 the Commission was alone in the field, and perforce went straight to the documents and their owners and custodians. Nowadays we are vastly better served, with qualified archivists in well-found record offices, and powerful bodies such as the British Records Association, the Business Archives Council, and the Society of Archivists exercising continual activity and vigilance." But it is doubtful if all the realities of the present-day archives situation were read aright in the conclusion that "in 1869 the Commission was required to do the job, since 1959 it has been required to see that the job is done".[66] In the vigorous archive world of the post-war period the need for co-ordinated action had been frequently canvassed. Usually it resolved itself into locally arranged compromises. Where outside stimulus was effective it often came from a body like the National Register of Archives with a clearly defined, practical function of its own which brought it into natural and well-informed contact with local conditions: "adaptability and sensitivity to the demands made of it were the Register's hallmarks".[67] It would seem unsatisfactory to substitute for these pragmatic activities the panurgic ambitions of a remote body, however "impartial, enduring and authoritative": local situations usually require intimate knowledge and diffidence in decision as well as "skill and sound judgment". As constituted, the Historical Manuscripts Commission seemed inadequately staffed and equipped to undertake its self-ascribed tasks.

In fact, in the face of financial and archival realities, these tasks appear to have been voluntarily circumscribed. By 1969 the aims of the royal warrant itself were seen as unattainable; the infinite space of seven years earlier had shrunk to a nutshell:

> New enterprises of any magnitude or duration cannot be absorbed by existing staff. . . . Should the Commissioners demand, and press for, an establishment three or four times the size of the present, in order to be able to carry out, in full and independently, all the tasks enjoined in the Warrant? The Commissioners, taking a realistic view, believe that this course is not only impracticable but not even desirable; it would, in fact, defeat its own aims by turning the Commission from an assisting to a competing body . . . if Oversight be taken as the function of the Overseer, this appears in retrospect as an overstatement . . . neither the Commissioners nor their staff have any power to order people about . . . the Commission stands as (so to speak) an extra-parochial district with a wide view in all directions. . . . It is perhaps symbolic that other bodies with related interests regularly hold their Council and Committee meetings in the Commission's Conference Room.[68]

Contrasting sharply with the panoramic purposes of the Historical Manuscripts Commission warrant of 1959 were the severely practical intentions of the Local Government (Records) Act of 1962. Before 1962, although some local authorities had obtained local acts allowing them to maintain record offices, others were doing so without specific authority. Archivists had long wanted legislation on local records and the new Act regularized the position by giving the council of every county or county borough the power to acquire records, in addition to its own official records, by purchase, gift or deposit. This power can be extended by ministry order to councils of county districts or metropolitan boroughs. In addition, the Act empowers authorities to make records available for study, and to index and catalogue them; to publish guides, calendars, and other summaries of the records; to arrange exhibitions and lectures; to lend the records for study in another repository; and to deposit records with another institution and make a grant towards the cost of keeping them there.

The Act was professionally welcomed as "a new charter for the local archivist".[69] After it had been passed the Ministry of Local Government sent a circular to local authorities encouraging them to exercise their powers under the Act to the fullest extent. However, the Act was not, of course, mandatory, nor, as some archivists perhaps hoped, did it introduce any central supervision over local record offices. Hence there still remains the wide disparity between different offices in methods, facilities, staffing, and accommodation which most archivists regret.

3. THE ARCHIVES SCENE

A QUICK impression of the current provision of record offices in this country can be got from the booklet, *Record Repositories in Great Britain*, published by the Stationery Office for the Historical Manuscripts Commission, third edition, 1968.[1] This contains particulars of 304 repositories, compared with 270 in the second edition of 1966, nearly 250 in the first edition of 1964, and 155 in the *List of Record Repositories in Great Britain*, published by the British Records Association in 1956.[2] Even in 1966 the editor of *Archives* thought "the figures might suggest that we are nearing saturation point, yet the creation of new repositories continues";[3] and in other quarters, too, considerable feeling exists that there are too many archive repositories in England: "having sprung up wherever and in whatever form the antiquarian interest of successive ages has seen fit, or has been able to obtain funds, to create them, record repositories exist there . . . at a greater average density than in any other country in the world except Belgium and Switzerland."[4]

English record offices occupy almost seven-eighths of the pages of *Record Repositories in Great Britain*, 1968; the remainder is devoted to Wales, Scotland, Northern Ireland, the Isle of Man, and the Channel Islands. English repositories are listed firstly under London (which occupies one-third of the booklet) and then under counties (one-half) arranged alphabetically. An idea of the *variety* of English record repositories can be gained by looking at the sixteen-page London section. This is arranged by type of repository, beginning with (i) *Government, Parliamentary, etc., Archives*: eight repositories are listed here, starting with the Public Record Office, and including Customs and Excise, the General Post Office, the House of Lords, and the Principal Probate Registry at Somerset House. Next follow (ii) *National Libraries and Museums*: eleven repositories, beginning with the British Museum, and including the India Office Library (European Manuscripts Section), National Maritime Museum, National Portrait

Gallery, and Victoria and Albert Museum; (iii) *Religious Archives and Libraries*: nineteen repositories, ranging alphabetically from the Baptist Missionary Society to Westminster Cathedral, and embracing Lambeth Palace Library and the Society of Friends Library on the way; (iv) *Societies, Colleges, and Institutions*: eighteen very miscellaneous repositories, beginning with the College of Arms, ending with the Wellcome Historical Medical Library, and including the libraries of the Inns of Court, the archives of St. Bartholomew's Hospital, and the library of the Royal College of Surgeons; consultation of the archives of some of these repositories is restricted, for instance in the Middle Temple Library where "permission to study the MSS. is granted to persons with suitable references and academic qualifications"; (v) *University Libraries*: five repositories; (vi) *Public Utilities, Banking, and Business*: eleven repositories; again, access is sometimes limited, as at Coutts & Co. where "the confidential nature of the Bank's business, and of the customers' records, enforces certain restrictions on research, and the permission of descendants of customers, or of the Directors of the Bank, is required"; (vii) *City of London*: the Corporation of London Records Office, the Guildhall Library, and nearly seventy livery companies, of whom the majority have deposited their records in the Guildhall Library but some have made special arrangements for access; (viii) *Greater London Record Office*: London records at County Hall, Middlesex records at Queen Anne's Gate Buildings; (ix) *London Borough Libraries*: eighteen repositories.

The next section is one of twenty-five pages devoted to the English counties. It is dominated by the almost all-pervasive county record office: only diminutive Rutland and the sprawling West Riding of Yorkshire are without one. Occasionally, as in Bedfordshire, Dorset, and Northamptonshire, the county record office is the only repository in the county, but often there is a considerable miscellany of repositories. For instance, Hampshire has seven: the county record office at Winchester; city record offices at Winchester, Portsmouth, and Southampton; the university library at Southampton; Winchester cathedral library; and Winchester college muniments. Sussex, Warwickshire, and the North Riding of Yorkshire also have seven repositories each, Kent has eight, the West Riding of Yorkshire has twelve, but pride of place goes to Lancashire with sixteen.

English archive repositories are thus both thick on the ground and very assorted: they include central government archives, national libraries, national museums, local museums, public and university libraries, county record offices, borough record offices, business firms, the Church of England, the Roman Catholic Church, nonconformist churches, colleges, hospitals, societies, and miscellaneous institutions. Some of these repositories are patently more important than others, with the British Museum and the Public Record Office at one end of the scale, and X public library, Y society, and Z county record office, perhaps, at the other. Exception by critics is, indeed, taken not only to the excessive number of repositories but also to the "proliferation of inadequate facilities", with many of the new record offices "operating on marginal budgets, precluded by circumstances from any possibility of serious development and often able to offer no more than minimal services"; the roots of the problem are seen to lie in the antiquated framework of local government as it is at present, with smaller authorities setting up rudimentary records sections "as the means of providing an 'extra' service—at least on paper".[5] Finally as if fecundity and a natural diversity were not enough, the vexed critic is confronted by an archive sport—the specialized repository: "in many ways the most disturbing element in the situation, for whereas local authority and university repositories will usually take a collection entire, the specialized repository is interested only in a part. Even the part is apparently to be fought over. The 1964 *List of Accessions* shows no less than three repositories solely devoted to collecting military records. . . . Will someone explain why all these are necessary?"[6]

Yet, in spite of all this proliferation, some forward-looking archivists believe that more, not fewer, record offices are needed. Thus, Mr. Edwin Welch thinks the plaint should be not "Too many repositories", but "Too many poor repositories", or "Too many local authorities": "the two difficulties in this field are surely that some local authorities which could afford efficient record offices are failing to do so, and others which need a record office are too small to provide one".[7] Another archivist of the same school, Mr. Michael Cook, feels that there are "vast areas of public life in Britain" where no archive work is done, namely, the great industrial and urban areas: "it is almost true to say that organised local archives offices cover the whole country *except* the most important areas. And yet these are also the areas which could most afford archival services, and which indeed stand to gain most from having them."[8]

Reaction to the multiplicity of record offices thus ranges between generally disapproving noises and proposals for the reorganization of local government. Dr. G. R. C. Davis, somewhere in the middle, thinks that English archivists must soon put their own house in order or "a new generation of reformers" will do it for them, and perhaps make confusion worse confounded by imposing yet another pattern of repositories. However, although he does not elaborate his remedy, Dr. Davis appears not to be against every sort of external agency, and, indeed, seems to regret the absence of an "official umpire, in the shape of some effective form of central direction or control". Strangely enough, it was almost exactly at this time that, as we have seen,[9] an attempt was being made by the Historical Manuscripts Commission to suggest itself in just such a role of gentlemanly arbiter as is prefigured by Dr. Davis. He approaches the complex English archives situation with his sympathies whole-heartedly engaged on behalf of the historian. He is quite sure that the English have "no respect for ideologies or for bureaucracy . . . they regard archives neither as documentary arsenals of the administration nor as national shrines, but simply as granaries for the historian". A little amused by the "wrangling, overlapping, and sometimes even . . . piracy" between record offices—"to the English, at all events, such a state of affairs is both natural and agreeable"—yet, as a spokesman for historians who want orderly access to their sources, he is a shade irritated that competing archivists should have "devised elaborate rules, rituals, and taboos for dealing with archives which are as unintelligible to the uninitiated as the laws of cricket", and he compares this "somewhat recherché national game" with "the staid and serious-minded profession that it has become elsewhere".[10]

Historians play a variety of roles in the archives world. Sometimes they are among the most vigorous critics of the professional establishment; occasionally they are refugees from it; frequently they sit on records committees; often they edit documents, to which they may have been given privileged access. Archivists themselves have usually trained as historians, and have historian friends to whom they give information about accessions and discoveries. Thus historians are not necessarily impartial observers: they are naturally chiefly concerned with their own convenience. Dr. Davis pictures English archives as so much "port wine", maturing undisturbed, awaiting the connoisseur's accepting nod. But, in fact, the archivist has obligations not only to professional historians ("scholars") but to non-professional historians ("antiquarians") of all kinds—teachers, schoolchildren, genealogists, amateurs—to his authority, to his depositors, to his community. Removal of local records to regional repositories *may* be the right thing to do, but it should not be done simply out of regard for certain historians' convenience. The metropolitan *cognoscente* is not seeing the English archives scene whole if he thinks the English archivist is "primarily . . . a scholar". Local archivists, while perhaps having the inclination, do not have the time to be "primarily" scholars.

The most realistic hope for archive reform might appear to lie in the reorganization of local government: "the boroughs seem to be the chief source of complaint at the present time and it must be admitted that their standards are in general very low. . . . The problem of the municipal boroughs and their archives can only be finally solved by local government reform".[11] Reform of English local government would, no doubt, radically affect the distribution of record offices, but whether their health would automatically improve might well be questioned, judging by the effect on record offices in Greater London of the London Government Act of 1963. Inheriting considerable quantities of records from their predecessors, and receiving the current records of the services they took over from the county councils, the large new boroughs (some with a population as big as that of Coventry or Nottingham) created by this Act became major record-producing bodies on a par with county councils and county boroughs. The new authorities clearly needed trained archivists immediately, preferably to be employed in the Town Clerks' departments; but, given a simultaneous demand for at least thirty-two archivists and a contemporary acute shortage in the archives profession, it was understandable that they should appeal in the first instance to their librarians (who already had some records in their charge), and that, in turn, the librarians should recruit from their own staffs individuals who could be "dubbed archivists and left to wrestle with the situation as best they may". Miss Ida Darlington, Head Archivist of the Greater London

Council, recommends that the archives profession adopt a generous and helpful attitude to these "librarian archivists", to show that "we are concerned not with restrictive practices but with professional standards", and she is hopeful that eventually good archival principles will be accepted, and that these officers will be recognized, as *borough* archivists. Nevertheless, the general significance of this particular "archivally unhealthy" situation is plain: the possibility, "with major local government changes imminent, that a similar pattern may emerge in areas far removed from London".[12]

Although, as we have seen, Mr. Welch feels that the final solution of the problem of municipal boroughs and their archives lies with local government reform, he believes that, in the case of other urban areas, self-improvement is possible now: "the county and London boroughs should be encouraged to provide proper facilities and appoint qualified staff"; it is an "ancient myth" that they cannot afford record offices. Mr. Welch would like these offices to be independent, not "poor relations of the county record offices".[13] Other commentators on the archives scene, however, like Mr. Maurice Bond, Clerk of the Records of the House of Lords, see county record offices in precisely this role of benevolent uncle. Mr. Bond makes a sympathetic but not altogether successful attempt to knead the yeasty welter of smaller repositories into an "integrated service" of English archives. He proposes a two-tier system of local record offices, in which "the relation of the senior and the smaller repository would be . . . that of service". For the nonce, he briskly lights on county record offices as "the wiser choice" (than, say, universities) for seniority in his hierarchy; for the future, he descries, faintly but fondly, a century hence, among those national bodies (especially a transformed Historical Manuscripts Commission) "which are emerging today as the centres of this new profession", "some sort of official articulation between the national and the local record offices . . . a general inspectorate".[14]

"Small independent groups of archives exist, are increasing in number, and will continue to increase", says Mr. Bond.[15] Indeed, whatever reform may materialize, the pragmatic nature of English archives should be recognized, and the localness of local records preserved. If an English house is lifted from its foundations and removed bodily to the United States cultivated reaction is a mixture of

amusement and distaste: where the house was, there is a feeling
of loss; where it now is, one of artificiality. Local archives are
as much a local growth, as much a part of the local scene, as a country
house. To drain records away from a locality is to inflict cultural
amnesia. That many localities are unaware of their rich archival inheri-
tance does not make it any the more proper to sleight away their
records. County libraries are rightly praised for their work in pumping
printed matter into rural areas; local record offices should at least
consider what they can do to preserve written remains as near to their
birthplace as possible, and certainly not sell the pass to regional
offices. Mr. Bond, in fact, makes much the same point: "records are
not simply raw material for the professional historical student. If
they were in fact considered purely in this light, there would be much
to be said for placing the entire national documentary resources in one
or two, or at the most half-a-dozen, great regional centres. The
archivist, however, has not only the professional historian to consider,
but also the local student and antiquary and, still more important,
the actual owner of the documents."[16]

"Archives for all"![17] If Mr. Emmison's extravagant clarion is to
ring even moderately true it will require a policy of restraint and
genuine co-operation on the part of larger record offices. It will mean
resisting the temptation to swallow smaller offices; it will mean even
more than the munificent provision, advocated by Mr. Bond, of repair,
photographic, and cataloguing help. It may be easier to get increases
in staff and accommodation by pointing to mounting accessions in
one's own repository, but a maturer policy is the encouragement of the
growth of other offices. Mr. Bond speaks of "the network of county
offices"[18] covering almost the whole country, but we have seen that,
on the contrary, "local archives offices cover the whole country *except
the most important areas*".[19] It is impossible for the record office of a
large county to know intimately the archive situation in each of its
numerous boroughs. Because of this lack of local knowledge, and equally
because of the absence of disinterested advice and help, important
collections of urban and industrial records have been lost. It is the local
archivist, with local contacts, who can persuade a local owner to
deposit his records. The approach may have to be informal, unconventional. This point was made by the librarian of King's College

London, when replying to criticism of his policy of collecting military records: "it may be argued that such papers should have been directed into the Service museums or the Public Record Office, but there was evidence that many private owners were reluctant to hand their papers over to an official repository because of the sensitive nature of their content."[20]

The existence of a record office is the manifestation of a need fulfilled. No doubt the pattern of offices is not ideal, but "it is there". As Dr. Davis says, competition is not necessarily a bad thing. Where more than one repository exists in a locality it may mean that more provision is being made for archives than would have been possible under one roof. Of course, rivalry needs tempering with co-operation. If areas of interest can be defined so much the better (though gentlemen's agreements can break down when gentlemen leave); but *coups* need not bring bitterness if they are accepted as an expression of superior liveliness—and if archivists publish frequent lists to let students know what is where: "the essential thing is that . . . records shall be preserved and that their location shall be known."[21]

4. THE ARCHIVES PROFESSION

As MIGHT be expected in a "new" profession like archives, its members are rather self-conscious, constantly asking themselves and each other, what are archives?, what is an archivist?, what are an archivist's proper functions?, where is he going?, what is his status?, what is his image?, what sort of relations should he have with his employer, with his public, with historians?, how much of a historian is he himself?, how should he be trained?

This continual self-questioning is evident in numerous professional articles published during the last twenty-five years, but, as usual, the classic statement is by Jenkinson, this time in a lecture, "The English archivist: a new profession", which he delivered when inaugurating a diploma course in archive administration at University College London in October 1947.[1] The very title of Jenkinson's talk catches the excitement of archives in those early post-war days. There were, of course, "archivists" already in England, and had been for practically a century —most of them in the Public Record Office where, however, they preferred to be known as "assistant keepers of the records". Jenkinson referred to the profession as "new" presumably because of the more scientific approach to archive administration which he himself had helped to introduce during the previous generation, and also because of the growth of interest in local records before and after the Second World War. Along with this interest went an attempt to establish local record offices, and it was to help supply the consequent demand for qualified archivists that the London course in archive administration was established. More than an inaugural address, Jenkinson's speech was the consecration of a new order.

Only in the late nineteenth and early twentieth centuries, says Jenkinson, did "the wealth hidden in Local and Private Archives" become fully apparent. A "small body of enthusiasts" was already sufficiently alive to the dangers of dispersal and destruction to which they were exposed to be drafting proposals for protective legislation. The practical pioneer was G. H. Fowler in Bedfordshire who persuaded his county council to set up a modest but properly equipped record office, and a few other authorities followed his example. Thus a new point of view gradually emerged, that of "the person interested not so much in the contents of Archives and their exploitation as in the earlier and more instant problem of their preservation and in the technical processes of arrangement, care and conservation which follow". The profession of archivist "may be said to have arrived"; a course in archive administration was, therefore, necessary to create "a body of Men and Women particularly qualified" to serve it: "the question arises—What are we to teach them?"[2] Jenkinson's answer to this question occupied the rest of his lecture.

The archivist's most important qualification, says Jenkinson, is respect for archives as "Material Evidences"; all the evidential value of his documents, including, perhaps, some which is imperceptible, must be preserved intact while they are in his keeping: all subsequent operations—arrangement, repair, make-up, access—are subject to this "delicate task".[3] Next, since the archivist must be able to read and understand his documents, he will need a knowledge of palaeography, medieval Latin, Anglo-Norman, Middle-English, diplomatic, and, embracing all these, administrative history.[4] On the practical side, the archivist needs to be "something of a Jack-of-all-trades. He must be skilled in Sorting, Arranging and Listing and in the mechanical processes connected with them; neat-handed by nature or training; more than a little of a Bookbinder and Repairer, with a touch of some of the allied crafts; a good deal of a Photographer; something of a Fireman; and a little of an Architect, Builder, Chemist, Engineer, Entomologist and Mycologist."[5]

Jenkinson's audience must have smiled disbelievingly at this point; and it is unlikely that any candidate for an archives post has ever been asked to produce evidence of such qualifications. Admittedly, in some cases, Jenkinson does moderate his requirements: accepting, for instance, an ability "to talk and listen intelligently . . . find the appropriate books or make the necessary contacts"; but in others he insists on a knowledge of "the points at which Archive requirements may compel a modification in the ordinary methods of the professional

Scientist", and an ability to convey his needs to the professions concerned—architect, builder, engineer—who, in all probability, are as yet ignorant of them;[6] and in bookbinding, repair, and photography he must be a "fair executant" because he cannot direct craftsmen on a basis of theory alone.[7] In a similar vein, when Jenkinson comes to consider the archivist's public relations and asks himself, "What qualification, besides intelligence and good nature, must we require in him?", he gaily replies, "omniscience", because "the quantity of topics of human interest which may find illustration in Archives is unlimited".[8] In the fervour of sighting a new archives world Jenkinson endows his "modest"[19] local government officer with the universal qualities of renaissance man; at the end the vision is apocalyptic: the archivist "exists in order to make other people's work possible. . . . His Creed, the Sanctity of Evidence; his Task, the Conservation of every scrap of Evidence attaching to the Documents committed to his charge; his Aim, to provide, without prejudice or afterthought, for all who wish to know the Means of Knowledge . . . the good Archivist is perhaps the most selfless devotee of Truth the modern world produces."[10]

Mr. R. H. Ellis, then an assistant keeper at the Public Record Office, helped to design the course in archive administration which Jenkinson inaugurated in October 1948. In a paper, "The British archivist and his training", 1967, he examines the syllabus of twenty years earlier and ponders what sort of curriculum he would advocate now, in the light of the changes which have taken place in the archives world.[11] In 1947, he says, the "focal point of archive theory and practice" was still the Public Record Office. The new archives course was designed almost entirely by its officials, whose experience was largely derived from "the scholarly arts of palaeography, diplomatic, heraldry, sigillography, chronology [and medieval administrative history]". Politicly, Mr. Ellis disclaims any intention of criticizing a course which "was, and still is, a Course of great value and distinction"; his concern is for the future. The course, he says, "has proved sufficient for twenty years", but that is "no guarantee that it will remain so for twenty more". What developments have prompted this doubt? Firstly, the enormous increase in both quantity and variety of records; and secondly, a great upsurge, and an increasing specialization, in historical studies. What are the implications for archivists? In the first place, fewer and bigger record offices: the local archivist has become too accustomed to the small office in which he plays a jack-of-all-trades— "janitor, fatigue party, search room attendant, document repairer, editor, palaeographer, records manager, specialist adviser to world-renowned historians, and in addition . . . polished and worldly enough to meet upon their own level the nobility, gentry, and captains of industry whose records he hopes to preserve". In the second place, Mr. Ellis would like to see the appointment of non-graduate archivists ("a feature of archive work more familiar abroad than in this country") like the Executive Officers of the Public Record Office, to whom "medieval and Tudor records may be a closed book", but who "make themselves the leading authorities on modern departmental records".

Given this new situation, Mr. Ellis finds the traditional course in archive administration wanting: it is "scholarly and thorough", but it covers only "a steadily diminishing part of the constantly increasing archive field". He therefore sketches an alternative syllabus. Although training in the *care* of archives may, and indeed must, be common to all archivists, when we come to *knowledge of their contents* we must accept and provide for specialization on a scale not yet attempted. For this reason the syllabus should be in two parts, each carrying a diploma: firstly, a basic course in archive administration, without reference to any particular records; and secondly, a choice in the specialized field between a medieval or a modern course.

As we have seen, Mr. Ellis excuses himself from explicit criticism of the 1948 course in archive administration, because any judgement he might pass would be with "the superior wisdom of hindsight". In fact, however, the course of 1948 was criticized from the start by both archivists and students as being over-influenced by the Public Record Office. Moreover, Mr. Ellis (who confesses to traces in himself of the lay heresy that archives consist exclusively of "all those old parchments") over-emphasizes the novelty of the problem of modern records in suggesting that it was not pressing in 1947—a surprising claim in the light of Jenkinson's description of concern about departmental records at the Public Record Office in the nineteenth, let alone the twentieth, century. There is a similar belatedness in the detection of "new" varieties of records: those which land-owning families "now" generate—"not medieval deeds and seventeenth-century rentals, but tax and revenue forms, returns, correspondence with local authorities and Government departments, and highly complex accounting records"; and those which "a generation ago were barely visible upon the fringe of the archive spectrum"—business records, the records of scientific and technological research and development, and the records of institutions, political parties, trades unions, and local societies. In fact, the importance of most of these records was well recognized by 1947; the kinds of private document noticed by Mr. Ellis were already common enough among nineteenth-century estate papers; the Business Archives Council was established in 1934; and public libraries have collected the records of societies and institutions since the late nineteenth century. Modern institutions naturally produce modern records. May the absence of any attention to modern records from the archive administration syllabus of 1948 have been due not so much to a lack of awareness of the existence of record-producing institutions in the first half of the twentieth century as to an assumption that, since archivists are scholars, their essential concern is with "all those . . . parchments" of the past? If so, it seems likely that the need for a change in the training of archivists springs more from a reassessment of their function in the modern world than from any supposed alteration in the variety or even the quantity of the records they are called upon to deal with.

Along the lines suggested by Mr. Ellis, and evidently aimed at recasting the character of the archives profession, a fundamental alteration in the syllabus of the London diploma course in archive administration was decided on in 1968–9, to come into effect in 1970–1. Of nine examination papers, three only were now to be compulsory: record office management, records management, and preparation of finding aids. The remaining six options, to be selected from a total of fourteen, would allow a student to specialize in either medieval or modern archives; and Latin would no longer be compulsory, except for the medievalist. *Business archives*, listing the contents of the new syllabus,[12] claimed that the change would "make the Course much more relevant to the needs of modern records management, including business records, than it has been hitherto", and the Society of Archivists welcomed "this effective extension of the facilities for training archivists", including overseas archivists, "for whom the present course contains little of immediate relevance and application".[13]

The function of the archivist has been another fruitful subject of recent professional discussion, the field dividing between traditionalist preservers like Mr. F. Hull and exploiting modernists like Mr. E. K. Timings. Mr. Hull believes that "we must be ourselves".[14] Archivists are often called "jacks of all trades", but the dangerous corollary of that is "master of none". Archivists are archivists and not, "despite a proper interest in education", educationists, nor historians, "despite our proper interest in historical research". Mr. Timings, on the other hand, is an activist who sympathizes with the development of liberalizing attitudes at the Public Record Office towards "literary" inquirers— from the obstructive in the mid-nineteenth century, through the permissive in the early twentieth century, to the co-operative of today.[15] For Mr. Timings, as for members of the Committee on Departmental Records of 1959, "the making of adequate arrangements for the preservation of its records is an inescapable duty of the Government of a civilized state", not simply for administrative purposes, but also for "some vaguely envisaged 'cultural' end". He politely qualifies Jenkinson's axiom that an archivist's primary duty is the preservation of his records, and provision of access to them only a secondary one. He agrees that the archivist's first responsibility is the proper custody and arrangement of his records, but the archivist should not forget "his *purpose* is not some sort of archivistic ideal—but to make accessible the raw material of history to the enquirer". He even goes so far as to claim that "the primary duty of the archivist is to know about his archives" so that he can help his public. There is now a great call for the archivist's help from historians, from young students, both pre- and postgraduate, and even from intelligent schoolboys engaged on useful research. Where there is a demand the archivist has a duty to meet it: even schoolboys cannot be sent away with a dusty answer. Ivory tower archivists are really pure research workers and only archivists by the way. They are "still living in the nineteenth century and have quite missed the significance in the changing role of record offices". Mr. Timings quotes approvingly from T. R. Schellenberg: "In general, an archivist should help inquirers in every way possible . . . he should give his knowledge about records unstintingly, even at a sacrifice of his own research interests."[16] Against this unequivocal tenet of a modern pragmatist it is instructive to set the coy plea of a great purist of yesterday: it would be hard, says Jenkinson, if the archivist were denied the pleasure of following up interesting discoveries; "the appropriate motto seems to be . . . 'Thou shalt not muzzle the ox that treadeth out the corn': we must allow him (one has allowed oneself in one's time) a few mouthfuls; while reminding him that his primary duty is to tread; and hoping that he will not, in the process, tread on any, or many, toes."[17]

5. MODERN ARCHIVES AND BUSINESS ARCHIVES

Modern archives

Though young, the archives profession has its generations. Recently, a spry group of archivists has been examining the profession's image, with some distaste. "One of the most popular [fallacies] confuses our work with that of the archaeologist. . . . This is bad enough, but there is a worse fallacy that we are only concerned with *old* documents . . . [with] no interest in anything which happened in the present century."[1] The archivist's image is "probably that of a dusty greybeard poring over faded parchments in a dim back room, seeking obscure information for some obscure contribution to the local antiquarian society's *Proceedings*".[2] Rejuvenation, however, is to hand: in the sea of modern records which, since the Second World War, has threatened archivists with immersion, some reformers see the opportunity of a second baptism.

As society becomes more developed and more sophisticated its records increase in volume and complexity; increase in population leads to increase in governmental activity. Most governments of the world produce far too many records: in 1954 the English government had 600,000 linear feet; at the same date the U.S. Federal Government had about 23 million cubic feet, and has probably created more records than all other modern governments combined. As records increase, archives become more important, both as precedents for the administrator and sources for the historian. But archivists are bound to become involved in the problems of modern records for other reasons. On the one hand, administrators "are becoming aware of the efficiency and economy which flow from good records management"; on the other, "archival methods . . . are developed, to a large degree, in relation to current record management practices"; since the archivist must accept the arrangement given to the records by the administrator, he should try to "promote management practices that will effectively serve both the immediate needs of the government official and the ultimate needs of the private citizen".[3]

An apt English illustration of this dual involvement of the archivist in historical research and records management is provided by the case of the London County Council. According to Miss I. Darlington, the Council's archivist, stimulus for the establishment of an effective system of departmental records control came in 1946 when the Council's library, specializing in London history, topography, and local government, was reopened, and work was resumed on the *Survey of London*.[4] It soon became clear that, if the needs of historical research were to be adequately met, a more scientific approach to the management of the modern council records was also required. Nevertheless, the lead and the opportunity for reform in London records were provided by developments in central government, namely the Treasury enquiry of 1951, which revealed that government departments were holding 120 miles of material destined for permanent preservation, the appointment of the Grigg Committee in June 1952 "to review the arrangements for the preservation of the records of Government Departments . . . in the light of the rate at which they are accumulating", and the publication of the Committee's report in 1954.[5]

As we have seen, this problem of modern records was new in size only: the question of their disposal had exercised the minds of nineteenth-century record keepers. The Public Records Office Act of 1838 contained no provision for elimination, yet before the Office was built the question of overcrowding from "unnecessary survivals" was being discussed.[6] However, the matter was not taken up seriously until 1875 when the Deputy Keeper proposed a committee "to consider what portions might be destroyed, without detriment to the public service, to individual rights, or historical investigations", and the Public Records Office Act of 1877 was the first measure to empower the Master of the Rolls to make rules for the destruction of "documents of not sufficient public value". The fact that the Grigg investigation was necessary showed how unsuccessful these nineteenth-century measures were. They were inadequate on two grounds. The system of preservation and destruction evolved after 1877 was one of listing, or "scheduling" as it was called. The principle was to "relieve the Public Record Office from the encumbrance of useless matter", while taking care to exclude from the schedules any document which could "reasonably be considered of legal, historical, genealogical or antiquarian use or interest, or which give any important information not to be obtained elsewhere". In 1910 the Deputy Keeper told the Royal Commission on Public Records that the effect of the system had been not only to stop the Public Record Office from being encumbered with valueless documents, but to substitute in government offices "destruction and preservation of documents according to well considered and approved principles" for arbitrary and inexpert destruction. But, says Jenkinson (and his comment is revealing on more than one score), "this perhaps rather masks a difficulty which will always confront those responsible for a policy of destruction—that of predicting the needs of the future . . . in a large majority of cases records are not ultimately used for the purposes for which they were originally drawn up and preserved . . . many of those now most highly prized have survived only by accident —because no system of destruction was in force at the time they were put away".

The scheduling system proved inappropriate also as a means of sorting departmental records for transfer to the Public Record Office. The reason was the invention of the subject file. Old classes based on form—in-letters, out-letters, minutes, accounts, etc.—were replaced by the dossier system, which arranged by subject, and produced innumerable files containing every kind of document, important and unimportant, and of every form. Weeding thus became a far more responsible job than had been envisaged by the Master of the Rolls' Rules. The elimination procedure evolved from 1877 onwards was "perfectly satisfactory"[7] when applied to documents capable of being listed individually or by entire classes. But now, strictly, every paper in a subject file ought to be scrutinized by an experienced officer, and this was something the Public Record Office could not do. The result was to throw "back on Departments a greater share in the decision as to what shall be kept than was contemplated in the Master of the Rolls' Rules";[8] or, more bluntly, "the actual operation of selection has hitherto had to be left entirely to Departmental officials".[9]

Weeding practice among departments varied between extremes of mercilessness and ultra-caution. According to Mr. J. H. Collingridge, however, it would be a mistake to believe that all departments had great hoards of documents, unreviewed for many years (although one ministry did have arrears of forty years' standing).[10] The main troubles were unsystematic reviewing, which resulted from overflowing records stores or departmental removals, and reviewing which concentrated on series which were most easily weeded. On the whole, most departments made "very creditable efforts": generally they kept too much rather than too little. Nevertheless, the operation could be very rough and ready. Mr. Collingridge once found a boilerman weeding legal documents in a departmental records store; on being asked how he was going about it, he replied, "The parchments we keep, and the paper we throw away."[11]

The Grigg Report solved the difficulties of file-weeding and historical assessment by killing two birds with a double-headed sledgehammer; saying, in effect, get rid of all papers of short-term value in as summary a way as possible, and make the file the unit of review. The over-riding aim was to narrow to the utmost the field to which a historical criterion of preservation would need to be applied. This could be achieved by a double review. The first should take place not more than five years after papers had passed out of active use; it should take only administrative usefulness into account, in the belief that any papers which a department can dispense with at so early a date can be safely assumed to have no usefulness for research either. Papers not destroyed at this review should be subjected to a second and final review when about twenty-five years old, but this time usefulness for research as well as the department's own purposes should be considered. The first review would be entirely the responsibility of a record officer within each department; the second would be the joint responsibility of the departmental record officer and an inspecting officer from the Public Record Office.

The Report got over the difficulty of weeding subject files by recommending the use of titles which would give a description of their contents sufficiently accurate to make examination of individual documents unnecessary. However, Mr. Collingridge found that this was not always possible, and so it seems as though stripping files of ephemeral papers, which the Grigg Committee thought uneconomic except in the case of files selected for preservation, must continue in some departments.[12]

The proposals of the Grigg Report were embodied in the Public Records Act, 1958. Under the Act primary responsibility for selection rests with the departments; general control—i.e. co-ordination and supervision—is vested in the Public Record Office as guardians of the interests of research. This duty of departments to make proper provision for selection and preservation is now, under the Act, mandatory, and not permissive as under the provisions of the old legislation. This was the main reason why it was necessary for the Public Record Office to sever its old association with the Master of the Rolls and be placed under a minister of the Crown.[13]

Little information is available in print about the extent to which local authorities generally have concerned themselves with their authorities' modern records. A county archivist is likely to take good care, of course, of the records of the Clerk of the Council's department, to which he belongs, but how systematically he has investigated the records of other departments will depend on local circumstances, particularly the strength and status of his records staff. According to Mr. F. Hull, "the County Archivist still holds an anomalous position as regards modern administrative records. In relatively few instances has he any control over records of departments other than the Clerk's Office, though his advice may be sought." In Mr. Collingridge's opinion, many of the Grigg recommendations (which, in the case of central government records, have proved "workable and effective") can be "adapted to the conditions found in the offices of local authorities, nationalised industries and other non-Government bodies"; indeed, the opportunity of the local archivist to use the Grigg principles successfully is more favourable than that of the government archivist whose field of operation is so wide.[14] The Grigg Report made an immediate impact on a few archivists who were already heavily engaged in modern records management, and their comments have appeared in a number of professional articles. Thus, Mr. Hull thinks the Report can be related to local government, but suspects that some of its features will startle local archivists: notably, the acceptance of destruction on a basis of files and not of individual papers; the acceptance of departmental administrative requirements as a criterion which would substantially cover the much more nebulous historical criterion; and the acceptance that "some material will undoubtedly be destroyed which the historian of the future would wish to have preserved". Mr. Hull believes that these principles of the Report are expedient in view of the growth of modern records, but admits that they mean a re-orientation of outlook in archivists—the acceptance of the need for destruction, and of criteria which would have been unacceptable to many archivists twenty years ago.

The local authority which probably made the most thoroughgoing provision for its modern records was the former London County Council, perhaps because it was, from the first, almost entirely an urban area and so was early confronted with a mass of detailed records.[15] Gradually, the Clerk of the Council acquired explicit control over the records of other departments, and record assistants who were respon-sible to the Clerk took charge of departmental record rooms. Yet, although the machinery was good and flexible, the results were "largely negative":[16] it was clearly an early attempt at modern records control which lacked the application, the drive, and the great attention to detail, which later experience has shown to be necessary on the part of the archivist. The interdepartmental committee set up by the Council in March 1955 revealed great variation in standards of records manage-ment. Many departments were retaining records long after they were needed for current purposes. In other cases, there had been indiscrimi-nate destruction of whole groups in an attempt to clear storage space in a hurry. Moreover, the introduction of new office methods and mech-anical equipment, and the general deterioration in the quality of paper, inks, and drawing office materials had revolutionized the formation of departmental records: files of papers, card indexes, loose-leaf sheafs, punched cards, ribbon wage slips, etc., were now the rule, in place of the strongly bound volumes of a generation or so ago, and these flimsy modern records were more vulnerable both to purges and to "new brooms".

The recommendations of the interdepartmental committee—a senior administrative officer in each department to supervise the re-cords; routine work done by trained records assistants; each depart-ment to draw up a scheme for the regular disposal of its records; records destined for permanent preservation to be transferred to the central record room when no longer required for current use—were successful and produced a large amount of clearance, weeding, destruction, and transfer to the central record room. The archivist, Miss Darlington, drew several important morals from her experience. One was that a scheme of records disposal drawn up for a particular department must be based on a detailed analysis of the actual records being produced in that department; schedules couched in general terms are no substitute.[17] But the most important factor in the situation is the records staff:

> The archivist and/or record keeper must have training, knowledge and experience. He must be prepared to keep abreast of the administrative developments of his own authority as well as of the trends of historical scholarship and of modern archive technique. He must be willing to advise on the preparation of a long-term programme of records disposal and on day-to-day problems and be able to put his point of view to hard-pressed and hard-headed administrative and executive officers. In addition, there must be a sufficient strength of subordinate records staff to see that the agreed policy is, in fact, carried out. Good records management like liberty can only be secured by eternal vigilance.[18]

Articles written by archivists from repositories with a tradition of modern records preservation have not exhausted the interest of the subject for, particularly, a group of younger archivists. A symposium on records management, arranged by this group, was held at Cambridge in January 1968.[19] By temperament, perhaps, and certainly by experience, these archivists are impatient of the traditional, almost exclusive concern with the archives of the distant past and near-contempt for the records of the present. But their proposals extend beyond the mere addition of modern records to the archivist's repertoire: for them, modern records mean the disappearance of the old-style antiquarian archivist, and his replacement by a new-style archivist-records manager. The classical activities of an archivist—care of older archives, publication of historical research—are, no doubt, part of our duties, says one,[20] but they are only a part. The archivist's other duties are assistance in managing his authority's modern archives, and advice to others on record problems. This sounds like a call for a return to the grass roots of archives management in this country, for archivists often began as records clerks and only became archivists with the spread of historical and educational interest in local records.

The techniques in which most archivists have been trained, continues Mr. Welch, can be applied to modern files just as easily as to medieval rolls; moreover, they are "the only people with the necessary skills and knowledge to do this". In fact, in looking after modern records, the archivist has advantages denied him as a keeper of old archives: "we have no control over what was destroyed in the past; we can and must control what is destroyed in the future". The archivist can control archives-in-the-making by advising on materials, storage, elimination. If he shirks this responsibility he will reap the consequences in two few records, or in too many produced in unsuitable materials. A further danger awaits archivists if they fail to take action now: "other professions are ready to rush in where we fear to tread".[21] Prominent among these rivals, Mr. Welch sees "some librarians" who already consider themselves well qualified to advise on records management: "Universal Decimal Classification and subject classification now threaten the modern archives as they once threatened the ancient". A second profession endangering the archivist's right to control modern records is that of "efficiency experts"; Mr. Welch sees them as having "a more legitimate interest in the field of records management [than librarians] but they propose systems which will ensure that any modern Domesday Book is destroyed long before it reaches the archivist".

Another archivist who senses a threat from record managers is Mr. Michael Cook, whose article, "Regional archives offices: some reflections", October 1967,[22] deals not, as one might at first think, with the hoary controversy about local versus regional record offices, but with a deeper, more interesting consideration of the contemporary archives scene. Mr. Cook believes that the first phase of archives work in this country—loving concern with old documents—is now over. His conception of new functions for record offices springs from his feeling for the overwhelming importance of modern records. The present-day archives profession has failed to fulfil expectations—for instance, in the field of business records—because it has "a very restricted view of its functions . . . and of their value to society". There are "vast areas of public life in Britain" where no archive work is done, namely "the great industrial and urban areas. It is almost true to say that organised local archives offices cover the whole country *except* the most important areas. And yet these are also the areas which could most afford archival services, and which indeed stand to gain most from having them."[23] Mr. Cook's radical solution is a regional archives office, with a "large staff of highly professional people", providing a wide range of services.

It would have at least seven specialist departments: records management, archival field work, search-room control, indexing and finding aids, repair and preservation, publications, and education; each specialist officer would control resources far greater than the majority of present-day archivists-in-charge. It is not surprising that of all Mr. Cook's departments easily the most important and revolutionary in conception is the one concerned with records management. In a fully developed region the records management officer would control a very large network of organizations, which ultimately would provide almost the whole intake of the archives office.

These regional offices would be records centres maintained either by individual, or jointly by several, local authorities. Business firms could maintain similar centres, or they might take advantage of a "commercial records management service" provided by the local authority centres. The records management officer would organize the establishment of these centres, supervise the compilation of destruction schedules, and advise the constituent authorities as a consultant. Mr. Cook sees one other department as of outstanding importance, and, significantly, it is again connected with modern records: the department devoted to technical finding aids. It is essential, says Mr. Cook, that the archivist of today make use of new technical and scientific developments. "An archives or records office which cannot employ them . . . will cease to be used. Some other body with a parallel function will emerge—a 'documentation centre' perhaps—probably with lower academic standards—and archives will become static collections of 'historical' material."[24]

Are these proposals practical possibilities? Well, says Mr. Cook, the growth in the size and complexity of modern administrative and business records has "spontaneously generated thought on the problem of records. This can very clearly be seen in the U.S.A., where commercial records consultants are now accepted as part of the group of management experts required by a large organization."[25] But, also in the U.S.A., the danger can be seen of allowing public needs to dictate methods: "what we must strive to avoid is the situation where records are controlled by commercial records managers, with archivists as extras out on the fringe. Records managers may have no adequate training or background to deal with archival problems."[26] Mr. Cook finally considers the financial aspect of his proposals. He submits that many organisations hide their records expenditure under a general budget for buildings, office equipment, and clerical staff. Only in the largest institutions (and he instances Pilkington Brothers Ltd.) has expenditure on records come out into the open. He decides that the vast majority of local authorities in England and Wales pay more in misuse of office staff, space, and equipment than they would if they maintained a professionally controlled records service. A public service records centre is, therefore, a financially viable project.

Confrontation with modern records has thus had a deep and liberating effect on at least some English archivists. Implicit in their proposals is a wish for a fundamental change in the character of the archives profession: "with the increase in staff and work the professional archivist will need training in management, because the record office will then be part of the administrative machinery, and not a non-essential annexe to be placed below libraries and museums in the local government hierarchy."[27] In other words, since it is unlikely that a specialized cultural service like historical archives will ever take precedence in the eyes of local authorities over larger and better established institutions such as libraries and museums, why not cut the Gordian knot by making the archives service something quite different: an intrinsic, indispensable part of modern administration and modern business techniques?[28]

Such a transformation would mean the end of the traditional archivist—the man or woman with, in the main, a reflective, historical cast of mind, and, at the extreme, an antiquarian, research-worker's approach to archives. But is not, in fact, the most satisfactory archivist one who combines scholarship with administrative ability; who can judiciously mix the attraction of personal research with a liking for people and a wish to help them? Of course, archivists should not be interested simply in old records of immediate historical interest. By accepted definition, archivists are concerned with the preservation of records of administration: in Jenkinson's classic definition of archives, as Mr. Welch points out, "there is no mention of dates or antiquity, but an awareness of the archives of the present and the future".[29] Jenkinson had scholarly, historical, antiquarian interests, but his *Manual* shows him very much alive to the problems of archives as physical objects, and not merely as research material. For instance, as Mr. Collingridge says,[30] he gave much thought to the mechanics of record appraisal: he promoted the "limbo" scheme, established a Modern Departmental Records section of the Public Record Office, and even (unsuccessfully) advocated a system of segregating ephemeral papers within files so as to facilitate early elimination.

Mr. Welch's comments about the relative status of archivists prompts one to wonder to what extent, despite the suggestion that "the pressures of modern society . . . are changing the character of the work we do",[31] cause and effect are not the other way round; how far, that is, desire for a change of status sees in the challenge of modern records the means of effecting it. How far it is possible to jack up the image of the archives profession is difficult to say. Its role is always bound to be a minor one. To the extent that its desire to alter its image is simply due to a wish to be rated above libraries and museums it is likely to fail; but in so far as it takes a natural part in the enlargement of local government it may succeed. Even so, the prospect of any profound change in the character of the archives profession is not necessarily a happy one: it would be a pity to cast away its educational role in pursuit of administrative prestige.

Modern records are influencing archivists increasingly towards an interest in records management as distinct from archives management. In T. R. Schellenberg's words in *Modern Archives* (one-third of which is devoted to records management) discussion of the management of current records is necessary because "public records are the grist of the archivist's mill. The quality of this grist is determined by the way records are produced and maintained while in current use, and by the way records are disposed of."[32]

This interest in records management is evident, for instance, in an article by Miss I. Darlington, "The weeding and disposal of files", October 1955.[33] Miss Darlington's reproduction of a memorandum circulated to all departments of the London County Council containing the main *desiderata* in any scheme for the formation, weeding, and disposal of office files is an excellent example of an archivist so effectively involved in the practical problems of modern records that she is able to offer acceptable advice on their formation.

It is clear that the tranquillity of archives thought in this country has been ruffled by the urgent difficulties of modern records: in the words of the chairman of the Cambridge symposium of January 1968, "there was much common feeling that the pressures of modern society were making these matters of greater importance, and changing the character of the work we do".[34] The agitation has been stimulated by ideas flowing in from countries more whole-heartedly concerned with modern records, notably the U.S.A., Australia, Canada, Rhodesia, and other African countries. What their ultimate effect in this country will be is not yet clear. At the moment Mr. Cook's proposals have an air of fantasy, but may they appear more realistic following a reorganization of English local government into larger units? The Cambridge symposium thought that, despite a number of attempts to apply the principles of the Grigg Report to local record offices, it was "noteworthy that after a year or two these attempts tailed off".[35] This seems to ignore, for instance, the apparently successful application in London described by Miss Darlington, but no doubt there is something in the symposium's contention that size is an important factor: "a basic premise of the Grigg system is that the originating departments are big enough and complex enough to develop a sophisticated records management function, capable of carrying out a sensible selection policy. These conditions may perhaps be found in central government, but they do not exist elsewhere."[36] Increase in the size of local government units would perhaps remove this difficulty.

An aspect of modern archives management which is not yet clear is the extent to which computer-produced records will replace traditional style documents. They are already well established in treasurers' departments, but how far will they spread elsewhere in local government? Little has been written on the subject in the professional archives press, presumably because the problem has so far been little encountered. At the moment, "computer techniques can be used for financial accounting, such as the preparation of staffs' pay, the writing of cheques and the keeping of accounts; for statistical purposes, such as the splitting of payments into budget heads, and costing by, for example, different types of houses or trades; and for technical purposes, such as the solving of arithmetical equations". But in the future the computer may be "used in local government administration for the planning of vehicle routes, and in the preparation of records of teachers' service".

However, at present, the main line of development is "towards the integration of various stages of work—in bringing together processes heretofore done by separate sections".[37]

So far, it seems unlikely that executive departments using computers have much considered "the preservation on tape of material of historical or sociological importance . . . as a long-term archive problem as distinct from an administrative one".[38] The trouble for the archivist is that "every time a tape is used it creates another tape, so that every time a record of payments is brought up-to-date the previous one becomes valueless".[39] "In the course of business these records are continually updated, and past transactions are lost when further entries are made."[40] Thus in the normal course of computer accounting original records are not kept unaltered. Computer fraud (i.e. the illicit alteration of a computer's working instructions without fear of identification) is possible and has already occurred. From a business point of view "there should be stringent rules on the documentation . . . of computer programmes".[41] It is interesting to learn that, in the meanwhile, "most companies are still keeping many of their old clerical records in parallel with computer files", but "clearly this cannot continue".[42] The archivist may have to make do with such documentation plus the final tape. In special cases he may be able to ensure the retention of earlier unaltered tapes, though even here, because of "the continuous introduction of new types of computers" it will be "essential to reproduce exact copies of tapes for use on current equipment".[43] There is every indication, thinks the editor of *Archives*, "that before very long computer record-keeping will make obsolete some of the time-hallowed classes of accounting records, and probably others. Business and economic historians will need to learn, as auditors have already had to do, how to cope with magnetic tapes and what are the limitations of these as records."[44]

In the meantime, however, there is still plenty of scope for the enterprising archivist among modern records of more traditional appearance: there are "vast areas of public life in Britain where no archive work" is being done: "the great industrial and urban areas . . .".[45] It is certainly true that, because of the way local archives administration has grown up in this country, urban areas have been neglected. Because of the exclusion of county boroughs from the administrative competence of county councils, county record offices have become disproportionately identified with rural life: their typical archives come from quarter sessions, landed estates, and rural parishes. Only in very recent years have county record offices attempted in any systematic way to broaden their repertoire to include industrial and business records, and even now they are hampered by local authority boundaries. The natural collecting agency in a borough is a borough record office, but such offices are still rare; most archivists employed by urban authorities are attached to libraries. In default of a borough record office a library is the most relevant body to collect modern business and local authority records (even though this function has not always been adequately performed in the past—for instance, by the archivist of a great city library who meticulously catalogued medieval deeds while enormous oceans of modern records, totally unexplored, serenely swelled outside his particularizing walls). During the last decade or two the situation has slightly improved, but on the whole the response has been ludicrously inappropriate to the challenge; and, unfortunately, county record offices, while not themselves in an effective position to collect modern records in urban areas, have been loath, or unable, to help libraries do so.

Business Archives

The problems of business archives, though naturally involved with those of modern archives, have a fascination of their own. Business records are the most difficult to collect, and so are richest in anecdote. An archivist once tried to persuade a senior executive in a great tobacco company of the importance of his firm's records. "We are not interested in what happened five years ago, even what happened last year", said the executive. "We are interested in what is happening this year and what will happen next year." Had he ever considered having the history of the firm written, if only for commercial reasons? Diffidently but deftly he opened a drawer in his desk and drew out a number of old pipes and a bundle of newspaper cuttings. "Yes," he said, "I'm thinking of doing it myself. Perhaps you'd like to look at my materials." In another case the managing director of a medium-size engineering firm readily agreed to hand over all his company's records. The company secretary, however, had other ideas: the archivist came away with order books, engineering drawings, and patents; but the hard core of accounts was missing. Accounts are often the sticking point: a small lace-machinery firm, *in process of liquidation*, offered a long series of letter books, but refused the account books, because "they might contain entries of bad debts of firms still in existence, contracted when the lace trade was bad". Thus the archivist can finish up with collections of peripheral miscellanea, lacking the heart of the matter which gives them meaning.

The response of the business man to the archivist is frequently compounded of a total misconception of what records are, an incredulity that they can have any significance compared with the glossy publicity which has been compiled without reference to them, and suspicion of the archivist's intentions. A letter out of the blue soliciting the deposit of records is of little avail in most contexts, and least of all in the case of business records. The archivist must have personal contacts. To create these takes time, but he may be lucky. On one occasion a chartered accountant rang to ask if the records of a firm whose liquidation he was superintending were of any monetary value. Although the archivist said no he still got the records, and, having made an interested friend of the accountant, the records also of other liquidated companies; they were good to have, though no doubt they painted a rather gloomy picture of English commerce. As well as personal contact, the archivist should have as much information as possible about the history of the firm he is approaching. Although most companies are not interested in academic economic history they respond sympathetically to factual details about their past. One institution which has adopted this method with some success is Hull University, where a research worker in the Economic History Department has produced potted histories of a good many Hull firms and then approached them about their records, subsequently holding an exhibition of some of them.

Business records are a particularly colourful illustration of the central ambiguity in the traditional English concept of archives. Jenkinson's definition of archives accepts administrative convenience as the only determinant of their existence; the historian has no say in the matter. This definition is perfectly valid from the point-of-view of the administration which produced them. Two considerations, however, make it of little general value. One is that, given time, an administration makes itself independent of its records. The second is the importance of archives for the historian—an importance which increases as their significance for their creator declines. Jenkinson himself admitted that, ultimately, archives are used for purposes quite other than those for which they were produced. And yet it is an axiom still accepted (confidently by the Grigg committee, but reluctantly by some archivists) that administrative convenience subsumes the historical criterion. There does not seem to be any theoretical reason why this should be so, and business methods demonstrate that in practice it is palpably not so. It is quite clear that, without the intervention of a historically minded archivist, the survival of records is dictated by the business's response to bulk rather than to careful consideration of the relative administrative value of particular records. This is true even of the most efficient, record-conscious organization. The firm which claims to destroy 96% of the records it produces is prouder of that 96% than of the 4% which it preserves. Who can say that none of the 96% was of historical interest? And how long will the 4% be sacrosanct? Will the time not come when, as far as administrative purposes are concerned, that too could go? If it is retained, will it not be for "extrinsic", i.e. historical (or sentimental) reasons. Many businesses demonstrate that they can exist without the long-term preservation of any records at all. The historian may have to be glad to settle for 4%.

It has been argued that, although all business records before, say, 1900 should be preserved, modern records are of little interest when so many commercial and financial statistics are published. Business history, however, surely consists of more than simply national figures and trends. The historian needs to see how particular firms fit into the general picture; he also needs to fill out the statistical skeleton with the flesh and blood of actual human beings—with their motives, their decisions, their dealings with each other. Even if lavish statistics existed for eighteenth-century commerce one would not expect economic historians to decline the use of correspondence and accounts of individual eighteenth-century entrepreneurs. Because of the difficulty of collecting business records an archivist does not usually decline any that are offered. If it were possible to collect all the business records in a great city, then, of course, he would have to select—say, a small, a medium, and a large example of each type of firm. If he received enormous deposits of business records he would also have to consider weeding; but, as things are, time normally takes precedence over space, and the archivist gratefully accepts the records he is given.

6. ARCHIVES IN LIBRARIES

AN ARCHIVIST was once appointed to a library whose considerable manuscript collections had previously been tended by librarians. He found the underside of the public counter solid with parcels of documents stuffed away unopened and unloved. Loose manuscripts which *had* been dealt with were either bound into volumes or, more recently, inserted into folders and then into boxes which stood vertically on the strongroom shelves. In fact, the library had no archive collections in the style familiar to a record office: no original bundles of documents, no boxes whose contents may look untidy but which, even when sorted, preserve a precious, organic archival order. Clearly, the library had attempted to make its archives look as comfortably like books as possible; those which did not merit, or could not easily be given, this expensive treatment, were best put out of sight. For his part, too, the archivist felt uncomfortable in the presence of documents in this unfamiliar guise: he was tempted to strip them of their artificial finery, and make honest archives of them once again. But the moral lay deeper. What was important was not so much the treatment meted out to the archives which the library already had, as the crippling effect which this attitude towards archives had on its policy of collection. The library's real understanding was of books, at best of literary manuscripts; archives lay outside its traditional cognizance. Therefore archives were not sought, merely received. The enormous efforts needed to identify, never mind acquire, the huge masses of records of a great city were not even appreciated, let alone undertaken.

And yet, in the words of Jenkinson, "It would be difficult to exaggerate the debt which the cause of Records Preservation owes to the Librarians".[1] In this country, in contrast to the Continent, local records have remained outside central control; hence the lack of systematic organization in the past, and the large number of local repositories deplored by many archivists today. For three centuries after the earliest, abortive, attempt by the Commons to establish county record repositories in 1547, nothing particular was done about local records: the great parliamentary record inquiries of the eighteenth and early nineteenth centuries were preoccupied with central government. This was the position in 1850 when William Ewart introduced the first Public Libraries Bill and, in his speech, referred to the needs of local history. Libraries established under the Public Libraries Act of 1850 quickly began "local collections"—anything relating to their locality, including books, illustrations, maps, pamphlets, and manuscripts. By 1927 a government inquiry found that 247 public libraries had such collections, with notable ones at Birmingham, Liverpool, and Manchester.

In 1908 Liverpool Public Library published a catalogue of its local collection, *Liverpool Prints and Documents*,[2] which in many ways, and especially for its time, was a considerable piece of work: it got quickly into print a great deal of detailed information, and the inquirer, though very inadequately served by a two-page "subject index", could usually find what he wanted. Unfortunately, while distinguishing between "literary" and "pictorial" records, the catalogue did not separate primary from secondary material, and so, in the section "History and materials for history", original documents were mixed up in one alphabetical sequence with printed books and articles. However, one's main criticism would be, not of what was done, but of what, as a result of the failure to distinguish between the important and the less important, was left undone. All energies were devoted to painstaking, individual, undiscriminating cataloguing, one piece of information as significant as another; the approach was to the general and the antiquarian inquirer, not to the research worker. Meanwhile, in cellars completely outside the purview of the catalogue, the rich deposits of Liverpool's civic and commercial records vegetated, and sometimes decayed: there was no understanding of the need for systematic, comprehensive collection of large accumulations of archives.

The climate which would eventually foster this understanding was, in fact, being generated elsewhere. In 1869 the Historical Manuscripts Commission was appointed to inquire into unpublished manuscripts in private possession and in the hands of institutions, and began publication of reports on hundreds of collections of local archives. Another ominous cloud, no bigger than a man's fist, appeared on the horizon in 1888: county councils were established, assumed custody of quarter sessions records, and, in a number of cases, began to take an interest in their arrangement and publication. Yet it remains true to say that, despite all the deficiencies of the old-style public libraries, and however miscellaneous and haphazardly acquired their local collections were, in the late nineteenth and early twentieth centuries, along with a few local societies, they were almost the only bodies actively engaged in preserving local historical documents.

In 1900 a committee was appointed by the Treasury "to enquire and report as to any arrangements in operation for the collection, custody, indexing and calendaring of local records, and as to any further measures which it might be advisable to take for this purpose".[3] The Library Association adopted a resolution "that the municipal public library authorities are the natural and best custodians of local records", and pressed this view on the Treasury committee. In its report of 1902, however, the committee said quite firmly "we do not recommend that local libraries should, as a rule, be used as depositories of records".[4] Their reasons were that libraries were not always fire-proof, that accommodation was often limited, and that the scope of a public library differed from that of a record office. The committee was in favour of establishing local record offices for civil records in county towns and in boroughs, and for ecclesiastical records at the cathedral town in each diocese. In fact, no legislation followed the report of 1902, nor that of the Records Commission of 1910. The *status quo* remained: public libraries were not deprived of the documents they had acquired, but neither were they specifically authorized to continue collecting. A step towards meeting the criticism that librarians were unqualified to deal with archives was taken in 1919 when the newly founded School of Librarianship at London University included a course of palaeography and archives in its syllabus. Secondly, from 1928, the examinations for the fellowship of the Library Association included palaeography and archive administration as an optional subject.

In 1924 the Law of Property (Amendment) Act abolished copyhold tenure. Manorial court rolls and title deeds to copyhold land thus ceased to have legal and practical use. So that these records should not be destroyed, the Act placed all manorial records under the charge of the

Master of the Rolls; he could direct that any documents not being properly cared for "be transferred to the Public Record Office, or to any public library, or museum or historical or antiquarian society, which may be willing to receive the same".[5]

This period saw also the beginning of county record offices, starting with Bedfordshire in 1923. Although public libraries, too, were readily recognized as manorial repositories, county record offices had an additional *raison d'être* in the preservation of their official records. The hope of systematically preserving all local records in a network of official local repositories, first envisaged in 1547, now began to materialize. In 1932, with the support of the Public Record Office, the British Records Association was formed under the presidency of the Master of the Rolls, one of its aims being to help the transfer of local historical records from private to public custody. Approval of a repository by the Master of the Rolls for the reception of manorial records encouraged it to collect all kinds of records within its reach. County record offices, with influence over specific geographical areas, and run by officers whose sole professional concern was with original historical records, would clearly have the edge over municipal public libraries, the geographical range of whose interests was less precisely expressed, and whose interest in archives was secondary. To hold their own public libraries needed to be especially active and perceptive.

Such was the position before the Second World War: on the one hand, county record offices gradually increasing in number, and an archives profession growing in self-awareness; on the other, public libraries somewhat on the defensive, with a long and honourable, but largely antiquarian tradition of sporadic records acquisition, staffs usually unqualified in archives, and little appreciation of the need for systematic and dynamic records collection. But new developments in archives after the war—a now rapid increase in the number of county record offices, the establishment of the National Register of Archives in 1945, the formation of the Society of Local Archivists in 1946, above all the explosion in accessibility of local records and an enhanced awareness of the dangers they were exposed to—began to affect public libraries. Their rising self-confidence was most dramatically evident in the counter-attack mounted on their behalf by J. L. Hobbs, whose *Libraries and the Materials of Local History* appeared in 1948, and by Philip Hepworth, under whose stimulus, in February 1951, the Library Association's Standing Committee on Archives sent out a questionnaire designed to secure up-to-date information about archive-keeping in libraries.[6] One hundred and forty-eight of the 626 libraries circularized replied that they collected archives. At about the same date (1953) *Local Records* contrasted the position before the war when, among public libraries, only Birmingham, Exeter, Leeds, Norwich, and Sheffield employed archivists, with that in 1951 when eighteen public libraries employed "special staff". However, during the same interval, the number of county councils in England and Wales which supported record offices had grown from thirteen to forty-six.[7]

In 1961 the Library Association conducted a second and fuller survey.[8] Of the 673 libraries circularized 214 reported that they collected manuscripts; of these, 108 had less than 1000 manuscripts, fifty-seven had between 1000 and 10,000, twenty-nine had 10,000–75,000, and twenty had more than 75,000. Once again, it is interesting to compare the progress of libraries with that of other repositories. In 1962, of 114 repositories reporting accessions of archives that year to the Historical Manuscripts Commission, forty were libraries; but in the first year that such statistics were published, 1930, there were twenty-one libraries among the twenty-seven institutions reporting.

When looking at the details of the 1961 survey it is perhaps as well to bear in mind two traditions of manuscript counting. In libraries in the past most manuscripts have been volumes. The bulk of a county record office's holdings, however, consist of separate documents. How can volumes and single items be meaningfully included in one total? In comparisons of manuscript holdings libraries were bound in the past to be at a disadvantage; but as soon as they begin to acquire large collections of loose papers, their numbers immediately look more respectable.

The survey of 1961 was not comprehensive because a number of libraries did not answer the questionnaire. Of the four national libraries only Wales replied; several university libraries with important collections—the Bodleian, Glasgow, Manchester, and Trinity College Dublin—did not reply; and "with one or two outstanding exceptions, libraries of learned societies, country houses, businesses, cathedrals, churches, schools and colleges were not reached by this survey".[9]

The best response was naturally from public libraries. Of municipal libraries, ten reported holding more than 75,000 manuscripts: Birmingham, Exeter, Gloucester, Leeds, Lichfield, Liverpool, Norwich, Plymouth, Sheffield, and Westminster. Eighteen held 10,000–75,000, and forty-five held 1000–10,000. Five university libraries reported more than 75,000: Bangor, Cambridge, Keele, Nottingham, and University College London; six reported 10,000–75,000: Aberdeen, Bristol, Edinburgh, Liverpool, London School of Economics, and St. Andrews. Miscellaneous libraries not fitting into any of these groups included three holding more than 75,000 manuscripts: Royal Botanical Gardens at Kew, the Wellcome Historical Medical Library, and the John Rylands Library. Other large collections were at Chetham's Library, the Royal Society of Arts, Exeter Cathedral, and H.M. Customs.

From a comparison of the results of the 1951 and 1961 surveys Mr. Hepworth concluded that "the tremendous growth of interest in local history has helped considerably to strengthen the collections of manuscripts in local public and university libraries".[10] Twenty-eight libraries reported increased collections in 1961 compared with 1951; forty-nine libraries, compared with twenty-eight reported collections of over 10,000 documents. Very large increases in deposits were reported by Hammersmith, Leeds, Liverpool, Norwich, Plymouth, Redditch, and York public libraries, and by Aberdeen, Keele, Liverpool, Nottingham, and St. Andrews university libraries. On the other hand, it is evident that, presumably as a result of the competition from county record offices, some libraries had fallen away: twenty-four had smaller collections in 1961 than in 1951; and some municipal libraries, such as Ipswich, Truro, and Winchester, and some county libraries, for instance, East Riding, Herefordshire, and Hertfordshire, had practically ceased to house manuscripts.

There can be no doubt that, as Mr. Hepworth says, the rise of the county record office stimulated either the formation, or the rejuvenation, of archive repositories in public and university libraries; in one case the chain reaction extended to the creation of a county record office in response to renewed library activity in its area. A second point is that only when a library can get a foot in one of the big archive fields is it able to register dramatic growth. Thus, at Sheffield City Library, although, in the words of the foreword to the *Guide to the Manuscript*

Collections (1956), "when the present Central Library was built in 1934, adequate accommodation was provided for the preservation of manuscripts according to accepted principles of archive administration", the quantity of archives remained small until, "with the accession, in 1949 and succeeding years, of the Wentworth Woodhouse Muniments, the Wharncliffe, Crewe and Spencer Stanhope papers, and many smaller groups, the collections administered by the Department of Local History and Archives have become one of the largest and most important in any public library in the country; for among these recent accessions there are great numbers of papers of national as well as local interest".[11] The records of these families occupy, in fact, three-fifths of the *Guide*, and since its compilation the Library has acquired the large Norfolk archive relating to Sheffield.[12]

Liverpool provides an interesting comparison with Sheffield. Sheffield has been able to acquire a large corpus of family muniments because of the absence of a county record office in the West Riding of Yorkshire: it is the accepted repository for archives for south Yorkshire. Liverpool, however, is restricted to collecting archives within its own boundary. In the past there have been landed family estates in Liverpool, and the City Library has the records of some of the smaller ones. But the records of the two most important families of Liverpool's past, the Stanleys of Knowsley and the Molyneux of Sefton, are in the Lancashire Record Office. As a result, the Liverpool Record Office has been encouraged to concentrate on business archives, of which, according to its *Guide*, Sheffield City Library has few, and on corporation records, of which Sheffield appears to have none.

In 1957 the Council of the Library Association adopted a statement of policy on the place of archives and manuscripts in libraries, which begins: "The acquisition of archives and manuscripts is a legitimate purpose of libraries serving the interests of scholarship and research."[13] Mr. Hepworth, too, makes considerable use of the scholarly associations of this side of libraries' work: "Neil Ker's *Medieval libraries of Great Britain* (1941) reveals that the great heritage of illuminated manuscripts is still mainly preserved in libraries of all kinds. . . . The vast majority are still in national, university, college or civic libraries all over the world."[14] A reviewer of Mr. Hepworth's pamphlet, however, retorts that "of course the meaning of the last seven words [of the Library

Association statement of 1957: 'serving the interests of scholarship and research'] is the vital point. Do they not exclude 95% of the public libraries in this country?''[15] It might be agreed that the Library Association's wording is unfortunate. Its statement is axiomatic in the case of manuscripts, but not of archives. In the end, county record offices exist because they hold the administrative records of their authorities. Public libraries might well aim to do the same. As is clearly happening in the case of the recently enlarged London boroughs, libraries, if they are to stake an undisputed claim to the acquisition of archives, must become the custodians of their corporations' records. The Library Association's first principle might, therefore, tentatively be recast to read: "It is a proper function of public libraries to serve as the custodians of the records of their local authorities. The acquisition of archives and manuscripts is a legitimate purpose of libraries in the interests of scholarship and research."

The attitude of an archivist towards the claims of librarians to deal with local authority records is well expressed by Miss Ida Darlington, head archivist of the Greater London Council, in writing about the problems of the new boroughs created by the London Government Act 1963.[16] Miss Darlington thinks that "there can be no doubt that these new local government authorities need staff trained in archives principles and techniques. . . . The right place for such staff is in the Town Clerk's Department but, unfortunately, at this time when at least 32 archivists are needed for these boroughs there is an acute shortage in the profession"; and so, "we cannot blame the London borough councils for turning for help in solving at least part of their problem to their reference librarians, most of whom already have some records in their charge. Nor can we blame those librarians who . . . look round for enterprising members of their staff who can be dubbed archivists and left to wrestle with the situation as best they may."

Miss Darlington sees the solution of a problem which "may emerge in areas far removed from London" arising out of a number of possibilities: the acquisition of archive qualifications by these new "librarian archivists"; the friendly help and advice of established record offices; the recognition of library archivists as *borough* archivists in charge of *borough* archives. As a matter of fact, as Miss Darlington finally points out, the problem of the absorption of formally unqualified archivists is one familiar to the profession: "no professional qualifications are required for membership" of the Society of Archivists; this is "an obvious source of weakness in building up professional standards . . . but it is probably inevitable in a young profession which is still largely in the hands of those who have learnt by doing". There is thus an avenue of acceptance into the archives profession for the "unqualified librarian archivist", and Miss Darlington welcomes it as an advantage: he can "seek admission to the society, and can learn something of archive principles at meetings and official visits to other repositories, and in talking to established archivists. Here is an opportunity to show that as a professional society we are concerned not with restrictive practices but with professional standards, that the basic principles relating to provenance, custody and the preservation of the archive group really matter."

In criticizing the archive collecting activities of public libraries, county archivists concentrate on the qualifications of librarians to deal with archives. In the case of university libraries, however, the county archivist's principal concern is fear of general encroachment. Geographically and administratively, county record offices neatly divide up the country; apart from county boroughs, there is no room for any other institutions which systematically collect archives. In fact, most modern university libraries have not gone in for purposeful archive collecting. If more academic than public libraries, they have been equally casual in their manuscript collecting, with perhaps a particular interest in the papers of literary or political notables which have sometimes provided material for research but have often lain dormant. There has been little dynamic interest in archives: the interests of university librarians have usually tended in more scholarly, literary directions. At least two university libraries have declined historically important archive collections because there was "no room for them". Nevertheless, some university libraries have been affected by the gathering enthusiasm for archives since the war. Mr. Hepworth instances Keele, which, in spite of a newly built county record office at Stafford, acquired more than 75,000 manuscripts in its first dozen years, and Liverpool, which received "very large increases in deposits in the decade [1951–61]".[17] It may be, however, that in such cases the increase has been due to the receipt of one or two considerable collections, for instance the Sneyd papers at Keele, and the Rathbone papers at Liverpool. Durham and Nottingham are probably the only modern universities which have actively and systematically engaged in the collection of archives in the manner of a county record office.[18]

In addition to the general historical argument which Mr. Hepworth advances in support of the claim of libraries to collect archives, there are more practical reasons: thus libraries have longer opening hours than county record offices (which usually close at 5 p.m.), and they often have considerable local and reference collections in the same building. That archivists are sensitive to these points was shown in Mr. Kirby's review of the first edition of Mr. Hepworth's *Archives and Manuscripts in Libraries*: the argument about opening hours was "an old stick used by librarians to beat archivists . . . archivists would no doubt agree that longer hours of opening are desirable, if not quite so vital as many other things".[19] Some of these "other things" would probably include such matters as storage and staff. For example, library buildings have not, in the past, normally provided strong-room accommodation. But if a library feels strongly enough about its right to house archives and manuscripts it can fairly easily build a strong room. This was done, for instance, when Liverpool Record Office was created in the Liverpool City Library in 1953 and approval was sought as a manorial repository. A further argument against storage of archives in libraries may be that the official records of the corporation are thus being housed away from the departments which produced them. Yet this can be so in the case of a municipal record office not connected with a library: "a record office may easily have to be somewhat remote from some of the departments it services, while municipal libraries are almost almost always quite close to the Town Hall".[20] In any case, the condition of borough records has been, and often still is, such that any initiative in housing them adequately is to be welcomed.

The attitude of county record offices towards libraries has, however, been mainly conditioned by a deep suspicion that librarians do not understand the essential differences between archives and books: between documents, which are "the product of activity"—impersonal, unself-conscious, objective, impartial—and manuscripts, which "represent conscious strivings . . . towards literary . . . excellence"—personal, self-conscious, subjective, partial; between a document, which is only part of a larger process—having a certain amount of meaning on its own, but not much more than that of a page torn from a book—and a literary manuscript—discrete, complete in itself, independent of other manuscripts. An archive and a literary manuscript are both unique, but apart from this quality literary manuscripts, in their nature and treatment, have much more in common with printed books than with archives. Various important differences in the treatment of archives and of books (whether manuscript or printed) result from the differences in their nature: especially in physical arrangement (classification) and in finding aids (cataloguing). Most of these differences arise from the collective nature of archives compared with the individual character of books. Archives, unlike books, do not have a subject, either as individual documents or *en bloc*; they are the written expression of an activity. An accumulation of archives, therefore, must be treated as a whole; this is the unit corresponding to the book.

Archives cannot be classified like books; they must be classified according to the organization which produced them—that is, according to their provenance. And because, as Schellenberg says,[21] archives have no author, title, imprint, table of contents, or index, they cannot be catalogued like books: archivists must find their own ways of describing, and producing finding aids for, the complex mass that is an archival accumulation. Archives and books require, in fact, basically different attitudes from those who deal with them. In Schellenberg's words,

> archival principles and techniques should be applied to records that are deposited in libraries. Librarians will not find this easy to do, for the differences between archival and library methods are difficult to bridge. . . . In order to manage records in their custody properly, librarians must literally change their thinking about methodology. They must learn to deal with collective units that have an organic significance.[22]

Misled, perhaps, by the superficial feature of handwriting common to archives and literary manuscripts, there is no doubt that some librarians failed to appreciate the fundamental dissimilarity between archives and books. But this lack of understanding is increasingly a thing of the past, due partly to the persuasiveness of propagandists like Hepworth and Hobbs, and partly to the practical work of archivists employed in libraries. In seeking support for the right of libraries to collect archives modern librarians naturally accept those standards of housing, staffing, and treatment which are required by the archives profession. A library which has a lively and informed interest in archives, and a willingness to implement this interest in a professionally proper manner, can play a very useful and satisfying role in the preservation of local archives and their preparation for public use.

II. PRACTICE

7. BRINGING IN THE ARCHIVES

THIS is probably the most exciting, certainly the most satisfying, part of a local archivist's work. Nearly all archivists are instinctive collectors. They like to acquire collections of records; the bigger (preferably measured in van loads or, failing that, tons), the older, and the more important, the better. Then they can enlarge on them to their colleagues, demonstrate the mountains of them to their superiors, and hope to get an increase of staff on the strength of them from their employers. Less subjectively, the activity can be seen as saving the nation's past, and making it available to historians.

One writer says the subject can be summarized in one sentence, "Go out and *get* the records".[1] Some archivists are better go-getters than others. The best equipped are probably those with a good deal of nervous energy, a fair amount of aplomb, and a considerable layer of charm, the last being perhaps the most important. The same writer continues that "local archivists have to divide their attention between records they have and those they would like to have". In fact, this is one of the most important decisions an archivist has to make. The management of this side of his work calls for the right sort of temperament and a large amount of skill. It requires a fine manipulation of the various levers at the archivist's command. It does not do, for instance, to be too successful in getting in large quantities of records if staff are not available, or unlikely to be available, to cope with them. A worth-while ploy is to nurse simultaneously the prospects of both a new deposit and a new member of staff, and then use the actual deposit to clinch the appointment.

Once a deposit is received it should be brought to the attention of the archivist's chief and of his records committee. Depending on its size and importance, a deposit may be made the occasion of a sherry party, a lunch, or even a dinner with speeches and a large exhibition. If the record office is well staffed and equipped the archivist will then produce, as quickly as possible, a list or catalogue of the collection, and

79

send the first copy to the owner. He will make the existence of the deposit known to students through his annual report and through the good offices of the National Register of Archives. If possible he will index the collection, and will display its exhibition-worthy items on all suitable occasions.

At each of these stages the archivist must be careful not to get bogged down. For example, he must be sure not to promise the owner, as an inducement to deposit, a more detailed catalogue than his office is capable of producing. And once having obtained a deposit he must keep its treatment in proportion: he has other collections to attend to and he must not neglect them for too long. Exhibitions take a lot of work and time; he must not let them take too much. Finally, he must be keeping an eye open for other deposits.

Archive collecting in virgin territory is relatively easy. Immediately after the war, with the decay of the landed gentry, the propaganda of the National Register of Archives, the activities of local archives committees, and the rise of county record offices, deposits came in very readily. But in circumstances where a considerable quantity of work is waiting to be done on existing deposits, and where a good deal of the available records appears to have been already acquired, the soliciting of new deposits can take a disproportionate amount of time. If the archivist's resources are small he should be continually asking himself if it is worth all the effort, or whether he should be spending more time on what he already has. Yet there can be no doubt that a healthy turn over of accessions is good for everyone, and certainly looks well in the archivist's annual report.

An archivist needs continually to keep his ears and eyes open for information about records ripe for deposit. In the words of the writer in *Local Records*, "the more an archivist moves about his area the more records will he gather in. Personal contact should be established by the archivist himself and if his area is a large one he must have a car available."[2] Business records are notoriously difficult to collect. The archivist must have contacts either with business men or with those who have. Business men are often suspicious of academics and it may be necessary to establish contact through social activities like golf or scouts. A good research worker can be a source of valuable information about the location of records but is unlikely to help in their acquisition.

The archivist needs fine judgement in deciding when to approach an owner about his records. It is possible to be over-cautious. The great difficulty is choosing between a direct, personal approach, and the casual stealth of third or fourth parties. The archivist needs to sense when the indirect approach will take too long: one of the sympathetic middlemen may die before anything has happened. But a frontal on-slaught out of the blue, like a circular to a business firm, or a letter to an owner the archivist has not met, is usually no use at all. In general the most successful collecting archivist is probably an extrovert, sociable type who can meet gentry, business men, solicitors, estate agents, and parsons on a non-academic level. The reclusive archivist tends to approach owners either too timidly, or boldly in a gauche way.

If an owner is unwilling to deposit his records he may be prepared to have them listed; the archivist should welcome this opportunity. The owner probably realizes it is the archivist's hope and intention that the documents should ultimately be deposited, and he is capable of playing the archivist along, making use of him as an unpaid, part-time, private archivist. The archivist should be careful not to commit himself to too much work for one individual away from his office; the extent of his commitment will depend on his assessment of the person-ality of the owner, the importance of the collection, and the likelihood of ultimate deposit. In a shrewd article on this subject of looking after family records in the house of the owner, Mr. Francis Steer stresses the virtues of courtesy and tact in an archivist's attitude towards an owner.[3] The relationship between owner and archivist in today's social circumstances makes, in fact, for interesting experience: the archivist encounters all gradations from aristocratic hauteur to youth-ful bonhomie, including the slightly awkward friendliness that flickers in deserted servants' halls and private corridors.

After a collection has been deposited a relationship will continue between owner and archivist. It may be impersonal, conducted through the owner's agent or solicitor. In the case of a small estate, where the agent is much less influential, the relationship may be a personal one with the owner. Or it may be a mixture of the two, with requests to the archivist coming bewilderingly, and sometimes contradictorily, from both owner and agent. Whatever the arrangement, the amount of attention required of the archivist by the owner will vary a great deal.

Some owners leave their records in the hands of the archivist and never see them again or trouble him about them again; nor do they particularly want to be troubled about them again. On the other hand, the owner may be personally interested in the history of his family, and frequently write to the archivist or ring him up asking for information or documents; the archivist must tactfully see that all borrowed documents are returned. The agent may also want the same service; if it can be supplied quickly and efficiently both owner and agent may feel confirmed in the wisdom of having deposited the records in the first place.

The deposit may be controlled by a specific agreement drawn up by solicitors, by an informal letter, or merely by a verbal arrangement. An agreement may stipulate the length of deposit, the amount of insurance, arrangements about consultation, publication, photography, and repair, and an understanding that the collection can be reclaimed at short notice. Consultation of the records will probably be at the archivist's discretion, but he may have to seek the owner's permission in the case of photography or publication. Sometimes, the owner may eventually allow the archivist to use his discretion about photography; once permission is given for photography it may be difficult to control publication.

The views of owners on this subject are not frequently heard, so the comments of Mrs. E. J. Mockler, who has deposited family records in the Berkshire Record Office, are interesting.[4] She makes the point that the phrase, "permanent deposit", may deter a potential depositor and suggests that archivists should find a more diplomatic description. Alternatives offered in the subsequent discussion included "indefinite loan", "semi-permanent loan", and (from Sir Hilary Jenkinson) "deposit of a substantially permanent nature". A fixed term of years would seem a satisfactory arrangement: as an owner is, in any case, entitled to reclaim his records whenever he wishes, he should be given a regular opportunity of explicitly renewing or revoking the deposit. Mrs. Mockler appears to favour detailed terms of deposit: "a simple receipt might leave the archivist without specific authority to do what he needed, such as repairs"; owners usually accept repairs thankfully, "but care should perhaps be taken to do nothing too drastic". She is also concerned about the use made of family papers by historians:

"where any question of publication arose, the owner had a right to refuse, and a scholar's wish to print deposited documents should be referred to the owner through the archivist; permission was likely to be given most willingly, if nothing derogatory to the owner's family was involved."

Important deposits of records are often insured by archivists. Although documents, once destroyed, cannot be replaced, their insurance is a token of the value an archivist attaches to an owner's property, and a guarantee of at least monetary refund. One archivist, however, thinks that "a policy of selected microfilming, spending a sum equivalent to the annual block insurance premium, might be more realistic and more acceptable to depositors".[5] The same archivist makes the rather awkward suggestion that "a moral obligation also rested on the archivist to see that records in his charge were not misused by being made available to someone who might use them to harm the depositor, e.g. in litigation". This may be difficult to do in all circumstances, but certainly, when the position is clear cut, as for instance in a case of footpath rights, it seems only courteous for the archivist to consult the owner, and to tell the inquirer that he is doing so. At Guildford one of the record office's regulations requires owner's consent if documents are investigated for legal purposes.[6]

Final comment on the subject may, perhaps, be left with another owner of family records. Deposit in a record office, he finds, is convenient for both researchers and owners. The advantage in the one case he does not discuss, but as far as owners are concerned, they are spared the trouble of correspondence with researchers, and the problem of entertaining them.[7]

8. DESIGNING AN ARCHIVES REPOSITORY

MOST archivists would like to have an independent, physically separate repository. There are sufficient practical justifications for this, but underlying them is a strong, unspoken motive: the natural wish of an archivist for an orbit of his own. The local archivist in this country is a new man, fighting for recognition of his profession and his status. Translated into mundane terms, this becomes a matter of relations with his superior: whether, for instance, he is to have his name on his notepaper; and, on a more elevated plane, the setting and the quality of his record office.

The case for a physically separate record office can be based on the special nature of archives, and hence the special precautions which must be taken in looking after them: precautions which are not fully possible if the office is part of a larger building, in which it is likely to occupy a subordinate position. This special nature of archives stems particularly, of course, from their uniqueness: if a document is destroyed a piece of historical evidence (admittedly of variable value) has gone for good. If a printed book is destroyed it is sad, but it need not be tragic: other copies usually exist. Then there is the relative fragility of archives; their peculiar response to unsatisfactory conditions of temperature and humidity, and to atmospheric pollution; and, often, their oddities of form. Preservation is thus at the heart of archive administration. Awareness of it is much livelier in an archivist than in a librarian: in his conscious thought about his duties, in his unconscious behaviour (the eternal concern with keys), in the way he handles his material. A much bigger proportion of archive than of library literature is devoted to preservation. It is significant that the principal textbook for local archivists in this country is called *Local Records: Their Nature and Care*: nothing in this title about *use*. Librarians, on the other hand, are predominantly concerned with the use of their materials: a book

84

like J. W. Clark's *The Care of Books* has a specialist, antiquarian flavour.

Physical separation of an archive repository is, therefore, an initial desideratum. But, though it is the duty of an archivist to press for it at every suitable opportunity, he is unlikely to achieve isolation merely for the asking: few separate repositories have so far been built in England. This means that the archivist must be prepared to accept the best possible compromise, whether in an existing building or a new building.

However an archives repository is arranged in detail the whole can be divided into three parts: strong rooms, public rooms, and administration. The overall design of an archives repository depends primarily on the relationship between these three divisions: what, in a given set of circumstances, is the best relationship, bearing in mind the safety of the archives, service to the public, and staff convenience? Archivists probably agree that the three departments should be clearly separated; firstly, because the peculiar needs of the archives demand special treatment; secondly, because the public should not have direct access to the archives; and thirdly, because the public do not normally need access to administration.

On the other hand, the staff must have convenient access to both archives and public rooms; and they must be able to transfer archives from the strong rooms to the public rooms, and back again, as easily as possible. The staff obviously act as link between archives and public, but this function is performed in a number of ways: reception of the public, oversight of the search room, transport of archives from strong room to search room and back again, reception of archives, transport of archives from reception to strong room, administration of repair room and photographic room, administration of general work room, oversight of exhibition room. Thus the role of the administration department is a varied and complicated one, and the layout of its area of the repository in relation to the other two sections will call for ingenuity on the part of the architect.

"The architect", because it is his, rather than the archivist's, job to suggest the disposition of rooms. Of course, before this stage is reached, the archivist will have supplied the architect with a catalogue of his basic requirements. This may take the form, firstly, of a statement of the purpose of the repository, the provision he needs to make for archives, public, and staff, and, in outline, the relationship he expects to exist between departments. There will then follow a list of the rooms required, with a brief description of the function of each, and a note of its area, the number of people it will have to accommodate, and any special features. Thus "Search Room" may read: "This room is intended to accommodate up to 20 research workers consulting archives at large tables. The room should have good natural light. Provision should be made of shelving for x ft. run of books. The room should include two cubicles, one for ultra-violet lamp and one for microfilm reader and typewriter. There should be easy access between search room and strong rooms. Total area 1,000 sq. ft."

After the architect has had time to mull over these requirements he will produce a first plan of the building, showing each floor divided into rooms according to the areas supplied to him, and including stairs, passages, lifts, etc. The archivist's first reactions on seeing the preliminary plan may well be dubious ones. He may feel that his original uneasiness has been confirmed: here is an architect without any experience of archives, who has certainly not designed an archives repository before; how much better would it have been if he, the archivist, had drawn the plans. But on looking at the drawings a second time the archivist may find his scepticism thawing a little. He notices that, yes, the architect has given the search room a good, sunny position; and, yes, he himself had not quite reached that idea of merging entrance hall with display area; and the architect has certainly arranged staff supervision of the entrance very neatly. In sum, the architect's expertise solves problems of room relationship which will probably surprise the archivist; and secondly, although he has no previous knowledge of archives repository design, the architect may well make suggestions which had not occurred to the archivist.

But, naturally, it is unlikely that the first plan will meet with the archivist's complete approval. For instance, the search room, although getting plenty of light and nicely adjacent to the strong rooms, is really too far away from administration. The photographic department, too, has been given good natural light where desirable, but its siting is unnecessarily prominent, too publicly accessible; it needs placing nearer to the repair room, with which it has numerous contacts. So perhaps photographic can move to the back of the building, and that will also allow the search room to be brought nearer to administration; then we should need to push the strong rooms round to take up *that* vacated space. . . .

At this point the archivist is tempted to produce a drawing embodying these alterations. But once again he must restrain himself, simply indicating to the architect the deficiencies, in his eyes, of the first plan, and emphasizing which relationships are most important. The architect responds with further plans, and so the interchange goes on until the best compromise (which is what it will have to be in the end) has been achieved.

9. THE ENEMIES OF ARCHIVES

No part of an archives repository determines its overall design more than the strong room. The aim of the strong room is to preserve the archives. To do so it has to repel two groups of enemies, one dramatic, the other insidious.

The Dramatic Enemies

Bombing

The danger to archives from warfare is one which has exercised archivists spasmodically in the past. No doubt many archives which were lost through bombing in the last war might have been saved had they been stored in deep shelters or, like the English public records, dispersed about the country. But in the circumstances of modern atomic warfare, when the protection of people themselves is conjectural, the possibility of preserving archives seems even more hypothetical and has not received extended consideration from archivists.[1]

Rain and flooding

An archives repository should, naturally, be completely weather-proof. If there are windows in the strong rooms they should not allow rain to enter even when open. The roof should preferably be apex, with the gutters outside the building. An uninterrupted roof is desirable because anything breaking its line, such as chimney stacks or gables, is a weak spot. Though floods are a less common hazard than simple rain the great damage they can cause was demonstrated in Florence in 1966, when the river Arno burst its banks, rushed into the basement and ground floor of the Uffizi Gallery, and soaked and coagulated with mud thousands of early printed books. The cardinal maxim for avoiding flooding is not to build a repository near a river, or, for that matter, a water main. Archivists in this country have a healthy dislike of basements for storing archives, mainly because of the danger of flooding from two internal causes: burst water pipes (either above the strong rooms or actually running through them) and the water used in fighting fires in the building. But flooding can also happen more surprisingly. One such case, showing the importance of roof design, occurred when autumn leaves choked the outlets from a flat roof surrounded by a parapet: water collected on the roof and poured through ventilation louvres into the strong room beneath.

Theft

The repository should be theft proof. If there are windows in the strong rooms they should be barred to exclude entry even when the windows are open. The strong rooms should have steel doors, and be kept under lock and key. Archivists are very key conscious and sometimes have key trouble, so there should be a simple, convenient, but safe system for keeping and supervising keys.

The monetary value of archives varies enormously. A humdrum document may have no sale price whatsoever; on the other hand, the Vinland map has been insured for £1½ million. Apart from special care taken with particularly valuable items, the most satisfactory course is to keep a fairly equal safeguard over all archives. To some extent the precautions taken by the archivist against theft are simply a demonstration, not least to the owners of the archives, of the seriousness with which he takes his responsibilities. Similarly with the insurance of archives: since they are unique they cannot be replaced, but indemnification may be some compensation to the owner.

Fire

Despite the comparative infrequency of fire it is regarded as the main dramatic danger to archives. Recently built repositories employ sophisticated methods of dealing with fire. Precautions against its occurrence are best made at the design stage. Because of the danger of spread of fire from neighbouring buildings a repository should preferably be isolated. Combustible materials, especially timber, should be excluded as far as possible. Strong rooms should be divided into compartments: there are fire regulations for the maximum space desirable for particular kinds of storage. The walls and floors of the strong rooms should be made of the best fire-resisting materials; all vertical airspaces, such as staircase wells and lift shafts, should be outside the fireproof walls. Because electricity is a frequent source of fire, there is a tradition on the Continent of excluding artificial light from archive repositories. The Public Record Office was originally built in this way, but, in the words of one assistant-keeper, it was tough on the archivists. All electric wires should be enclosed in seamless steel tubes, and all electric fittings should be fixed—loose wires can cause shorts.

Today there is a preference for steel-and-concrete repositories: older archive buildings, which had unprotected iron columns and girders, collapsed from the effect of fire. In Finland's national archives reinforced concrete has recently replaced an iron framework, and the building has been divided into sections separated by fireproof walls and doors. The division of strong rooms into small units, with fireproof doors kept open by metal catches which melt under heat, helps to limit internal fires. Other precautions against fire are: shelving made entirely of metal; the ability to cut off electric current from the building as a whole as well as from individual floors; fire alarms of various kinds; and fire-fighting apparatus (though this can sometimes be as dangerous to the archives as fire). There are two main techniques of fire detection: by heat, which causes a thin metal membrane to melt and establish electrical contact; and by smoke, which is the more usual system, and is in use, for instance, in the Leicestershire and Staffordshire record offices. In either case, the fire-warning is usually sounded not only in the repository itself but in the local fire station as well. In the new Essex Record Office the Minerva smoke-detection system has been combined with an arrangement for flooding the strong room with carbon dioxide gas within two minutes, and for simultaneously isolating the strong room's electrical circuits.

The Insidious Enemies

Light

Not much has been written about the effect of light on archives; Ingvar Andersson, Director-General of the Swedish Archives, says, "the question is well worth the attention of technologists".[2] In some countries light, especially sunlight, is felt to be a major enemy of archives because of its bleaching effect; indeed, it is said that the ultraviolet rays of the sun destroy paper. A good deal of consideration has been given to the problem in the U.S.A., where many archive repositories, for example, the National Archives in Washington, have been built without windows. In France and Germany, where modern archive buildings tend to have a lot of windows, the approach has been rather to finding kinds and colours of glass which will inhibit the deleterious effect of light. The subject has not received much attention in Great Britain, presumably because the climate makes archivists more sensitive to the dangers of damp than of strong sunlight. Nevertheless, British archivists would generally be averse from unduly exposing documents to sunlight. The danger arises more in connection with exhibitions than with the normal storage of archives, when they are protected by containers; but in the case of strong rooms where archivists have no particular need for windows, it is possible that, like the Staffordshire Record Office, they might opt for artificial light.

Damp

Until recently, at any rate, damp was seen as the principal insidious danger to archives in Great Britain, with some areas, for instance the West Country, suffering from a particularly humid atmosphere. Three environmental factors are involved in assessing the impact of damp: humidity, temperature, and air-movement. Although humidity—the measure of the amount of moisture vapour in the atmosphere—is the "single factor of paramount importance",[3] it is influenced by the other two. Consideration of humidity cannot, in fact, be separated from consideration of temperature. This is because the amount of moisture which the atmosphere can hold varies with its temperature: a cold atmosphere holds less moisture than a warm one. Coldness in itself is not harmful to documents, but when the temperature drops the *relative humidity* rises and condensation results: moisture is deposited on the documents and mildew is formed. Thus the danger to archives lies not in absolute, but in relative, humidity. Relative humidity (R.H.) is the ratio of the amount of moisture vapour actually present in any given volume of air (m) to the amount of moisture needed to saturate the same volume of air at the same temperature (M). This ratio is usually expressed as a percentage:

$$\text{R.H.} = \frac{m}{M} \times 100.$$

The archivist thus starts off with a desideratum in his strong-room construction: good insulation, giving even temperature. The building, that is, should conserve heat; for this brick is good, concrete is bad; if the building has a concrete shell it should be given an asbestos lining; windows, too, lose heat, so they should be double. That the problem of humidity control is not straightforward is demonstrated by the temptation to open strong-room windows on a warm, sunny, summer's day. It seems a natural thing to do, in order to give the archives a breath of fresh and, one might think, dry air. But, in fact, the warm outside air may conceal a high humidity, and opening the strong-room windows could result in condensation on cool walls and floors: this happens particularly in cellars, which keep cool in summer time. It is noticeable, in the case of a strong room which shares a central heating system, that when this heating is switched off in, say, May, the relative humidity of the strong room immediately shoots up. It is desirable, therefore, to heat strong rooms independently of the rest of the building.

Relative humidity is particularly important in the storage of archives because parchment and paper are both hygroscopic materials, that is, they tend to absorb or give up moisture in sympathy with the rise or fall in the relative humidity of the surrounding atmosphere. Over-dry parchment shrinks and cockles; desiccated paper becomes brittle. But too high relative humidity produces profounder deterioration than too low: "all the materials of archives are potential sources of nutrient for mould and bacteria *whose spores are everywhere.* . . . Cellulose of paper will be attacked by many so-called cellulytic organisms, whereas size and parchment will be attacked by even a larger number of other types of organisms. As a result of mould attack the fibres of paper will become soft, spongy and very weak."[4] Relative humidity should ideally be controlled at between 50% and 60% at a temperature of 60–70°F. It is a useful working rule that for relative humidities in the region of 60% a 1°F rise in temperature corresponds to a 2% decrease in relative humidity.

Several instruments are necessary to check strong-room atmosphere. A thermometer measures the temperature at a given moment, and a hygrometer the relative humidity at a given moment. (A hygrometer consists of two thermometers, one dry bulb and the other wet; the relative humidity is calculated on the basis of the differences between the readings of the two thermometers.) But it is clearly also desirable to record fluctuations over a longer period of time: this can be done in the case of temperature with a thermograph, and in the case of relative humidity with a hygrograph; or both can be recorded simultaneously with the same instrument, a thermo-hygrograph. On the other hand, a thermo-hygrograph is a fairly bulky, delicate instrument which is best left stationary; a hygrometer is necessary for snap checks in particular, perhaps rather inaccessible places in the strong room: high relative humidity can build up in localized air-pockets. To prevent the formation of such pockets it is essential to provide adequate air-circulation: if an outbreak of mould growth is discovered "good ventilation is the first-aid measure to adopt, although in special circumstances, e.g. accidental flooding, it may be necessary to use heater-fans so long as adequate air-circulation is maintained to remove the excess of water vapour and prevent the build up of a high relative humidity".[5] Dr. Anthony Werner, Keeper of the British Museum Laboratory, instances the case of a basement strong room in which, after flooding, the relative humidity of the general atmosphere was successfully reduced to 55%. Later, however, active mould was found in the spine of a book which had been standing next to a hollow steel shelf support: "a pocket of moist stagnant air had persisted inside the hollow support, because the original air circulation had not been maintained at a sufficiently high velocity; indeed, when the relative humidity of the air trapped inside the hollow support was measured, it was found to be no less than 83%."[6]

The traditional way of dealing with mould in archive repositories is to treat affected documents with thymol. The method is to place a small dish of thymol crystals in a sufficiently air-tight cabinet. (While there is no health risk in moderate inhalation of thymol fumes nor in handling the crystals each day when refilling the dish, the cabinet should be in a room with good ventilation.) An electric light bulb fitted beneath the saucer is lit for about one hour each day, and the warmth is enough to convert the crystals gradually to vapour. The mould-infected documents are placed on a lattice shelf above the crystals so as to receive the full benefit of the fumes. It is a laborious process because the pages of an infected volume must be meticulously turned each day if the treatment is to be fully effective. A more comprehensive variation, used at the Somerset and Staffordshire record offices, is to treat all suspected documents on reception in a large fumigation chamber: documents are taken into the chamber on trolleys, and heating is by electric light bulbs seated in a trench in the floor.[7]

A more recent method of mould treatment is to wrap infected, or potentially infected, documents in paper impregnated with a chemical which inhibits mould growth. In 1947 sodium pentachlorophenate was shown by H. J. Plenderleith, F. Armitage, and others to have "a remarkably wide range of effectiveness, and to be less volatile than thymol".[8] Marketed under the trade name of Santobrite, it was used on a large scale by government departments and record offices (notably the House of Lords Record Office.)[9] It proved extremely efficient, and the Staffordshire Record Office came to regard its fumigation chamber as merely supplementary to Santobrite; unfortunately, in recent years it has ceased to be generally available. Instead, the British Museum Research Laboratory now recommends sodium orthophenylphenate, marketed as Topane W.S.; almost as efficient as pentachlorophenate, "it can now . . . be accepted as the most generally effective fungicide available for use in record offices and libraries". The best method of applying Topane is to interleave infected documents with impregnated sheets of tissue. In rooms liable to mould growth lengths of tissue can be placed as lining on shelves and as covering to the tops of books and boxes "in order that a general *ambiance* of Topane may be built up". Mr. Bond and Mr. Baynes-Cope believe that fungicides are necessary because many record offices are unable to install either a full system of air-conditioning or even the very much less expensive dehumidifier units. Quoting Jenkinson, they point to the virtues of air-circulation, but stress that its effectiveness must be superintended: "paper and parchment do not get rid of humidity as quickly as they absorb it . . . not only must the archivist avoid having pockets of stagnant air in his repository; he must also keep a watch on the materials stored on the shelves to ensure that they do not possess a markedly higher moisture content than the surrounding atmosphere."[10]

Dr. Werner has no doubt that good ventilation is a better way of combating mould than fungicides: "chemical treatment can never be regarded as a substitute for good housekeeping. Only in tropical countries may the use of fungicides and insecticides be regarded as a necessity rather than a luxury"; "any local growths of microfungi can generally be made to disappear by increased ventilation".[11] Mr. W. H. Langwell, however, suggests that the virtue of ventilation has been exaggerated: "old-fashioned ideas about the desirability of paper being free to breathe were best forgotten: ventilation might introduce damp or sulphurous air".[12] The belief of mycologists that mould develops at relative humidities of 70–75% is, he continues, mistaken in the case of documents and is based on experience with foodstuffs: for rapid mould growth documents must be quite limp, with a relative humidity of as much as 90%. The real danger is from change of temperature, when cold documents may condense moisture from the warm air surrounding them; this is perhaps the commonest cause of mould damage to stored documents, and in such a case ventilation cannot help.

Mr. Langwell's faith in chemical agents leads him to explore treatments aimed at "a 100% kill": thymol he finds too volatile, insufficiently toxic, and more in the nature of a "fungistat" which retards development rather than kills fungi. But, apparently inconsistently, he stresses the extraordinary powers of fungi to survive in adverse conditions, and deduces that it is illusory to think of eliminating them completely: "a more practical way of dealing with them is to slow down their activities until the damage they cause becomes negligible."[13]

Mr. Langwell suggests that perhaps the simplest way to combat damp is to reduce the relative humidity by raising the temperature, and circulating the heated air round the strong-room stacks. This has been done in Ceylon: there, at a temperature of 86°F, the relative humidity can be 90%; by raising the temperature to 95°F the relative humidity is reduced to 70%; it may seem absurd to raise an already high temperature, but the reduced relative humidity makes the atmosphere more tolerable for people working in the store room than it was at the lower temperature.

Some authorities clearly view Mr. Langwell's ideas with scepticism. Thus Mr. F. D. Armitage criticizes him for underrating the susceptibility of paper to moulds—the practical experience of many archivists, he says, shows that microfungi spread very rapidly over papers and books—and for failing to point out that many biological agencies will break down cellulose in conditions of 70% relative humidity at elevated temperatures. In other words, the figures given by Mr. Langwell for permitted humidity and temperature are unreliable.[14] On the other hand, some archivists support Mr. Langwell. The archivist of the Ipswich and East Suffolk Record Office says that in his strong room, with a relative humidity of 70–80% and a constant temperature, no mildew has occurred;[15] and the Leicestershire county archivist reports that mould has occurred in his strong rooms even though the ventilation is mechanically controlled, and that he has had to install dehumidifiers as a remedy.[16]

However, traditional ideas about relative humidity, temperature, and ventilation probably predominate with British archivists. Thus the Clerk of the Records of the House of Lords speaks cautiously of the possible danger which might develop from latent fungus when papers are removed from the sort of temperature and relative humidity allowed by Mr. Langwell into an atmosphere favourable to their growth.[17] In spite of disillusionment at Leicester, too, air-conditioning continues to be seen as the best answer to atmospheric troubles: for instance, at the Staffordshire Record Office, built in 1960–1, where in winter the system provides complete control of strong-room climate, washing, drying, and heating the air; there is no refrigeration plant, so in summer the air is merely washed and dried, but, along with two air changes every hour, this is expected to maintain conditions which will inhibit the growth of mould.[18] Similarly, in the strong room of the even more recently built Essex Record Office (1964), although surprisingly situated in a basement, "temperature and humidity are maintained day and night at a constant level by five large electric air-conditioning units".[19] If full air-conditioning cannot be afforded the next best thing is to blow heated air through the strong room with fans; for safety's sake the heaters should preferably be sited outside the strong room, but if they must be inside then tubular electrical heating is desirable.

Air pollution

For generations damp has been considered the principal insidious danger to archives in Great Britain. It is only recently that the danger from acidity has been fully appreciated. Parchment is not involved: it is a relatively stable substance, relatively constant in quality, and has a slightly alkaline reaction, "due to the small amount of lime retained by the collagen fibres of the parchment during the liming of the skins".[20] Paper, on the other hand, is unstable, varies widely in quality, and is very liable to deterioration for a number of reasons. A most insidious form of deterioration is caused by acid. Small quantities of acid can have a catastrophic effect on the cellulose of paper: "cellulose is prone to a form of chemical attack called hydrolysis which occurs in the presence of acids; furthermore this reaction is also catalytic, i.e. the acid itself is not used during the hydrolysis, and, therefore, quite a small amount of acid can cause extensive hydrolysis, resulting in a degradation of the cellulose molecule; mechanical strength is lost and the paper becomes brittle and fragile."[21]

The source of acidity in paper can be either intrinsic or extrinsic. Intrinsic acid is introduced during manufacture, for instance in the form of alum added during sizing, or bleaching agents left in because of inadequate washing: thus deterioration is particularly marked in paper made after the discovery of chlorine in 1744. Archivists today, however, are more disturbed by extrinsic sources of acidity, the commonest of which is sulphur dioxide in the atmosphere. It is estimated that about 5 million tons of sulphur, mainly in the form of sulphur dioxide, a by-product of the consumption of coal and fuel oil, is released into the atmosphere of Great Britain every year. Pollution is naturally greatest in large towns and manufacturing areas. Sulphur dioxide is not in itself harmful to paper, but it readily combines with metallic impurities in paper to form sulphuric acid, which is highly destructive. These metallic impurities are found in nearly all modern papers and in many papers made after the mid-eighteenth century.

In 1958 the Technical Committee of the Society of Archivists, in collaboration with Mr. W. H. Langwell, tested air pollution in archive repositories situated in representative areas.[22] Test slips, in which the active ingredient was CO_2O_3 (higher oxide of cobalt), were placed in different parts of the repository—for instance, on walls, in volumes, in boxes, in offices and workrooms—and examined after a week. The slips, a dark mottled brown to begin with, were designed to bleach more or less rapidly and more or less completely according to the amount of sulphur dioxide in the air. In the atmosphere of an industrial district or large town complete change could be expected within a week, or even within 48 hours in the case of extreme pollution. In a dry atmosphere the slips would change to green, and in a humid atmosphere would bleach to white.

The experiment was conducted during two periods: July to September, and November to July. Pollution in the summer period was found to be slight or non-existent. In the winter period rapid fading of the slips was widely experienced. No repository reported complete immunity in all its strong rooms, but at the House of Lords Record Office there was no pollution in the air-conditioned section of the repository, where the incoming air, before entering the strong rooms, passes through Vokes resin wool microbiological filters, designed to remove solid acidic particles, and silica gel beds, which absorb acidic moisture.

From this experiment (which was later repeated on an international basis)[23] the archivists drew three conclusions: that the tests were simple but effective; that complete protection from atmospheric sulphur dioxide can be obtained by air-conditioning, even when the apparatus has not been specifically designed for that purpose; and (the conclusion of perhaps most practical significance for archivists) that virtually complete safety is provided by boxing, even in conditions of high acidity (although, to allow air circulation to deter mould growth, the boxes should have loosely fitting lids, and documents should be placed in them unwrapped; items, such as books, which cannot be boxed should be loosely wrapped). The Committee, however, entered two caveats: firstly, that since the content of the atmosphere is constantly changing, due, for instance, to air movement, seasonal variations, wind direction, and rainfall, one satisfactory test does not necessarily indicate permanent immunity. Secondly, boxes and wrappings themselves in time acquire an acidity which they will transmit to the papers they are designed to protect; so archivists must be prepared to dispense with them even before they have outlived their apparent usefulness.

In October 1961 two chemists, F. L. Hudson and W. D. Milner, reported on an investigation into the tendency of papers, especially book papers, to pick up sulphur from the atmosphere.[24] Their results confirmed Langwell's conclusion that copper and iron in paper help to fix sulphur by catalysing the oxidation of sulphur dioxide to sulphuric acid; and also confirmed the traditional value put on high-quality rag paper, which picked up much less sulphur than, in particular, mechanical pulp paper. But, interestingly in view of Langwell's suggestion for reducing relative humidity by simply raising the temperature, they believe that temperature is important in the tendency to pick up sulphur. Books should, they feel, probably be stored in the cool, dry place which is so often suggested for organic materials generally, but which can only be obtained by an air-drying system, and most conveniently by refrigeration.

Acidity and alkalinity of dilute solutions are measured on a so-called pH scale. From study of a large selection of paper manuscripts it has been established that serious deterioration occurs in nearly all cases where the pH value lies below 5; "this has now been accepted as the critical limit by conservators".[25] Yet the actual concentration of acid involved is extremely low; for instance, in the case of sulphuric acid, a pH value of 5 corresponds approximately to a concentration of 0·00005% of acid. Tests of acidity in paper formerly resulted in destruction of the sample. Recently, however, a quicker and simpler method has been introduced which uses a flat glass electrode in a drop of water on the surface, and leaves the sample intact. As Dr. Werner says, "it might be highly desirable if the determination of the pH value of paper documents were to become an established practice in archive work."[26]

If the pH value of a paper is found to lie below the critical value of 5 the acid present must be removed to safeguard the life of the paper. W. J. Barrow has devised the following process of deacidification: the paper is first immersed for 20 minutes in a saturated solution of lime water (concentration *ca.* 0·15%) and the acid in the paper thereby neutralized. The paper is then transferred to a bath of calcium bicarbonate (concentration *ca.* 0·15%) and left for a further 20 minutes: in this second solution any excess of lime water in the paper is converted into calcium carbonate (chalk) which is deposited as a fine precipitate and held in the fibres of the paper. After the process the pH value is usually about 7·3, i.e. slightly alkaline. At the same time the chalk deposited in the paper will protect it against any future extrinsic source of acidity.[27]

Although deacidification is thus often desirable on its own account, it has become closely associated with a particular technique of document repair—lamination. So long as the Public Record Office remained "faithful to what are known as traditional methods of document repair"[28] and rejected lamination, it was unlikely to practise deacidification extensively. In April 1959 Mr. R. H. Ellis was saying "in passing, but with emphasis, that Mr. Barrow's technique of de-acidification seems a wholly admirable development which deserves wider study and use",[29] but in his description of repair methods at the Public Record Office in October 1961 Mr. D. B. Wardle makes no mention of deacidification,[30] and by the time of the Office's tentative adoption of lamination in October 1962, Mr. Wardle was welcoming a method of deacidification which no longer "necessitated a preliminary process of immersing the documents in alkalising baths and then drying them".[31] In fact, Mr. Ellis had himself spoken of documents "weakened by immersion in the de-acidifying bath";[32] but at the British Museum, where the Barrow process of lamination was actually used, it had been found that any document which, although extremely fragile, was still capable of being handled, could be treated by this process if it was laid between two pieces of tissue paper and then placed in bronze wire-mesh carriers. Indeed, says Dr. Werner, far from weakening documents, there is evidence that deacidification actually causes a slight *increase* in their strength.[33]

Before carrying out deacidification it is essential to check that the ink resists wetting. This can most simply be done by pressing a small piece of damp blotting paper on to the ink to see whether any ink is transferred. If the ink does prove susceptible to water a partial deacidification can be achieved by dusting the document with fine chalk, and leaving it for some time under light pressure.

Insects

Conditions of infestation

Because the materials of archives are almost wholly of organic origin they are liable to attack by forms of life, such as moulds and insects, for which they provide nourishment. There is some difference of opinion among experts about the role of humidity in insect infestation. A. W. M. Hughes suggests that dampness encourages attacks certainly by psosids and possibly by cockroaches: under war-time storage conditions, he says, archives were affected by damp, and "it is often in these circumstances that insect attack occurs".[34] Plenderleith, on the other hand, thinks "the presence of insect parasites is largely independent of atmospheric conditions". He concedes that "the life cycles of insects may be affected profoundly in duration by elevated temperature, moist conditions of packing materials, etc., and even by the existence of mould growths". But his central point is that the presence of insects, compared with the presence of mould, is fortuitous. Moulds grow inevitably when the atmosphere is above a certain relative humidity; insect infestation is largely a matter of chance. The contents of one box may be attacked while a dozen adjacent ones are unaffected. Insects are liable to be discovered unexpectedly; satisfactory hygrometer charts are no evidence of immunity.[35]

Moreover, whereas fungoid growths tend to be widespread and so readily recognized, insects specialized in their food material usually operate locally. The prolonged action of moulds results in general staining, disfiguration, and disintegration, but insect parasites cause local destruction of an irreparable kind. Insects may be active in storage boxes of the best and most modern repository: their attack is thus the more insidious.

As with clothes, perhaps the best protection of archives against insect attack is frequent disturbance. If they are regularly moved and dusted the dangers of attack are negligible; a vacuum cleaner is a useful weapon. Books, especially, should never be jammed together tightly on shelves: this invites attack from both insects and fungi.

Signs of infestation

Small holes are frequently found in the bindings, especially the hinges, of archive volumes—for instance, in open-spined nineteenth-century account books which have been stored away undisturbed for years in estate office cupboards. If the volume is tapped vertically on a table eggs and excreta pellets shower down the inside of the spine: evidence of the activity of the clothes moth. Holes and dust in woodwork reveal the presence of woodworm. Silk may occasionally be noticed, spun by a caterpillar when making a cocoon. Sometimes a moth will be found on the wing. Sometimes all that may be seen are the hurried movements of a creature across the floor, particularly the flash of a silverfish.

Types of insect

Brown house (or false clothes) moth
(*Hofmannophila pseudospretella*)

This is probably the worst enemy of books. The larva (popularly known as bookworm) attacks both leather and cloth bindings, and may bore its way through the pages as well. Its usual location is in the back of the volume where it is perhaps attracted by the gum or glue. The excreta pellets vary in colour with the material on which the larva has been feeding. Eggs are oval and pearly white, slightly over $\frac{1}{24}$ in. in length. The full-grown larva spins a cocoon in which it turns into a chrysalis. This is often found at the base of the back, and sometimes between books that are seldom moved. Adults are moths with dark brown wings, and are about $\frac{1}{3}$-in. to $\frac{1}{2}$-in. in length.

Common furniture beetle or woodworm (*Anobium punctatum*)

This insect, too, damages books, nearly always as a result of the adult beetle's trying to escape from woodwork, for example a bookcase, and boring through a book which happens to be in the way. Hughes once found a beetle which, having bored through one volume of 700 pages, "lost heart and died in the middle of the next massive tome".[36] The beetle is also, understandably, found in wooden deed boxes.

SILVERFISH (*Lepisma saccharina*)

Silverfish feed on starchy materials. They sometimes damage books but it is normally paper which they attack and which, if left long enough, they can reduce to the texture of insubstantial lace. When seen, silverfish are usually darting at tremendous speed across a floor. One visible specimen may betoken scores lurking unsuspected except by the nightwatchman who has passed by night through the deserted library and "observed with amazement how these tiny denizens of the skirting boards disport themselves in the midnight hours".[37]

COCKROACH

There is very little which cockroaches will not attempt to eat. Damage to leather-bound books is normally in blotches, where the surface has been shallowly removed. Cloth-bound books look as if the dressing has been removed in patches. Two kinds of cockroach are common in this country; both attack paper and books. The Common Cockroach (*Blatta orientalis*), often called the Black Beetle, is a long insect which usually lives in warm places, for instance near boilers and in hot pipe ducts. The German Cockroach or Steam Fly (*Blattella germanica*) is much smaller and more agile, and is often found in crevices.

PSOSID

While dampness is probably an added inducement to attack by cockroaches, this is certainly the case with psosids (otherwise known as book-lice or dust-lice). They feed on fungi and mould, and it is thought that they sometimes damage paper, leather, cloth, and parchment in eating the mildew.

Protection

If dead insects are found inside a box of documents it is not advisable to empty the box and dust the contents in the muniment room. Dead insects *may* mean that all life is extinct, but very improbably: some insects, for example the furniture beetle, never look very lively. Eggs may be hidden away, larvae may be active in the bindings, and the net result of such cleaning may be to spread infection.

BOOKWORM

The archive insecticide most generally used in this country is paradichlorobenzene. In crystal form it passes straight to vapour without artificial heat, although a temperature of 70°F is desirable. The crystals, in the proportion of 1 lb to 10 ft³, are put in the bottom of an airtight box; a steel deed box can be used if it is made as nearly airtight as possible, for instance with gummed paper. The affected volumes are put in the box and left in the vapour for a fortnight or three weeks. Loose documents can be given long-term protection in their storage boxes by placing with them several foolscap envelopes, each containing 2 oz of paradichlorobenzene; the end of each envelope should be torn off, and the boxes made as airtight as possible.

An alternative to paradichlorobenzene is carbondisulphide. This has even been applied by brush to the affected parts of a binding: the volume is then kept wrapped in greaseproof paper for a month. The more usual way, however, is to put a saucer of carbondisulphide, in a proportion of 10 oz per ft³, in a sealed box for about a fortnight. Carbondisulphide forms an explosive mixture with air, so it must be used in a room with no naked flame, no smoking, and preferably no heating. For this reason archivists prefer paradichlorobenzene.

The most effective method of dealing with bookworm on a large scale is vacuum fumigation. The National Archives, Washington, and the Huntington Library, California, use a mixture of ethylene oxide and carbon dioxide in this process. Vacuum fumigation with hydrocyanic gas is used at the British Museum, but only for ethnographic material: apparently the Museum does not encounter much bookworm and when it does, uses a saucer of carbondisulphide in a sealed box.

WOODWORM

Cuprinol, although very inflammable, is very good for immunizing furniture timber against woodworm. More elaborate measures are necessary in the case, for instance, of a wooden binding. Plenderleith describes finding a volume with a beechwood binding from which wood dust was falling on to the shelf. Having wrapped up the volume and taken it away, he damped the end papers and removed them from the boards, revealing extensive tunnelling. He blew out the dust with a pressure blower, and then treated the book with carbondisulphide for a fortnight. Finally he strengthened the wooden bindings by painting them with a dilute solution of vinyl acetate in toluene.[38]

If a wooden binding is found to be punctured with woodworm holes when the manuscript is received, a close watch should be kept to see if dust is deposited from the holes; if not, it can be assumed that the woodworm has gone.

SILVERFISH

The Natural History Museum formula is 1 part by bulk sodium fluoride to 6 parts by bulk flour. This powder can be got into the finest crevices by using a horticultural blower. It is a stomach, not a contact, poison, so that spraying a running insect may have its nuisance value, but is not necessarily lethal. Another method is to spread powdered borax along the backs of shelves.

COCKROACH

More potent insecticides are needed for cockroaches than for silverfish. Some suggested chemicals are poisonous to human beings. Plenderleith mentions two chemicals in use in spray form at the British Museum: pyrethrum and lethane. Though these are stomach poisons they act virtually as contact poisons because cockroaches, who like to be immaculate, constantly comb themselves with their front feelers drawn across the mouth.[39]

GENERAL

When insects are affected by contact poisons there is no need for chemicals to come into contact with archives. This is particularly desirable in the case of commercial insecticides, whose composition may not be stated, and which are very unlikely to have been tested in contact with manuscript materials. Gaseous treatment is generally safest: the vapour of paradichlorobenzene and carbondisulphide acts quickly and evaporates after its work is done. Experiments have also been made in incorporating insecticides in the tissue used in the lamination method of document repair.

10. SHELVES AND BOXES

Shelves

Shelving is a subject which engages archivists' attention less than it used to. This is perhaps because many local record offices are now well established: archivists, having investigated different kinds of shelves, have chosen a particular type and remained fairly content.

One or two archivists, however, for example Mr. I. P. Collis of the Somerset Record Office, maintain an especially lively interest in practical topics like shelving and are very ready to strike off in new, unconventional directions. It seems worth while for more traditional archivists to keep note of what they are doing because occasions arise, such as the equipping of a new strong room or even of a new repository, when an archivist can profitably re-examine his assumptions.

Basic considerations in comparing the relative qualities of different kinds of shelving are: strength and rigidity; resistance to fire and to damage by insects; the absence of features likely to damage records, such as rough surfaces, rusting, and sharp edges; provision of free circulation of air; ease of cleaning; adjustability. The materials which have most commonly been used for shelving are: soft timber, hard timber, slate, aluminium alloy, and steel.

Soft timber is usually rejected immediately by most archivists, certainly for permanent storage. It can be painted with fire-resisting paint, but this increases its cost. It can also be immunized against insects, dry rot, etc., by treatment with Cuprinol, but this is very inflammable. However, an archivist may be forced to use soft timber for temporary purposes. For instance, a large deposit of documents may be suddenly received, which is in a very confused state and in poor condition. It will be convenient, and perhaps desirable, to keep and sort such a collection away from the repository's other archives. In these circumstances it may be worth temporarily installing slatted wooden shelving up to the ceiling of a suitable room, getting in as much as possible. Such shelves are relatively cheap, can be assembled rapidly, and can be quickly dismantled and stored when their immediate use is over.

Soft timber is perhaps the cheapest material available for shelving. Hardwood shelves, for example batons of teak held together by cross pieces, are certainly not cheap today. There are such shelves in the Public Record Office; they do not burn easily, are immune from insects, and are very hard, strong, and durable. On the other hand, they are very thick and heavy. The modern archivist is unlikely to contemplate teak as a material for his shelves. Similarly with slate: an even more unlikely sounding material, it also has been used in the past by the Public Record Office. Strong and fireproof, it is enormously heavy, does not allow air-circulation, and encourages condensation. Aluminium alloy is light and does not corrode. There is, however, some doubt about its lasting quality, tensile strength, and rigidity. The Caernarvonshire Record Office has used aluminium alloy shelving, but, according to Mr. J. R. Ede, "the circumstances of this installation were . . . rather exceptional".[1]

In the end, whatever material may be theoretically suitable for shelving, the archivist will "normally be limited to shelving made of steel, for the simple reason that for a given degree of strength and rigidity steel is much cheaper than anything except, perhaps, timber".[2] The fact is that the cost of equipment like shelving comes down with the quantity manufactured. Record offices are never likely to be a sufficiently large market for the manufacture of shelving to their special requirements at reasonable cost, so they must accept what is already available. In steel the choice lies between shelving made for industrial storage (for which there is a large and continuous demand) and shelving made for library storage (for which the demand, though relatively small, is sufficient to interest a few specialist manufacturers).

Industrial shelving

The essential characteristic of industrial shelving is assembly from standard parts to suit individual needs. A bay (the basic unit of shelving, complete in itself) consists of four vertical angle-post uprights, supporting the required number of flat shelves which are adjustable on 1-in. centres by means of holes drilled in both flanges of the uprights. The shelves are attached to the uprights at eight points (i.e. to both flanges at four corners) by means of bolts and nuts. Bays can be fitted back to back to provide double-sided shelving, and any number of bays, whether single- or double-sided, can be lined together to form stacks. Further rigidity is provided by flat cross-braces at sides and back. This is one of the strongest and cheapest forms of adjustable steel shelving. The open sides and backs allow free circulation of air, and since it is unnecessary to use back braces for every bay it is possible, say in alternate bays, to use the full depth of two shelves, back to back, for storing rolled maps and other large documents.

There are, however, two disadvantages. Firstly, the shelves are not quickly adjustable: it is necessary to unscrew eight nuts every time a shelf is moved. Mr. Ede says this need not be a serious drawback if the archivist forecasts his storage requirements accurately;[3] but archivists in general like to keep their archives on the move. Secondly, documents and boxes are liable to catch against the projecting flange of the angle-post uprights and against the ends of bolts (although it is possible, at some extra cost, to substitute flat-section uprights for the standard angle-post uprights; another alternative is uprights of solid sheet steel, with a tubular or squared front edge, but these impede circulation of air).

A final type of industrial shelving is made of slotted angle lengths, of the sort patented by the Dexion Company. Dexion is made in 10-ft lengths, with a choice of four thicknesses depending on the load to be carried. A special feature of Dexion is the perforations of various shapes in the angle lengths which make it possible to adjust the shelves in close increments: it is sometimes useful to have a finer adjustment than the 1 in. available in standard steel shelving. Lengths of Dexion can be cut easily to the required size with a special cutter, and can be joined together by splicing or overlapping.

The Somerset Record Office has used Dexion extensively, starting with a rack for rolled maps, and progressing to one for deposited Quarter Sessions plans, which are large and flat and difficult to store. This second rack was constructed in very wide bays, each 7 ft high by 6 ft wide by 3 ft deep and consisting of four uprights without cross braces. Lengths of Dexion 10 in. apart were placed across the bays in place of solid shelves. The only disadvantage is that the conventional 1-in. thick shelf is replaced by a 2¼ in. flange, so that the height of the shelving needs to be increased proportionately.

Dexion is very adaptable. For instance, the Somerset Record Office has used it for bridging over stairs and gangways, thus utilizing all available space. It can be easily erected, and it allows plenty of circulation of air and penetration of light. The conclusion seems to be that Dexion is particularly useful for special purposes. At the time of erection the cost of Somerset's "double-entry" 6-ft-wide bay was £16; conventional shelving would have cost considerably more. However (and this seems surprising), there is no saving in cost if Dexion is used, as it can be, with 3-ft solid shelves, or (as suggested by the Dexion Company) with chip-board shelves. Dexion shelving is especially adapted for the storage of large items; smaller items, like volumes and small boxes, tend to slip off the skeletonal support provided by a mere framework of Dexion: of course, extra pieces of angle can be inserted, but that is to approach uneconomically close to a fully solid shelf.

Library shelving

Sheet panel uprights

The essential characteristic of library shelving is ready adjustability. In the sheet panel type the shelves are supported on adjustable lugs which fit into holes drilled 1 in. apart in the sheet-steel uprights. The lugs can be moved more readily than nuts and bolts, and do not catch on boxes and documents. The cheapest version of library shelving has uprights made of single sheet panels, with tubular front edges, and flanges at the back to take cross braces. Another slightly more expensive type uses double sheets for the upright panels, giving greater strength and improved appearance; however, additional space is taken up by the width of the double panels, and they may tend to harbour dust and insects.

Bracket shelving

In this type of library shelving the shelves are supported on brackets, the backs of which are hitched, by means of projecting hooks, on to strong steel central uprights perforated on 1 in. centres. Free-standing stacks must have diagonal bracing and, especially if they are of any length, lateral supports overhead. The uprights can be made of sufficient strength to carry the loads of many concrete or steel floors. Multi-tier installations of bracket shelving have been successfully erected even in old buildings, the steel uprights passing through the old floors to carry the new, load-bearing floors.

With its central uprights bracket-type shelving gets right away from the cupboard-without-a-door appearance of panel-upright shelving, and its extremely open nature allows excellent air-circulation. The tray-like shelves are very easily adjustable: for instance, two people can move a shelf complete with contents, and even one person can do it by adjusting the shelf a hole at a time. On the other hand, the bracket sides of the shelves become rather loose in time, and the archivist can find himself clutching a cascade of disintegrating components, rather than comfortably holding a complete shelf. Luxfer shelving of this type, in pale yellow, has a pleasing appearance, in search rooms as well as muniment rooms. Since less sheet steel is used, the cost of bracket shelving is rather less than that of other kinds of library shelving.

Mobile shelving

Where accommodation is limited, and the floor can stand the extra load, mobile shelving has obvious advantages. However, archivists have had reservations about its usefulness, perhaps because of the cumbrousness of older, less mobile types. There is indeed one outstanding hazard: it is clearly not safe to allow documents to overlap the edges of the shelves. In fact, mobile shelving is really not suitable for outsize or awkwardly shaped items: to cater for these it is necessary to install conventional fixed shelving, as has been done at the Staffordshire Record Office, which uses mobile shelving for most of its storage.

Apart from this disadvantage, one writer thinks "there seems no objection, and every advantage, in installing mobile shelving when space is precious", and he quotes, with apparent approval, a maker's claim that the closing-up of the steel units provides extra protection for their contents against fire.[4] Ede, however, lists five further disadvantages of mobile shelving: high cost of installation; high and increasing cost of maintenance; vibration and noise in movement; poor ventilation; and inaccessibility.[5]

The best known mobile shelving in this country, Ingold-Compactus, was invented in 1949 by a Swiss engineer; the sole manufacturing licensees in Great Britain and the Commonwealth are J. Glover and Sons. The system has double-sided stacks up to 21 ft long, made up of the type of shelving required. Small stacks up to 9 ft long are operated by hand, longer stacks by a ¼-h.p. electric motor. The installation in the Staffordshire Record Office is in units either 15 ft or 12 ft 6 in. long; most of the racking has shelves 2 ft 6 in. wide and 3 ft deep, loadable from front or back, but a proportion has shelves 2 ft deep, designed to take books.

Another system of mobile shelving, the American Snead system, has been little used in this country. It consists of a triple bank of double-sided shelving, with a fixed centre row, each face having attached to it a row of hinged double-sided bays. There are thus six layers of shelving between gangways, each outer bay being swung outwards like a door into the gangway to give access to the inner shelving. The system has been adopted in the Archives Nationales in Paris, with a 50% saving in space. The basic cost of materials is probably about the same as in Ingold-Compactus, but the cost of assembly may be higher.

In general, the feeling in repositories in this country (for instance, in the Hertfordshire, Middlesex, and East Suffolk county record offices) seems to be that the installation of a small amount of mobile shelving may help to postpone an accommodation crisis, but that its universal use is not necessarily the most satisfactory long-term answer to problems of archive storage.

SHELVING DIMENSIONS

It is desirable to have a standard length of shelf, to accommodate standard sizes of boxes. The standard length of shelf at the Public Record Office is 3 ft, and this has become normal in English record offices. The optimum depth of shelf will vary with the type of record. Most volumes are comfortable on 12 in. The average file is 14 × 9 in.

(or 15 × 10 in. if boxed). If files are standing they fit conveniently on a 12-in. shelf, but if they are lying on their sides they need deeper shelves. The Public Record Office, which has many depths of shelf, considers 14 in. the best compromise dimension (though it is too deep if there are a lot of volumes). A certain amount of deeper shelving is necessary, for instance for maps and for eighteenth-century deeds written on whole parchment skins. For this specially large material shelves about 3 ft deep are desirable. The shelving in the Nottingham University Manuscripts Department is mainly 15 in. deep, with some 12 in. and some 18 in. The 18-in. shelving is particularly useful when arranged in double stacks: in this way some shelves 3 ft deep are obtained, and these are very convenient for storing large, flat items.

Much of the material in a given collection of records is miscellaneous in character and size, including, for example, bundles, rolls, and volumes, as well as loose documents. The usual practice is to pack this material as conveniently as possible into boxes, omitting only items which are too large or too awkwardly shaped. If he works on this "container" principle the archivist is faced only with fitting mainly standard sized boxes on to his shelves. Up to the present, local record offices have not generally had to accommodate many files; but now that, as a result of increased activity in the fields of modern business and local government records, some offices are acquiring files in larger numbers, they may wish to reconsider the whole of their shelving policy. On the other hand, they may decide not to accord this newer material the standard of accommodation which they give to their older archives, and accept, for instance, the narrower passageways which result from laying file boxes on their sides and allowing them to jut out into the gangways.

In calculating shelving provision in strong rooms the basic dimension is rack + gangway + rack:[6]

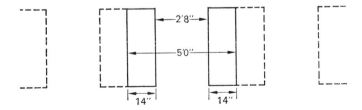

Gangways should have a minimum width of 2 ft 6 in. to 3 ft 0 in. Anything less makes for bad lighting, difficult access to top shelves, and indecipherable labels on bottom shelves. Using the Public Record Office's average shelf depth of 14 in. one arrives at a convenient average figure of 5 ft for the basic dimension of rack + gangway + rack.

The optimum maximum height for shelving is 8 ft. If a room is much over 13 ft high it should be possible to install two tiers, each of which requires a minimum headroom of 6 ft 6 in. If the room is between 8 ft and 13 ft high it will be necessary to have tall stacks to make economical use of the accommodation, but boxes on their top shelves will be difficult to reach (and electricians have been known to use them as ladders to get to the ceiling). On average, 8 ft high racks accommodate 5 shelves each.

From these figures one can now work out the approximate foot-run of shelving in a given strong room:

Top view of two racks, each having five shelves, with intervening gangway.

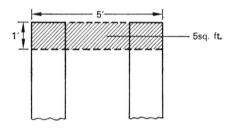

Total shaded floor area = 5 sq. ft. Run of shelving in this area = 10 ft. Foot-run per sq. ft of floor area (i.e. floor area actually covered by racking and gangways between racks) therefore = 2.

In a strong room with 8 ft high racks, each having 5 shelves 14 in. deep, and with gangways 2 ft 8 in. wide, there will thus be 2-foot-run of shelving for each sq. ft of floor space (racking between 12 ft and 14 ft high produces slightly over 3 ft run). This is a useful formula for a preliminary estimate of the amount of storage which a particular strong room will provide.

Further necessary calculations concern the weight of the records, and thus the weight which shelves and floor will have to bear. Records differ very much both in weight and bulk. Files are light; large volumes, such as registers, can be very heavy: they may weigh 20–50 lb each, so that 6 volumes at 40 lb each would result in a load of 2 cwt. It would clearly, however, be uneconomic to design shelving which could take a normal weight of 2 cwt or more. The Ministry of Works, which supplies the Public Record Office, reckons 40 lb per ft run of records, or 1 cwt per shelf of 3 ft length, as a safe average. Very heavy volumes should lie flat, with not more than two to a shelf, thus easing the strain on both bindings and racking.

The figure of 40 lb per ft run of records is useful in calculating the strength not only of shelving but also of floors. As we have seen, 8-ft-high shelving gives 2 ft run of records per square foot of storage space; 40 lb per ft run of records produces, therefore, 80 lb of records per square foot of floor area. Finally, allowing 20 lb per square foot for the racking itself, we arrive at a load of 100 lb per square foot for the whole room; a figure which the architect of a new strong room will be interested to know. In the case of an existing building the archivist will need to discover the safe loading of the floor before he begins to store records; the formula of 100 lb per square foot will then tell him the foot-run capacity of the room.

Boxes and Packing

The dimensions chosen for boxes—length, height, and depth—need to be carefully related to the dimensions of the shelves and to the type of records they are to hold. An archivist soon realizes that it is impracticable and uneconomic to have too many sizes of box: he must aim at the best compromise, and then make special provision for awkward items. Boxes should neither be so small as to waste shelf space, nor so large as to prevent the insertion of fingers at the side (otherwise, there is a strong temptation to pull a box out by the lid, which is thus soon broken; Essex Record Office solves the difficulty by wrapping a tape round each box and instructing its staff to use this to pull the box off the shelf). An optimum space should also be left between the top of a box and the underside of the shelf above: this will allow occasional lids to rise higher than normally owing to awkwardly shaped contents.

Nottingham University Manuscripts Department has only two box-sizes; until recently these were $15\frac{1}{2} \times 12\frac{1}{2} \times 6$ in. and $16\frac{1}{2} \times 16 \times 6$ in., both fitting conveniently on to standard 3-ft-long shelving. Experience, however, showed that the larger box was very heavy when full and difficult to handle on the higher shelves; it is, therefore, being replaced by a box $20\frac{1}{2} \times 15\frac{1}{2} \times 3$ in., four of which combine neatly with two of the smaller boxes on one shelf. The Department has some-times felt the need of a larger box, say 3 ft long by 16 in. wide, so that two would fit side by side on a through shelf 3 ft deep; it would have to be fairly shallow, say 5–6 in., to avoid undue weight. So far, however, the Department has put its bigger material—e.g. medium-size maps and large deeds—in plan-file drawers. It seems likely that a record office will feel an increasing need for a larger size box as it grows older, and opens up more and more documents which have previously been folded.

A box is more rigid if its lid reaches right down to the base. This requirement should be precisely stipulated when ordering from the manufacturer. The archivist should also be careful to indicate that all dimensions are external ones, and to ask that lids be fairly loose fitting—empty boxes with tight lids reaching down to the base can be frustratingly difficult to open.

Some repositories, for example the Essex Record Office, like to pierce holes through the sides of their boxes, on the theory that this improves the ventilation of the contents. Such a policy presupposes, of course, that the air being welcomed is clean air: as we have seen, one of the best protections of archives against atmospheric pollution is adequate wrapping. Moreover, holes in the sides of boxes will only ventilate documents which are contained fairly loosely; they will not introduce air to the insides of bundles or files of papers. The only satisfactory answer would seem to be frequent opening of boxes and airing of their contents, which implies either a well-used record office, or a habit of regular inspection.

Record office boxes used to be made of a type of cardboard called leather-board. This material has now, however, been found to have a comparatively short life: made by crushing fibres under great pressure, the board becomes brittle after the size has gone. The material now used in many record offices, including the Public Record Office, is container board: manufactured from repulped, miscellaneous paper, it is produced with less pressure than leather-board, and is lined with glazed kraft paper which protects it against deterioration.

Small boxes have board 0·08 in. thick, larger ones, 0·16 in. The boxes should be stapled with brass wire to avoid rusting. A drawback of staples is that they scratch tables very easily; perhaps a box could be designed without staples in the base. Container board boxes are not cheap; on the other hand, they are nowhere near as expensive as the buckram-covered boxes used, for example, by the John Rylands Library. A record office in a fair-sized city can find a satisfactory local supplier; one in a small town may have to go further afield. It is a good idea in the first instance to get quotations from a considerable number of firms, asking each one for a sample: there can be a wide range of prices. Since box-making firms are often quite small an archivist may get a lower quotation by indicating that he will have a steady, if smallish demand.

Record offices usually like to get most of their documents into boxes as soon as possible. In an emergency (like shortage of money), however, it may be necessary to wrap records in brown paper. This should be looked on as a temporary measure because brown paper has a relatively short life: it can absorb acidity from the atmosphere and pass it on to its contents while still apparently in good condition. On the other hand, some record offices, and particularly the Public Record Office, use wrapping for long-term packing, for example of repaired, rolled maps. For this the Public Record Office recommends binder's glazed cloth, or unbleached calico, both of which allow the air in.

Other materials used by the Public Record Office for various packing purposes are: strawboard (or pulpboard covered with glazed paper) for protecting large documents; manilla paper (a stout glazed paper) for making file covers for some documents, for example very large parchment documents kept flat in drawers of plan-files; tape or webbing, for attaching, for instance, to rolled maps or large portfolios; Italian cord, a strong string; labels and tags made of rope manilla, a paper which is very difficult to tear; and binder's cloth or buckram, for covering specially made boxes, cases, and portfolios. Containers hand-made in this way are naturally expensive, but very useful, for instance to protect medieval books in their original bindings; numbers were made in the Nottingham University Manuscripts Department by a repairer who was not only a professional binder, but had worked also as a commercial box maker.

11. THE ARRANGEMENT AND DESCRIPTION OF ARCHIVES

IN PREPARING his archives for use, an archivist has two aims: good order and ready availability. Having accessioned and shelved a collection, the archivist needs a record of where it is located in his repository, and what treatment he has given it; if it is an accession of some size the order of its parts should be quickly intelligible, both in general in the strong room and in detail on the shelves. Secondly, if the archivist wants to be able to refer easily to particular items in a collection it will need to be analysed to varying degrees. Schellenberg calls these two processes "arrangement" and "description".[1] Arrangement embraces accessioning and classification; description involves cataloguing (of various types) and indexing.

Arrangement

Accessioning

(i) ACCESSION RECEIPT

When an accession of (particularly, private) records has been received the archivist will want to express to the owner his thanks for the deposit or gift. In his enthusiasm he may be tempted to promise a list or catalogue by a certain date, or perhaps "in the near future". The archivist should, however, resist this temptation: he has no idea what other pressing commitments he may have to accept, and even everyday administrative distractions will usually unhinge a hopeful schedule. Instead, but as a token of the value which he places on the accession, and in the nature of something on account, the archivist may well feel that an official, though attractive, receipt would be acceptable to the owner: the Warwickshire Record Office, for instance, supplies a foolscap receipt in hand-made, linen-rag paper, headed with the county's coat of arms.

(ii) ACCESSIONS REGISTER

The carbon copies of accession receipts are useful for reference purposes, but the archivist also needs a more formal record of his acquisitions: an accessions register in volume form. This should be fairly substantial, with plenty of vertical rulings. An accessions volume is expensive if specially made, but it is possible to adapt a standard account book. An accessions register in card form is not an adequate substitute for a volume: cards can get lost or misplaced or destroyed. The accessions register is, after all, perhaps the most important single record of the repository's activities: a methodical, chronological record of the receipt of archives. Beyond that, it has psychological value as an indication of the importance attached by the repository to the records it receives: it should be neatly kept, without alterations, and preferably written in one person's handwriting.

Schellenberg defines the primary purpose of an accessions register as providing "an immediate, brief, and permanent record of how material came into a repository"[2] (*Local Records* would also include record of where the material goes to in the repository.)[3] The "permanency" required by Schellenberg's definition is catered for by using a substantial volume. "Immediacy" means registering the details of an accession while the details are still fresh in the archivist's mind, so that the collection doesn't get lost sight of, or out of sequence. While registering the accession the archivist can also complete the first stage of its treatment: giving the documents a first dusting, perhaps, boxing loose items, noting documents which need urgent repair, and, having given the collection an identifying number, putting it away in a recorded part of the repository.

As for "briefness", the following details need to be recorded: accession number, date received, source, terms on which received, description (including covering dates), quantity, correspondence file, location, and classification. These details might be laid out across two open pages of a register as illustrated.

Frequently, more than one accession is received from the same source. *Local Records* advises cross-reference in the accessions register, and suggests, as the simplest method, a forward reference from the first entry to *all* additions, with later entries merely referring back to the previous one.[4]

In county record offices it is usual to keep separate registers for official and unofficial records. In addition, a register for temporary deposits and loans is desirable to cater, for instance, for outside documents being examined, or documents received from another record office for the convenience of a student.

A further useful, subsidiary register is one of correspondence, containing a daily record of all in-coming and out-going letters. It might take the following form, across the open pages of a quarto or foolscap notebook:

Date	From/To		Subject	File

In this dual purpose correspondence register in-coming letters are entered in black and out-going letters in red. A correspondence register is helpful in tracing a letter when its writer's name has been forgotten, and also in proving, to the archivist's satisfaction at any rate, that he has not received a letter which someone else claims he has.

A simple system of filing correspondence and other papers in a record office has three sections: I. Miscellaneous, containing all occasional correspondence, much of it from people wishing to visit the record office; II. Subjects, containing the office's general mass of papers, arranged by topic and ranging from, say, "Annual reports" to "Wills"; III. Collections, in which are arranged alphabetically the files of correspondence concerning particular accessions; correspondence negotiating an accession being transferred here from section I as soon as the accession has been received.

(ii) Accessions register

Acc.^{n} no.	Date of acc.^{n}	Source	Terms	Descriptions	Quan-tity	File	Locat-ion or Class-ifica-tion
128	16.6. 1971	Atlas Engineering Co., Ltd. Olympus Works, Barcheston (through Mr. G. Jones, Company Secretary)	De-posit	Accounts, correspondence, minutes, drawings, photo-graphs, c. 1868-c. 1950	5 boxes and 3 rolls	III Atlas	Strong room C

An accession itself must, of course, be labelled with its accession number. A good many accessions are quite small and can be put in either single envelopes or single boxes. If there is more than one item it is unnecessary to label the items themselves, simply the envelope or box that contains them; but, naturally, if an item is ever removed from the strong room, care must be taken to relate it to its container. If there are several containers it is useful to label them: Acc. 128/1, Acc. 128/2, . . ., Acc. 128/8 (end).

It is convenient to allot part of a strong room to unclassified accessions, so that they can be kept in numerical order (though, of course, a single accession may fill a considerable part of a strong room and so disturb the sequence). As collections are classified they are normally removed from this location, but small accessions, which it would be superfluous to classify, may well continue indefinitely in their accession order.

(iii) ACCESSIONS CARD INDEX

To complement the register it is useful to have a card index of accessions, so that the archivist can quickly locate a collection. This index may be an elaborate one, recording not only much of the information already in the register, but also the various stages of treatment of the collection, such as stamping, cataloguing, calendaring, indexing, and dissemination of catalogues. However, it is also worth having a simple index, giving the name of each collection and its location in the repository, arranged by classification marks: this helps to keep a check on the allocation of these marks.

Classification

It is a usual practice today for archivists to arrange a collection physically in classified order, and for the catalogue of the collection to follow the same order. This operation, called "classification" by Schellenberg and "sorting" in English record offices, involves, of course, to some extent, imposing order on the collection; but, to guard against excessive rationalization (or "methodizing", as it was called in the nineteenth-century Public Record Office) the archivist is all the time looking for the natural, organic order—the manner, that is, in which the records were created. There is an older, more cautious procedure which simply accepts any arrangement existing in the records when they are received and lists them document by document, from the first container to the last. This method has two disadvantages. Firstly, in listing document by document, the archivist is tied to a detailed description of the collection: he cannot proceed by broad groups in case other related documents turn up in other parts of the collection. Secondly, a collection treated in this way presents a confused picture both on the shelves and in the catalogue; the archivist can never have the satisfaction of embracing *all* the household accounts or *all* the medieval deeds; he is continually taking boxes down to extract isolated documents. Similarly, since most inquiries are for runs of documents from particular archive groups, it is easier for the searcher if he can see these runs listed consecutively in the catalogue.

Collections are rarely received by the archivist in the order in which he will decide to arrange them. This may seem to contravene the maxim that the archivist must preserve the original archive order; but what, in fact, he is trying to do is to revive or reveal this order. It is a subtle, delicate process, but, like a surgeon, an archivist must be firm, while remaining sensitive to the nature of the organism he is operating on. From his first sight of a collection to the last catalogue entry he makes, the archivist adapts his treatment of the collection to an unspoken assessment of its character, its age, its comprehensiveness, its physical condition, its order, its housing, its use.

What the archivist will not disturb is the original bundle. He may find this tied round with string or tape, wrapped in brown paper, or contained in a tin deed box. These documents have been deliberately put together in the past because they related to a certain piece of property or a particular transaction. It is likely that the bundle will have a label, the parcel a note, the tin box a schedule, describing the contents of each bundle; in addition, the bundles may be numbered and there may be an inventory of them. The bundles, therefore, are clearly organic units, and the archivist must preserve them as they are; he will, in fact, bring similar bundles, parcels, or tins into proximity with each other so that they may form one of the classes (for example, deeds or correspondence) or sub-classes (for example, vouchers) of the collection.

The condition of an accumulation of records when they are received into a repository varies enormously according to the attention they have been given in the past. They may be in good order, or, more likely, some parts of the collection, for instance, those in recent use or those with attractive bindings, may be in better order than others. Many collections of family and estate records come into record offices at a time of depleted staff, so it is possible for a collection which was once well ordered to show signs of recent neglect or disorganization. It may also be the case that the records have been through the hands of an intermediary, perhaps a historian, who has imposed his own artificial arrangement. For whatever reason, then, it is almost certain that the archivist must, to some extent, restore the archive order.

How does an archivist set about sorting (or classifying) a medium-size collection which has lost most of its organic order? As Mr. Francis

Steer says, archivists have different notions about size in archive accumulations,[5] but the collection imagined here would not be too embarrassing; not too big, that is, to stack, when received, in one large sorting room, leaving enough space for tables and for manoeuvring. Ample sorting area is essential. A good idea, employed at the Staffordshire Record Office, is to have plenty of large pigeon holes around the walls of the sorting room. Also useful, for sorting long series of small documents, is a smaller, movable frame of pigeon holes, say 5 ft × 4 ft overall, with eighty holes each 7 × 5 in., which can be hung on the wall. Such a frame was used in the Nottingham University Department of Manuscripts for sorting 5000 medieval deeds connected with thirty counties; under each pigeon-hole was a strip of plastic on which place-names could be written with a crayon and then erased. In the absence of pigeon-holes a considerable number of tables is necessary; these can well be trestles or stacking tables, to be stored away when not in use.

The archivist, then, looks round his store room at a jumbled mass of volumes, bundles, maps, tin boxes, cardboard boxes, and parcels. He sees similar types of records in different parts of the room, and he may decide to move like things near to each other, but it is not essential and he may not have space. Since his aim is to classify, arrange, and list the accumulation as a whole, and he cannot be completely certain about everything that is there until he has looked at the last item, the archivist cannot start listing until he has come to the end of sorting. What he does instead is to insert into each volume or bundle, as he deals with it, a projecting slip of paper on which he writes brief details of the item.

Perhaps the best items to start on are the volumes since they can be worked through more quickly than, say, bundles. The archivist thus makes an earlier impression on the collection, and this is always psychologically helpful. Having collected the volumes together, the archivist begins to examine them one by one. As he identifies volumes of accounts, of rentals, of surveys, etc., he notes this information on the slip which he inserts in each volume, giving also locality and covering dates. He may well at this stage put a classifying letter at the head of the slip; this will help him to sort the volumes later on. Two such slips would then appear thus:

```
┌──────────────┐        ┌──────────────┐
│      A       │        │      R       │
│  Wollaton    │        │              │
│  Household   │        │  Wollaton    │
│  1573-82     │        │  1713-25     │
└╌╌╌╌╌╌╌╌╌╌╌╌╌╌┘        └╌╌╌╌╌╌╌╌╌╌╌╌╌╌┘
```

where A = accounts and R = rentals.

When the archivist has gone through the volumes in this way he can sort them into classes (e.g. accounts) and types (e.g. household), arrange them chronologically within these groups, and pile them away on a side table or on the floor. He does not, however, list them at this stage because other similar volumes may turn up in boxes or parcels.

After the volumes have been gone through, it is a matter of personal preference which class the archivist turns to next; perhaps an attractive group of estate maps engages his attention. If the number of maps is considerable they may take some time to identify and record. Large and, particularly, rolled maps are rather awkward to handle, so the archivist needs a good-size table, and lead weights to keep the maps flat while he is examining their details. As rolled maps acquire a column of dirt down the innermost margin it is worth while giving them a preliminary wipe with a duster (treatment which is desirable with volumes and bundles, too, at this stage, looking at the same time for evidence of mould and insects).

Eventually, of course, the archivist will want to catalogue his maps, giving details of size, scale, surveyor, area, special features, etc. For the moment, however, all that he is concerned with is date and locality; if the area covered by the map includes parts of several parishes their names should be noted, or, alternatively, the area can be identified by the name of that part of the estate. These details are then written in pencil at one end of the outside of the rolled map, and can remain there for convenience even after listing. The maps are probably best arranged alphabetically by principal place, and within that chronologically; minor places will appear in the list, and should ideally be picked up in an index.

Deeds form a considerable part of most estate collections. Detailed cataloguing and calendaring of deeds comes later. At the listing stage the technique for deeds is the same as for other material: to slip a note under the string of the bundle or parcel, giving the covering dates and the places referred to. How the bundles and parcels are then dealt with will depend on their quantity and the structure of the estate. The Middleton family archives in the Nottingham University Department of Manuscripts contain two distinct groups of deeds. The first group consists of 5000 medieval deeds: documents which, having been long dissociated from each other, can be treated as single items and arranged as seems most convenient to the archivist: actually, firstly by county, secondly by parish, and thirdly by date. The second, larger group comprises post-medieval deeds, made up in bundles, with each bundle referring to a particular piece of property or a certain transaction (for example, a marriage settlement). In this case the deeds clearly have to be arranged by existing bundles: as a large proportion of the bundles fall into groups relating to particular parts of the estate, they are conveniently listed firstly by these areas and then chronologically, the date of each bundle being determined by its earliest document.

When the archivist has eliminated volumes, maps, and deeds, he will have dealt with a fair proportion of the whole collection, but he may still be confronted by a considerable mass of miscellaneous bundles and loose papers. At this point he is in danger of getting bogged down. If he approaches the documents one by one he is liable to lose his way in a jungle in which he cannot tell the wood from the trees. There are two methods of getting out of a forest: one is to chop down each tree until there is no forest left; this method, though thorough, can take a lifetime; the other is, by climbing the tallest trees, to feel one's way systematically and expeditiously towards the edges of the wood.

Applied to a mass of estate papers made up in bundles, the moral for the archivist is not to read, identify, and list each individual document, but to flick through a bundle, noting as he goes the dates of the earliest and latest documents, and the subject, or principal subjects, referred to. Of course, this way he will miss some of the subjects, but even if he read every document he would still, because he is not a research worker, miss much of the matter. At this stage the archivist is not aiming at a calendar of the documents, but simply a descriptive list, that is, a list which will give to an inquirer an idea whether the documents fall within his period, his locality, and his subject. The archivist can build up a fair speed in this method of dealing with bundles of papers.

By now, probably most of the collection will have been gone through, but one considerable group, manorial records, may remain. Once again, these can be listed quite simply: by type (court rolls, bailiff's accounts, etc.), by manor, and by date.

When the archivist has dealt with the whole collection in this summary fashion (depending on its size the operation may take him a few days or several weeks) he will finish up with bundles, rolls, and volumes piled more or less neatly about the room, each pile a related group of documents, and each item with a projecting slip bearing a brief description. To each of the groups he has given a letter: A for accounts, D for deeds, E for estate papers, M for manorial records, O for official papers, and so on. He now arranges the groups in alphabetical order, very likely beginning with accounts; if the accounts are a largish group he may wish to divide them into types, e.g. household, personal, estate, but if they are very miscellaneous he may decide simply to arrange them in chronological order, identifying their contents in his list. Having arranged the accounts in the order he prefers he proceeds to number and list them. The beginning of the first page of his list may therefore appear thus:

ACCOUNTS
A
1	1525–36	Wollaton: household, estate, personal
2	1536–48	Wollaton: household, estate
3	1550–56	Wollaton: estate, personal

In a similar way he continues through the remaining groups of the collection.

Mr. Steer has described the method he adopted in listing the very large accumulation of family records of the Duke of Norfolk at Arundel Castle. When he began work he "vainly attempted to sort the archives into classes so as to get all the accounts together, all the letters, all the manorial documents, all the inventories, and so forth, in the hope that they could be catalogued as separate groups". Because of the size of the collection he found this system unworkable. Instead, dealing with each document as he came to it, he noted its details on a card, gave

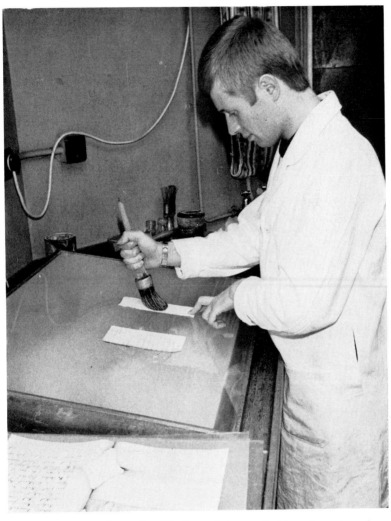

Fig. 1. Paper repair: pasting. The letters being repaired have been charred by fire. At the bottom of the illustration are completed repairs.

Fig. 2. Paper repair: drying. Hanging up repaired paper documents on the drying rack.

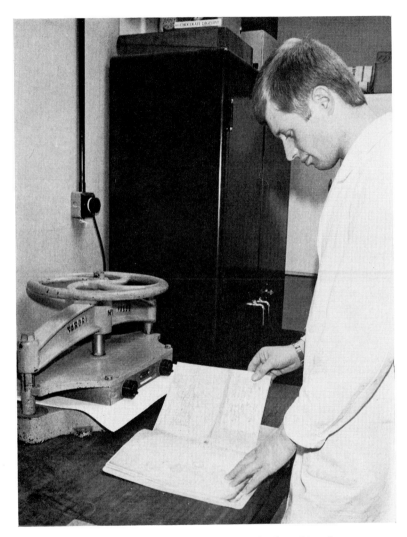

FIG. 3. Lamination. A paper document is being laminated in a hot press. In front is a made-up volume of laminated documents.

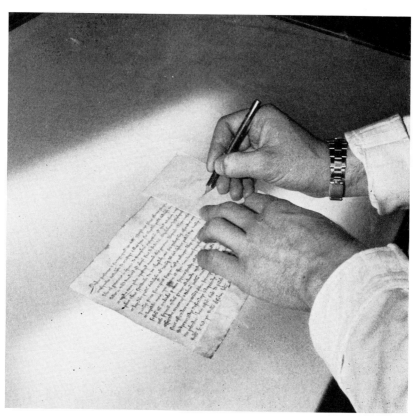

Fig. 4. Parchment repair. Outlining the area to be patched, over an illuminated glass plate.

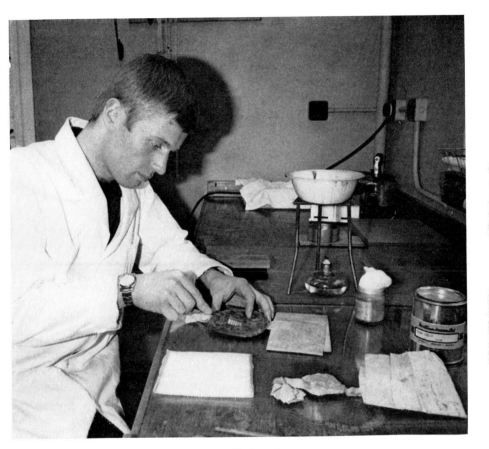

Fig. 5. Seal repair.

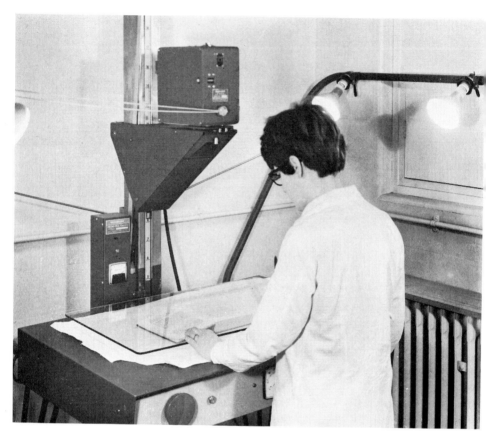

Fig. 6. Microfilming. This Recordak Micro-file Camera, MRD-2, is capable of microfilming large documents up to $36\frac{3}{4} \times 26$ in.; it can be used for photographing newspapers.

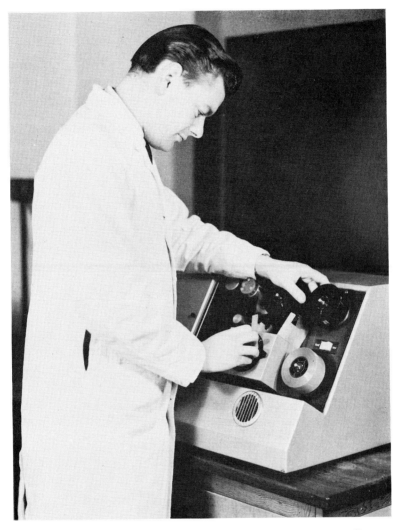

FIG. 7. Making positive microfilm. Making positive from negative microfilm with a Caps-Kalvar printer-processor. A hundred feet of positive film is produced in about 15 minutes.

FIG. 8. Display board. A Nottingham University Department of Manuscripts mobile display board. The board, 6 × 4 ft, and made of Sundaela, can be readily unscrewed and mounted on a wall of the Department's exhibition room.

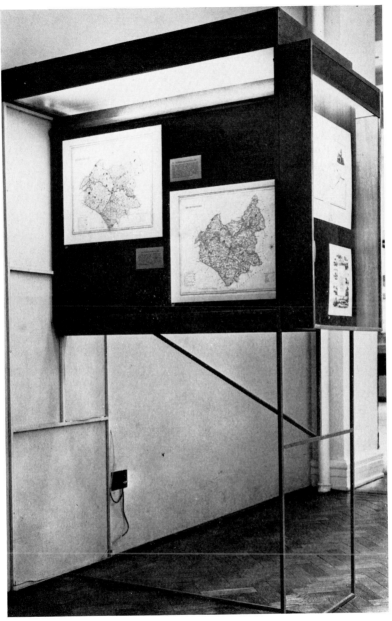

FIG. 9. Exhibition case. A Leicester Museum Archives Department exhibition case. Displayed items are kept in position by the pressure against glass of expanded polystyrene behind felt.

Fig. 10. A clutch of archive teaching units.

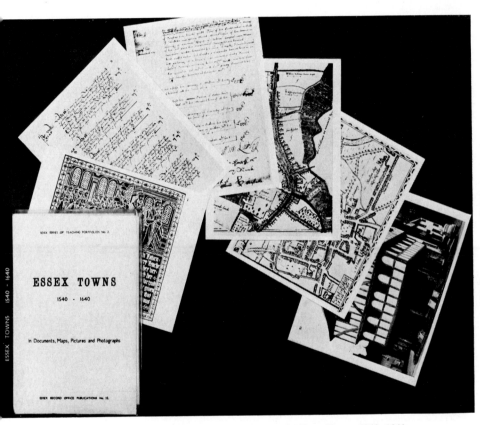

Fig. 11. Essex Record Office archive teaching unit, *Essex Towns, 1540–1640*. The illustration shows only a few of the unit's large and wide selection of well-produced facsimiles. Unusually, the unit caters for excercise in palaeography.

Fig. 12. University of Nottingham Department of Manuscripts archive teaching unit, *The Invasion of England in 1688.*

the document a temporary number, and replaced it in its box. At the end, when the cards had been arranged in classified order, the relevant documents could easily be found and given permanent number and storage: "by this means, one avoided having too much archive material lying about".[6]

Description

Both Jenkinson in his *Manual of Archive Administration* and Schellenberg in his *Management of Archives* devote considerable space to the description of archives. What they (and particularly Schellenberg) say is very detailed (and not always easy to follow) because they have in mind large masses of records, namely the national archives of their respective countries. Practice in smaller record offices will naturally be simpler.

For Schellenberg the description of archives involves two actions: firstly, identifying the "record unit", and, secondly, enumerating its essential qualities. He distinguishes three types of record unit: large, consisting of groups of public records, or collections of private papers; intermediate, consisting of series (or, as English archivists would say, classes) within groups or collections; and small, consisting of individual record items within series. According to Schellenberg, archival description techniques in the U.S.A. relate mainly to large and small record units, i.e. to groups (or collections) and to single items; particularly to the latter: the "literature on the description of private papers is concerned almost exclusively with cataloguing and calendaring single items. . . . Relatively little attention, on the other hand, has been paid to the description of series", yet it is these intermediate units which require the special attention of the archivist.[7]

Schellenberg finds that the terms used to designate various types of finding aids—guides, inventories, calendars, catalogues, lists, indexes, etc.—are "not well defined". During the formative years of the American archives profession the word "catalog" was used as the generic term, because of its library usage, but Schellenberg proposes the term "finding aid" to cover all types of archive description. The word "catalog", he suggests, should be used for a description in card form. "Inventory" should have the meaning it commonly has when applied to goods: a stocktaking of records. "List" should refer to a detailed description in which record items are identified and described. "Calendar" should apply to a chronological list of record items with a brief summary of the contents of each. "Index" should imply a finding aid in card form which shows where specific information can be found in record units; it should merely identify the units, not describe them.[8]

(i) INVENTORIES

For Schellenberg, the first operation is the compilation of an inventory. The inventory is an initial, provisional finding aid, primarily for internal use. Its preparation is also "a kind of discipline" for the archivist, because in compiling it he has to study the organization which produced the records.[9] The inventory's entries should be logically (e.g. organizationally) arranged, and should consist of (i) a title line, giving the record type (e.g. correspondence), its inclusive dates, and its quantity; (ii) a descriptive paragraph, specifying significant items, provenance, content (e.g. main subjects dealt with), and composition (e.g. files, bundles, volumes).[10]

Jenkinson defines an inventory rather more casually as "a summary but complete exposition on paper of the arrangement we have given to our Archives".[11] But English practice, as, in fact, described by Jenkinson, and as followed in numerous local record offices, is similar to the American. Thus, a typical inventory entry reads:

> County Bridges:
> Bridge Committees: 1821–1889; 2 bundles, 2 volumes of draft minutes (1821–51) and 2 volumes of minutes (1846–59, 1876–89).
> By order of Quarter Sessions (Mich. 1876) a standing County Bridges Committee was to be annually appointed.[12]

(ii) DESCRIPTIVE LISTS

Jenkinson says that in repositories of any size, in which part at least of the detailed work must often be postponed for many years, the inventory is an essential finding aid; but "the archivist dealing with a very small quantity of documents might find it possible to proceed at once to detailed Listing or Calendaring and dispense with the Inventory".[13] The experience of local archivists probably confirms this. The classifying operation described earlier produces not an inventory but what in England is called a descriptive list (or by Schellenberg simply a list). A descriptive list "may vary from the barest schedule to a form of catalogue only once removed from the calendar".[14] The feature, however, which distinguishes a descriptive list from an inventory is that the unit of description is not the series (or class) but what Schellenberg calls the item, i.e. a single document, bundle, file, or volume.

The technique of sorting and listing which we have advocated in a small repository leads, then, to the production of a descriptive list: for each item dealt with the archivist gives its nature (record type), the name of the principal places mentioned, the date or covering dates, the physical characteristic of the item (volume, bundle, file, roll) and the approximate number of documents in any bundle. This is a fairly expeditious, fairly (but not too) detailed way of dealing with a collection. The inventory stage is missed, though in fact it returns later on. The inventory example quoted earlier was actually from a record office guide. A guide is an assembly of inventories, and so to prepare one the archivist must condense his descriptive lists into inventories.

(iii) Guides

A typical entry in a local record office guide reads:

> Dodworth National School: treasurer's cash books, 1887–1904 (5). (*Guide to the Manuscript Collections in the Sheffield City Libraries*, 1956, p. 43).

A typical entry in the *Guide to the Contents of the Public Record Office*, 1963 (vol. 1, p. 75), reads:

> Memoranda Rolls (L.T.R.) (E368) 2 Henry III to 5 William IV. 804 rolls.

In these entries there is no attempt to distinguish the dates of particular volumes of rolls; i.e. they are characteristic inventory entries, as distinct from descriptive list entries. It is, however, difficult to make an inventory without first making a list. Hence, it is difficult to make a guide before all the collections in a repository have been listed, and this naturally delays its compilation. Yet a guide is generally recognized by archivists as the best introduction for a student intending to use a particular record office; one suspects, therefore, that parts at any rate of some guides are based on a summary examination of the documents. The Sheffield *Guide* is quite frank about this: "In order that the *Guide* might be as up-to-date as possible on publication, several collections which have not yet been fully listed and arranged for students' use, are included."[15] There is clearly justification for a certain amount of summary treatment in order to get basic information into the hands of research workers as quickly as possible; the information, however, will not always be accurate, or it may give a false impression of the amount of material which exists about a given subject or place. It is for this reason that Schellenberg describes the inventory as provisional, not necessarily correct in detail, and primarily for use within the repository. When the National Archives of the U.S.A. started publishing its inventories, "excessive attention came to be given to their composition and editing", and so the inventory programme of the National Archives became gradually bogged down.[16] Thus the archivist is on the horns of a dilemma when he is considering the publication of his guide. On the whole, there is much to be said for urging him to publish sooner rather than later—temperamentally, archivists (with some notable exceptions) are prone more to punctiliousness than publicity.

Schellenberg quotes an American archivist to the effect that "from the public's point of view, the guide is the first publication that should arrest the attention of the archivist".[17] Schellenberg has no doubt about the importance of guides and devotes twenty-four pages to them (six more, in fact, than indicated in his index). Strangely, however, despite the distinction of the Public Record Office's *Guide*, Jenkinson's *Manual* has only eight lines on the subject: "The first requirement may probably be held to be a General Guide to the contents of the Repository. This will be a small matter if the system of arrangement advocated above has been followed, for it will consist roughly speaking of a combination of all the Introductions and Notes from all the Inventories, condensed as far as possible, *plus* a modicum of information from the body of the Inventory as to dates and (in some cases) quantities."[18] Equally strangely, in view of the popularity of guides with local record offices in England, the word "guide" does not appear at all in the index to *Local Records*.

(iv) CALENDARS

Calendars have whetted a good many antiquarian appetites in the past, so it is not surprising that both Jenkinson and *Local Records* have more to say about them than about guides. Jenkinson defines a calendar as "a précis whose compiler endeavours, while economizing space, to achieve the same end as the Editor of a full text—that of making consultation of the original document unnecessary save in exceptional circumstances".[19] For *Local Records* "the ideal method of treatment of records is by the calendar and, for certain types of archives, notably title deeds, it is eventually almost the only practical method of cataloguing. This method, however, can hardly be applied to many other records . . . in repositories where economies of time and labour are of vital significance."[20]

However, once again, it is Schellenberg who is the most stimulating. He interestingly suggests that the technique of calendaring "probably grew out of the registry practices of English government offices. In such offices, documents are brought together into file units that are registered, i.e. identified by date, by the name of the person initiating a transaction, and by a brief statement of the content of the transaction."[21] English archivists began compiling calendars of records in the State Paper Office as early as 1825, and the first Deputy Keeper of the Public Record Office, Francis Palgrave, began a systematic programme of calendaring in 1841. Schellenberg then goes on to give a pithy statement of the nature, virtues, and deficiencies of calendars. They contain, he says, substantially more information about records than lists, and they are always concerned with individual documents, which are listed in chronological order, identified, where possible, by the names of writer and recipient, and described by a digest of their contents. On the other hand, calendaring is a time-consuming and expensive procedure which can only be justified for important documents with great research value. Jenkinson, as we have seen, says that the aim of the calendar is to make consultation of the original document unnecessary except in exceptional circumstances. But, claims Schellenberg, "a cheaper and more accurate modern way of doing this is to microfilm" the originals; and, from a research point of view, microfilming is better because it provides a full text, not merely an abstract. If, on the other hand, the calendar paraphrases the language of the main facts and ideas of the documents, then, says Schellenberg, "perhaps a better and more efficient way of providing information in regard to the documents is to compile subject lists of them. In such lists, documents are described in relation to subject heads, not merely enumerated in chronological sequence. The information provided in them about the record type, the provenance, the dates, and the content of individual documents is usually quite adequate to meet all scholarly needs".[22]

A second reason for calendaring, continues Schellenberg, is "to make records accessible that would otherwise be inaccessible because of their physical character", and he gives as "a perfect example" the calendars prepared by the Public Record Office of medieval rolls, documents that are difficult to use because they are cumbersome and sometimes in poor condition, and because (and here Schellenberg writes presumably as a modernist) "the writing in them is often almost indecipherable and in languages difficult for many present-day scholars to interpret". Schellenberg gives as a third reason for calendaring, the protection of "records of great intrinsic value" by reducing the need to handle the originals; but, he thinks, this purpose "can be accomplished as well and perhaps more cheaply by microfilming the documents".

Schellenberg concludes on a gently satirical note:

> Calendars have a peculiar appeal to historians. They provide information about documents in chronological sequence—the sequence in which historians must read them to understand how things actually happened. They provide enough information about documents to enable an historian to know if any one of them is pertinent to his enquiry. They almost relieve historians of note-taking, and often relieve them of the necessity of consulting the originals of documents.[23]

(v) INDEXES

One of the ways of judging the quality, or at any rate, the maturity of a record office is to look at the extent of its indexing. On the whole, an archivist cannot afford to engage in systematic indexing until his listing and perhaps his calendaring have reached a fair pitch; but there is a technique, practised in the past by the Nottinghamshire Records Office, of listing straight on to cards, which can then be arranged in index order. This sounds attractive, but there is some doubt whether it produces either satisfactory lists or decent indexes: it is as though the two disciplines require different frames of mind which are difficult to adopt simultaneously. The virtues of extensive and thorough indexing have been eloquently sung by Mr. Emmison who graphically portrays the miseries of record offices without them and the complacency of customers with them.[24] In the early years of a record office an archivist, perhaps with the help of an assistant, can usually recall his collections in sufficient detail to be able to refer readily to the relevant lists and guide inquirers in the right direction. With growth, however, this becomes gradually impossible and indexes come to seem inevitable. Yet they can never be all-sufficient. Just as a reader in a closed-access library can find the formal punctilios of the most detailed catalogue frustratingly inadequate, so a student confronted by cards full of references to names and subjects feels the need for some sort of evaluative comment before he calls for particular documents. Indexes will always need archivists as midwives. Nevertheless, there is no doubt that indexes satisfactorily narrow students' options and stimulate archivists' memories.

12. REPAIR

THE number of documents awaiting repair in any repository is likely to be large, and may sometimes be enormous. Since repair is slow the work needing a repairer's attention stretches into the indefinite future. All archivists are sensitive to the need for repair, but some are particularly attracted by the techniques and the craftsmanship involved. From an older generation one thinks, for instance, of G. H. Fowler, the influence of whose *The Care of County Muniments* (1923)[1] was seminal in the administration of local archives, and of Jenkinson, who has been described as the "archivist chiefly responsible" for the development of the orthodox method of repair.[2] The repair room has always occupied a prominent position in the local record office—if not in reality, then at least in the archivist's list of priorities for the future.

By means of practical courses of instruction, the traditional methods of repair have been generously disseminated by the Public Record Office to local record offices throughout the country. It is, of course, possible to train a repairer from scratch—from a neat-fingered boy; but it is better to take someone who has served his time as a bookbinder, and then give him further training in manuscript repair: the services of a skilled binder are, in any case, always valuable—for the repair of bindings, but also for the manufacture of special boxes, portfolios, and map cases. A trained binder will need to be paid trade union rates; in addition he will probably find the holidays and working conditions in a record office more acceptable than elsewhere. Because of its tea-brewing facilities the repair room frequently becomes the social centre of the office.

As with other archive topics, the techniques of manuscript repair have been matter for a good deal of amiable controversy between traditionalists and innovators: the one group having a natural stronghold in the Public Record Office, the other deriving its ideas largely from America and including several local archivists prepared to experiment. The principles of traditional repair were stated by Jenkinson many years ago: replace missing material by material of the same kind; do not take away anything which was there when the document was received; put into the document as few alien materials as possible; and, since no laboratory test can tell the effects of time, use only repair materials which have been tested for durability by experience. The practical expression given to these principles at the Public Record Office has been described more recently by Mr. D. B. Wardle: "parchment documents are repaired with parchment for the most part, and paper documents with paper; when the written surface must be strengthened, silk gauze is applied; only wheat-flour paste is used as an adhesive, and the size applied to paper documents is a gelatine size made from parchment waste."[3]

The principal controversy has centred on lamination, a repair technique adopted by the British Museum (which, unlike the Public Record Office, has a scientific department) and, with enthusiasm, by a good many local record offices. And such has been the influence of the modern resurgence in archives on traditional attitudes that, while apparently fighting a rearguard action against lamination, the Public Record Office has, in fact, both shifted its ground in this particular, and in general succeeded in retaining its position at the centre of repair practice in this country—by arranging, under its aegis, two or three meetings a year of repairers from repositories throughout England and Wales.

What a repairer decides to do with a document in need of repair will, therefore, partly depend on whether he (or his archivist) is a traditionalist or an innovator. Since, however, lamination is a technique advocated principally for dealing with large quantities of uniform-sized, second-class, modern records, the repairer will remain, in large areas of his work, dependent on traditional methods developed over many years in the Public Record Office, modified, through the use of modern materials, by unconventional archivists and ingenious repairers.

Confronted by a document on which he decides to employ traditional methods, the repairer has to consider the material of the document (paper or parchment), whether it is written on one side or both sides, the extent of the damage, and the cause of the damage. The document may have suffered from bad handling, damp, fungi, insects, burning, or acid pollution from the atmosphere. Of these agents the most frequent in this country is damp. If documents are still damp when they arrive in a repository they must be dried out as soon as possible, by putting them in a good current of drying air, and turning folios over frequently. When only a few documents are involved they can be dried by putting them between sheets of cartridge paper and pressing them; but this must not be done with parchment documents, which turn black if pressed when wet.

Damp documents are also likely to be affected by mildew. It is advisable to treat mildew quickly, to prevent its spreading. As soon as the documents are dry, therefore, they should be exposed to thymol vapour in a cabinet or a fumigation chamber. Similarly, at this stage, the archivist must be looking for evidence of the presence of insects, which should be treated in the ways already described.

So far we have been discussing preliminary, first-aid treatment of the records. Unless particular documents are obviously in danger of rapid deterioration the records will probably now be put away until the repairer is ready to attend to them. Since there is more than enough to keep a repairer occupied, it seems a good idea to diversify his work as much as possible by allowing him to move between various types of document—for instance, parchment deeds, maps, documents needing lamination—as he feels inclined. It is essential, however, that he work systematically through each class, so that the archivist can assume that all documents earlier in the catalogue than the point the repairer has reached are either repaired or are not in need of repair.

Superimposed on this basic programme the repairer will have an emergency programme. That is, he must be prepared to interrupt his bread-and-butter work to undertake pressing commissions—for example, items needed for photographing or immediate consultation, items frequently consulted, or items wanted for exhibition.

The repairer should keep a card index in class order of the documents he has repaired, and should keep a note of the total of each kind of repair operation—paper, parchment, seal, lamination, etc.—that he has carried out.

It is, of course, desirable that a repairer understand the nature of archives. Some of this understanding will be conveyed to him when he starts work at the record office; some will be got from his subsequent training, perhaps at the Public Record Office; the remainder he will pick up from methods, attitudes, conversations, which he sees and hears during his work. The archivist will gradually come to feel how much the repairer can be left to work on his own, and similarly the repairer will come to appreciate the occasions on which he needs to consult the archivist. If the repairer is a good one, he should be left to work as much on his own as possible, even though, occasionally, misunderstandings may occur.

Paper Repair

The repair of paper documents is conducted with both document and repair paper quite wet. This is because pasting will make the paper and parts of the document damp in any case, and the repairer has to ensure that the material of both expands and contracts uniformly. Similarly, the grain—that is, the wire-lines—of both document and paper must lie in the same direction, or cockling will result.

There are two basic methods of paper repair, depending on whether the document is written on one side or on both sides. If the document is written on only one side, then it can be backed, that is, pasted on to a whole sheet of repair paper. If there is writing on the other side as well (and this often covers a smaller area of the document, as in the case of an endorsement) then the document is framed, that is, a whole sheet of repair paper is pasted over the back of the document but a "window" is then removed from the repair paper to reveal the writing: removal is done by tearing, not cutting, so as to produce a feathered edge, and the boundary of the writing is indicated to the repairer by illumination from below through the glass plate in his repair bench. The open area of writing is then often covered with silk gauze to strengthen the part of the document which lacks the benefit of repair paper. When a document is particularly fragile it can be "double-framed" by employing this process on both sides. Occasionally a document is covered with writing right to the edges on both sides and in this case it may only be possible to sandwich it between two pieces of silk gauze since there is insufficient margin for repair paper to grip.

After the paper document has been backed or framed it is placed between waxed sheets and cartridge paper, and put under light pressure (a couple of heavy boards are sufficient) for 12 to 24 hours. When it is dry it is pressed hard between cartridge papers. Then it is trimmed and sized. The size is applied with a broad camel-hair brush, and is painted onto both sides of the document. The document is then hung on the wires of a drying rack, being moved occasionally to avoid sticking.

Parchment Repair

Parchment is a rather more contrarious material than paper. It is the reverse of paper in its tendency to suffer more from dryness than from damp (though extreme wetness makes parchment coagulate). If a parchment document is badly shrunk or crinkled by heat it needs to be folded in a fairly wet, soft cloth, in such a way that no part of the document is in direct contact with any other part otherwise there is danger of the whole deteriorating into a gluey mass.

As in the case of paper, a parchment document in need of repair is damped completely and evenly. The repair parchment has to be buffed, that is roughened, so that when pasted it will stick to the document. Buffing can be done with a file, but the Public Record Office uses a buffing machine. The methods of parchment repair are similar to those of paper repair—backing, framing, gauzing. The equivalent of feathering is achieved by paring the edges of the repair parchment with a knife having a bevelled edge. Backing of parchment is not as frequent as of paper because a parchment document often has more body than a paper one: patching and cornering are usually sufficient.

Parchment documents have some special features, however, which require special attention. Thus care must be taken not to press them hard when wet; special care must be taken in damping parchment documents which are illuminated or have coloured inks; and, in the case of documents with flaking carbon ink, silk gauze should be pasted over the ink to stop further peeling.

Public Record Office Experiments

The methods of paper and parchment repair briefly outlined here were introduced by the Public Record Office about fifty years ago and have, says Wardle, stood the test of time.[4] Nevertheless, although its self-confessed policy is one of caution and wait-and-see, the P.R.O. is, he claims, constantly on the look-out for safe improvements in methods, and more effective or more economical materials: many experiments have been made, and some have led to marked improvement in repairing technique.

Thus the high cost and often inferior quality of repair parchment since the war prompted the Public Record Office to search for a substitute suitable for documents not of the first importance. Since the material used must be as strong as the sound parts of the document, paper is normally ruled out. Linen and cotton are strong enough, but as they shrink when damp and expand again when dry (the reverse of parchment) a parchment document backed with closely woven linen or cotton ends by curling up. Jaconette, a cotton cloth of medium thickness, is, however, manageable and is used at the Public Record Office for backing large parchment documents which have to be folded. Loosely woven cotton mull can also be used if it is backed in turn with thin paper: the shrinkage of the paper in drying counteracts the curl of the cotton; but as additional material and an additional operation are thus involved the technique is uneconomic.

Of other materials tried by the Public Record Office as a substitute for parchment and finally abandoned, cotton organdie also produced curling, and bonded fibre absorbed too much paste and took too long to dry. And so, after numerous experiments, the *status quo* of repairing parchment with parchment has returned; except for one small innovation: in the case of documents of secondary importance filling-in is being done with hand-made bank paper instead of with parchment pieces. As the paper is simply pasted on and torn to shape, whereas parchment has to be cut to size and pared, there is a considerable saving in time.

The Public Record Office was also disappointed in its search for better paste. A long trial was given to paste made from wheat starch; more quickly made, very smooth, and easily worked up, it seemed a great advance on wheat flour; unfortunately, it proved not to have the holding power of flour paste, and was unsuitable, for instance, for backing maps which had to be rolled; it dried too quickly for some work; and it lacked the viscosity or "slide" which is especially valuable in parchment repair. Reluctantly, then, it was dropped; but, at W. H.

Langwell's suggestion, flour paste is now made in a pressure cooker, which produces an even consistency.

More successful was an experiment in strengthening modern paper records (now being received in increasing quantities) by a quicker method than applying normal gelatinous size, in which drying and subsequent pressing are slow. Following a suggestion by Langwell that a spirit solution of polyvinyl acetate, a synthetic resin used in glue and paints which is highly stable, permanent, and not subject to discoloration, would dry quickly and not cockle the paper, the Public Record Office made a trial on poor-quality, printed material, using a 6% solution of the adhesive "Heatfix" in industrial methylated spirit, to which 1% of magnesium acetate was added as an acid-acceptor. The size was sprayed on but could equally well have been brushed on. The papers thus treated with this synthetic size will be examined at intervals to see whether discoloration or other deterioration takes place.

When terylene and nylon were introduced after the war the Public Record Office hoped they might be useful as substitutes for silk gauze. Trials were made of fine terylene gauze and subsequently of non-woven terylene and other synthetic fibres, but none would stick securely with flour paste, and it was feared that chemical adhesives might prove unstable.

Nevertheless, because of this very property of non-adhesion with flour paste, terylene has proved an almost ideal material as a support for documents during repair. The traditional material, waxed tissue, can only be used two or three times, and also leaves traces of wax on the document which appears as "an unpleasant patchy sheen". Terylene, on the other hand, is very durable, can be rinsed out and used repeatedly, and is porous, so that air-bubbles are not so troublesome when the material is laid down on the bench; finally, a document can be dried out on terylene without fear of adhesion as long as excessive paste is not used on the supported side.

The terylene is used in conjunction with sheets of perspex laid over the glass window of the repair bench. On the completion of each repair the work, carried on the perspex sheet, is set aside to dry (Staffordshire Record Office has a rack in which several perspex sheets are held vertically) and thus the bench is left free for the next document. When the work is dry, and the terylene support has been peeled off, the document is already flat and so does not need pressing; the method is, therefore, especially useful for documents with applied seals since these are not easy to press.

Another recent change at the Public Record Office has been the adoption of thick blotting paper in place of cartridge paper for drying and pressing. It is more absorbent than cartridge paper, and if the document should stick at any point the surface of the document is not likely to be stripped when the two are pulled apart, as can easily happen with cartridge paper. Blotting paper does not last long, but, on the other hand, says Wardle, cartridge paper tended to be kept too long.

Lamination

Lamination is the sandwiching of a document between two sheets of supporting material. Lamination in a general sense has long been employed in conventional manuscript repair, for instance in enclosing a document between two sheets of silk gauze. But in current manuscript repair parlance it is identified with a technique of inserting a document between two sheets of plastic material.

This method was originated just before the war by the American archivist, W. J. Barrow. In his process the document, having been previously deacidified, is placed between two sheets of cellulose acetate film; a sheet of fine Japan tissue paper is then placed on each side, making a five-ply sandwich. The sandwich is passed through a laminator, a machine consisting of two thermostatically controlled plates, which heat to *ca.* 315–325°F, and a pair of calender rollers which can apply pressure varying from 300 to 2000 lb per square inch.

Exception to this process was taken by the Public Record Office. Thus R. H. Ellis, writing in 1959,[5] suggested that lamination is "only a very partial solution" of the problems of archivists in this country, who are concerned with a very wide range of problems: with parchment documents; with paper or parchment documents bearing painting or illumination and so requiring special care; with maps, plans, and other outsize documents; and with seals and bindings. Lamination, on the other hand, is suitable only for paper documents, and even then only those small enough to pass through the machine.

The orthodox repairer, says Ellis, regards each document as an individual case and varies its treatment to suit its condition: often only sizing will be needed; if repair paper is required he can vary the amount or the weight according to the extent of the damage; he can use silk gauze if needed, and again in varying quantity; he can thicken or dilute the paste, or size, before as well as after repair; and he repairs only the damaged part of a document. Lamination has none of this flexibility: the method and the materials are the same for each document. It is a process designed to deal with the whole of every leaf: lamination of one part of a document has not so far proved satisfactory.

Further, silk gauze and paper applied with flour or starch paste lie on the surface of the document and are not difficult to remove because they soak off easily. Acetate foil can certainly be dissolved away in acetone, but since it has been *pressed* into the document, are not the fibres of the paper possibly broken or bruised by the pressure and heat, or distorted by the intrusion of the melted foil?

However, the Barrow process of lamination was adopted by the British Museum. In April 1958 Dr. A. E. A. Werner of the Museum contributed to an article on the conservation of documents which took exception to silking, "the classical technique of lamination", because the silk deteriorates, has to be replaced every twenty-five years, and is difficult to remove. The writers thought the Barrow process "the safest technique yet offered for the protection of valuable documents on paper . . . [it] introduces nothing of a foreign nature to the paper that cannot at any time be removed with the greatest of ease". They concluded that "as a routine method for preserving bulk collections of letters and such like it is unsurpassed especially where the process selected is continuous and involves the minimum of strain".[6]

Ellis was swift to respond over the sensitive subject of silk, claiming that, during the fifty years the Public Record Office had used silk gauze, it had "certainly not been observed that it regularly requires replacement after half that time". The gap may well be one between generations. In the Barrow process lamination is only a part of the operation of repair: more fundamental is the previous deacidification. Awareness of the damage caused to paper by atmospheric acidity is, of course, recent; classical silking was applied to documents untreated for acidity. Ellis admits that if a document with a strong acid content is repaired with silk and not first deacidified then the acid will in a short time attack the silk as well as the document; but that, he maintains, is a different matter. In general, Ellis's stance seems somewhat uncertain. Thus, while saying that "Mr. Barrow's technique of deacidification seems a wholly admirable development which deserves wider study and use", he also claims that a document is "weakened by immersion in the de-acidifying bath"; and, although he saw lamination as "a repair process with great possibilities", yet he felt that "lamination (even if guaranteed permanent and harmless) still offers only a partial solution".[7] In a brief reply to Ellis published in October 1959 Werner claimed that Barrow had produced evidence that "deacidification actually causes a slight *increase* in strength", and said that this was certainly the experience of the British Museum.[8]

Ellis's hesitation was reflected in the practice of the Public Record Office. Writing in October 1961 D. B. Wardle underlined the Office's continuing allegiance to "what are known as traditional methods of document repair"; as far as lamination was concerned, "there is a possibility that the complex synthetic materials used may in time undergo changes which could frustrate the purposes of the repair". Nevertheless, he was careful not to close the door completely: lamination had "not so far been introduced" largely from caution, and the Office was constantly on the look out for safe improvements in methods.[9] In fact, a year later, in October 1962, Wardle was able to announce, in an article entitled "Lamination for all?", that the Public Record Office had been trying out Langwell's method of lamination on library and reference material "with promising results", and that the method "may well bring this process of document repair within the reach of the smaller record offices". Yet the final note was still a tentative one: the process must be regarded as "still in the experimental stage" and "on trial for a long time to come"; "it will have to be submitted to artificial ageing and other tests before its suitability for use with archival documents can be judged".[10]

Fear of deacidification was still present in Public Record Office minds, and Wardle noticed it as a "very important feature" of Langwell's process that the deacidifying agent was incorporated in the laminating tissue, thus avoiding the risk involved in immersing a document in alkalizing baths. This method of lamination, patented by W. H. Langwell and called the Postlip Duplex process, is the one now usually adopted by local record offices. Although the Barrow process had been successful its special roller press was very expensive, a rather high temperature was used, and the deacidification technique was tedious. Recent developments in synthetic plastics now give a choice of adhesives which can be activated at a much lower temperature than in the Barrow process so giving a very wide margin of safety. The Postlip Duplex process uses a tissue which "combines in a single sheet a strong fibrous tissue paper of undoubted permanence, a stable fusible polyvinyl acetate resin, and an acid-neutralizing salt such as magnesium acetate". This combination makes separate deacidification unnecessary, simplifies the process, and allows a low temperature of 185°F or even, by using a cheap solvent such as methylated spirit, an unheated press.[11]

Langwell claims that his process is very flexible because of four variable factors: the length of pressing, the temperature of the patens, the amount of pressure, and the presence of a small amount of moisture in the hot process (in the cold process the amount and nature of the solvent are also important factors). The apparatus is quite simple. For the cold process only a bookbinder's standing or nipping press is needed; while it requires more manipulative skill it is useful to the archivist who has only a few documents to repair and who does not wish to spend even a modest amount on a hot mounting press. It is probable, however, that local archivists, if they adopt lamination at all, will use the hot process; in this heat activates the adhesive, the duplex tissue softening at about 185°F: a standard, easily obtained, screw-operated photographic dry mounting press, capable of giving an even pressure of about 20 lb per square inch over a platen area of 200–300 in², is quite suitable, but should be fitted with an efficient thermostat.

For lamination by the hot method the document is first cleaned and flattened. A seven-decker sandwich is then built up as follows:

> Sheet of blotting paper
> Sheet of release paper
> Sheet of tissue
> Document
> Sheet of tissue
> Sheet of release paper
> Sheet of blotting paper

With a sheet of smooth white card, rather larger than the platens, placed under the sandwich so that it can be handled without burnt fingers, the sandwich is then pressed at full pressure for about 1 minute at 185°F. It is then removed from the press, the release papers stripped away, and the laminate (i.e. the laminated document) trimmed, leaving a small margin to ensure complete sealing. Variations of time, temperature, pressure, and moisture can give results which are better than those of the standard process. Thus increased pressure, says Langwell, gives excellent results with a thinly coated tissue, producing a laminate which is thinner and more flexible than usual. Even in the standard process Wardle advocates slightly moistening the document beforehand between damp blotting papers (in much the same way as parchment is softened for flattening), because some documents may be difficult to laminate dry; in the case of a document bearing soluble colours, the tissues should be moistened instead of the document.

In the cold process the tissue is first softened with a solvent and then built into a sandwich in the same way as for the hot process. After the sandwich has been pressed between boards under full pressure for 5 minutes it is removed from the press and the release papers are carefully stripped from the sticky laminate, which should be kept as flat as possible to prevent creasing and separation of the layers. When, after a few minutes, the laminate has dried out sufficiently for it to be handled safely, the free edges of tissue are lightly sponged over with a piece of cotton wool soaked in spirit, and any holes in the document are treated in the same way. Finally, the laminate is given a quick nip between release papers to seal the edges and so completely encapsule the document.

If a document is in several pieces these can be assembled in register on a sheet of tissue resting on a sheet of release paper. Each piece of document should be lightly touched with a warm tacking iron to fix it temporarily in position. The document is then moderately damped with spirit and the sandwich completed and pressed as before. If a document bears colours likely to run when damped, care should be taken not to flood the document with excess spirit.

After standing in the air for a few hours laminated documents can be creased and sewn for binding. If only one surface of a document requires protection both sides need not be laminated; one-sided lamination gives a very thin, flexible sheet. A very smooth-surfaced, heavily sized paper may not produce a perfect laminate under standard hot treatment, so the temperature should be raised to 212°F and, if necessary, the pressing time increased to 2–5 minutes; the Public Record Office method of damping may prove even more effective. Documents with applied seals can be laminated by the cold process by cutting a hole in the tissue to take the seal, and pressing with a rubber cushion arranged so as to give a soft bed for the seal. Both cold-process and hot-process laminates can be delaminated by soaking in methylated spirits, which leave the document unharmed.

Lamination has been successfully used in a number of local record offices and seems likely to spread. In the Nottingham University Department of Manuscripts it has been particularly employed for repairing a long series of archdeaconry presentments. These are documents which, though originally on file, are now loose, are normally of uniform, quarto size, are not too damaged but are frequently decayed at the edges, and generally lack body. Though sizing would have returned some of this body, the over-all nature and condition of the documents seemed to make them eligible candidates for lamination. After repair the sheets are guarded and filed in manilla folders, thus forming handy "books". There has been a little sticking of sheets after lamination (called "blocking") but this has been quickly eradicated by dusting with French chalk.

Lamination, while less expensive than orthodox repair, is not cheap. It was found at Nottingham that a quarto size sheet of tissue cost 2d., so that the repair of a "book" of archdeaconry presentments of 120 leaves cost £2 in tissue alone. However, it was also found that repair by lamination took only a quarter of the time of orthodox repair. Moreover, the equipment is cheap, the operation is simple, and the result seems very satisfactory. Each record office must decide for itself the merits of lamination.

Binding

The repair of bindings is not a major preoccupation of document repairers. *Local Records* says the repairer "should be capable of undertaking high quality hand-binding in the style of the original".[12] In a local record office, where there is already so great a demand on the repairer's time, it would clearly be disproportionate to ask him to spend hours rebinding a nineteenth-century account book. However, although most volumes in such an office are modern, sixteenth- and seventeenth-century parchment-bound account books are common, and these could fairly quickly be rebound in their original style.

County record offices do not normally have many literary manuscripts; libraries may have. If the manuscripts which need rebinding are held on deposit and have monetary value the library is likely to be in a quandary. Should a volume be otherwise in fair condition it may be best to leave its binding unrepaired: in this way, at least, its make-up may be visible. But if its leaves are decaying, and if the volume is in frequent use, the question of rebinding becomes more pressing. The whole status of the volume then requires careful consideration. In the moderate words of one owner "care should perhaps be taken to do nothing too drastic",[13] and the archivist would certainly wish to consult the owner before proceeding. The decision might well be to commission a distinguished binder: as, for instance, Sydney Cockerell in the case of some of the medieval and renaissance manuscripts in the Hunterian collection of Glasgow University Library. Aesthetic considerations then arise. Should the aim be a facsimile binding, or should the binder be allowed to produce a work of art in its own right? Consideration of this kind will not normally concern a county archivist, but they may easily arise in connection with the manuscript volumes of a university or large public library.

The traditional public library practice of binding loose papers into volumes is probably now dying out. At the Public Record Office and in local record offices the equivalent treatment is "guarding and filing". This is frequently done with documents which were originally kept in some sort of bundle or file, and is particularly useful in the case of documents of varying sizes, for example those in Quarter Sessions files or bundles. A piece of guard paper ("toned seconds" in the case of paper documents, and linen-backed paper in the case of parchment documents) is stuck to one edge of each document with flour paste, and the guards are then stitched or pasted into folders. Such a system keeps the documents neatly together, yet allows them to be readily taken apart, for instance for exhibition or for photographing.

When a document repairer has to repair a bound volume he will try to incorporate the original covers. If, as often happens, it is only the hinges that have perished, he may be able to incorporate the old spine too, with new leather hinges. Otherwise, his aim is to produce "an honest facsimile". Because of the fairly elaborate work needed in rebinding, some of which will be hidden when the work is finished, it is desirable (and this is advocated by Jenkinson)[14] for the repairer to attach to the inside cover of the volume a note of what procedures he has followed in rebinding. At the Public Record Office the general policy is to resew and rebind in account book style, i.e. with hollow back: in this way pages lie flat when open, which is convenient both for reading and for photographing.

It is interesting that *Local Records* has only twelve lines about binding (seven of them concerned with loose leaves)[15] whereas Jenkinson devoted several pages to it in his *Manual*:[16] evidently quite a lot of binding work goes on at the Public Record Office. Jenkinson summarizes his conclusions in an appendix "Repair of bindings".[17] He believes that rebacking should always be preferred to rebinding if the sewing is good and the boards sound. Old sewing is always preferable to new sewing; if new sewing is used it should follow the holes of the old as closely as possible. Stamps, labels, and any written or otherwise marked part of the old binding should, if they cannot be worked into the new binding, be cut out and pasted inside the front cover. The free parts of old end papers should be preserved and inserted; the parts stuck down should be preserved only when they are marked with writing.

Even if the binding of a book is sound the leather may be in poor condition; the surface of pigskin is particularly friable. Much can be done to preserve leather bindings and improve their appearance with a dressing such as that recommended by *Local Records*: lanolin (wool fat) 7 oz, yellow beeswax $\frac{1}{2}$ oz, cedarwood oil 1 fl. oz, hexane 11 fl. oz, neatsfoot oil 1 fl. oz; rub the dressing on with cotton wool, then let the binding stand for 24 hours before polishing with a soft cloth. Parchment and vellum bindings can be cleaned with a soft rubber, then sponged lightly with a soft cloth which has been soaked in milk and wrung out before use.[18]

Maps

The repair of maps presents difficulties if they are large, and they often are. These difficulties mainly concern paper maps. Parchment maps occur fairly frequently but they are usually relatively small because of the limiting size of a sheep's skin: their repair follows the normal course of repair of (rather large) parchment documents. Occasionally a parchment map may consist of two or more skins joined together, but these can be repaired separately and then rejoined.

Traditional map repair, developed at the Public Record Office and adopted by local record offices, is conducted flat on a table. Sheets of repair paper are damped down on glass and pasted. The map is evenly damped (on the back only, if it is coloured), laid on the repair paper, and boned down. A piece of repair linen is damped out and pasted. The paper-backed map is then boned onto the linen and framed with strips of repair paper to keep the edges flat. The map is left to dry out under cartridge papers, and when dry is trimmed and pressed for at least 48 hours; this pressing will usually have to be done under boards and weights.

The size of table needed for this operation may be of the order of 9 × 8 ft. Such a table is difficult to get hold of, and in any case a record office may not have a room large enough to take it. Whoever, then, thought of repairing maps vertically, as though dealing with wall paper, had a deceptively simple, revolutionary idea. The wall board on which the vertical repair of maps is carried out is made of hardboard mounted on a trellis-work of battens fixed to the wall. Since ordinary hardboard will not accept drawing pins a softer type, such as Sundaela, is needed, its very porous surface being first treated with polyurethane sealer to prevent furring from wear and dampness: numerous coats may be necessary.

The wall board should be as big as the available wall will allow. As hardboard is supplied in 8 × 4 ft sheets a convenient overall size could be 16 × 8 ft. The bottom edge of the board is fixed 10 in. above floor level. To get access to all parts of the board the repairer needs a low platform. Somerset Record Office uses two movable platforms made of Dexion, with wooden tops and plastic feet. In the Nottingham University Department of Manuscripts a platform, made of wood but fitted with a rubber mat to prevent slipping when wet, is hinged just below the board and can be lifted up and secured in position when needed.

In the Somerset Record Office method of wall repair, described by Mr. I. P. Collis,[19] as many maps as can be fitted economically on to a large sheet of backing linen are repaired simultaneously. Firstly, the backing linen is fixed to the wall board with brass drawing pins 5–6 in. apart, the linen being flat but not stretched. Sheets of 22-lb handmade paper, damped out and pasted on a table, are then applied to the linen using a paper-hanger's brush: fingers, palms, or fists should not be used because uneven pressure can cause air bubbles which may appear only after drying out. The paper sheets are laid so as to overlap each other by about $\frac{3}{4}$ in. and to protrude beyond the edges of the map to provide a protective border after trimming.

Maps should have their old backings removed before repair and be thoroughly cleaned with bread crumbs or artist's rubber. If pieces of map are flaking away they must be fixed in position, perhaps with silk gauze. Varnish can be removed with methylated spirits, but as the treatment is harsh it should be used cautiously. A valuable coloured map may be best entrusted to an expert picture restorer.

The back of each map, continues Mr. Collis, is now damped and pasted, left for 5 minutes to allow the paste to penetrate, and then applied to the linen. If the map is fairly large the repairer will probably need some help at this stage. A large map can be lightly folded like wall paper. Application is initially made near the lateral centre but towards the top, then gradually outwards, first with the fingers, then with a squeegee (an 8-in. photographic roller) applied to the surface of the map through a protection of lightweight polythene. The paste should be thin enough to allow the map to slide, again in the manner of wallpaper, over the backing for adjustment. The edges are then worked over with a bone folder to make sure they stick, and the map is left to dry out.

If any pieces of map have been lost the holes are now filled in with handmade paper. Heavier weight paper (32 lb) to match the thickness of the map is usually necessary, and in the case of very thick maps more than one thickness of patching paper may be needed. Strips of paper are also laid overlapping the border of the map, to prevent the edges lifting from the backing. A kind of *papier-maché*, made from shredded paper and paste, can be used for filling in small cracks and holes.

When the map is dry it is removed from the wall board and trimmed, with a 1-in. border, however, left on the long sides and on one of the short sides. On the other short side a wider "guard" should be left, its size depending on the method of map storage used: if vertical, perhaps 6 in.; if on a roll, a wider guard may be necessary; and at the opposite end a substantial width of linen backing is left to provide a wrap-around cover, to which tapes can be attached.

In the wall method of map repair it is noticeable that there are two periods of drying out: one after the repair paper has been applied to the linen backing, and the other after the map has been applied to the repair paper. These waiting periods appear to be necessary to allow the linen and paper to dry out taut and flat. In this respect the wallboard method of repair compares unfavourably with the table method, in which the repair is one continuous process. The outstanding virtue of the wall-board method, however, is that the map occupies no floor space in the room. During the waiting periods the map can be protected by a curtain of polythene. This allows even drying out, and protects the map from accidental damage. As Mr. Collis concludes, "the wallboard has proved to be a most effective piece of equipment and . . . for its size and effectiveness it is extraordinarily cheap to provide".

Seals

In the first edition of his *Manual* Jenkinson says that the preservation of seals is a vexed question which has given trouble "from the earliest times".[20] He contrasts the seal bags designed at an early date by the Public Record Office, the contents of which are "in most cases" dust, with large and frail seals which have remained intact elsewhere although kept without any precaution: for instance, a fine collection of seals at Pembroke College, Cambridge, where, in 1922, the documents were still kept loosely in the large old wooden chests in which they had been stored for centuries. Another old way of protecting seals at the time of their manufacture was to enclose them in skippets—boxes of the same shape and size as the seal, which can be made of wood or even silver but are usually of tin. Jenkinson finds that seals in skippets have usually not suffered even though fresh air has been almost entirely excluded; however, in other archivists' experience, Great Seals kept in tin containers of this kind have often been dry and broken.

Investigation of the problem of seal preservation was made in Sweden where the Royal Archives came to the conclusion that although seals, like documents, should be given plenty of air, their most harmful condition is contact with any soft material which will absorb the grease from the wax and so make it dry and brittle. The method devised by the Public Record Office, therefore, for protecting pendent seals was to make bags of cotton-wool contained in grease-proof paper. In an article published in October 1961 D. B. Wardle revealed that in the previous decade the P.R.O. had improved on this technique by making the bags out of cellulose wadding encased in polyethylene sheet.[21] The cellulose wadding is cut to shape with scissors, built up in layers to any desired thickness, then enclosed in polyethylene bags heat-sealed round the edges. Finally, tapes are laced round the mouth of the bag and tightened to the tag of the seal. To protect seals *en placard* a fold of polyethylene-coated paper is sealed to one end of a pad of wadding and polyethylene and attached to the document by paste or a stitch. Because of its wax-like texture, polyethylene sheet is quite safe in its contact with seals. The Public Record Office has its bags and pads made commercially in certain standard sizes, but in a small record office, they can, of course, be readily made by the repairer.

The great majority of pendent seals occur on medieval deeds. Thus, at Nottingham University the Middleton collection contains about 5000 medieval deeds, many with attractive, interesting, and early (e.g. twelfth century) seals. One of the repairer's set jobs has been to work his way through this large group of medieval parchment documents, repairing the seals as he goes along (and keeping a separate tally of the number of seals repaired). After repair the deeds are inserted singly and unfolded in stiff paper envelopes of standard size and without flaps. The envelopes are then stood on their edges in boxes, each box being only comfortably filled. In this way the wadding in the seal bags provides cushions throughout the box and no seals lie on top of each other.

The modern system of protecting seals seems very satisfactory. In the past a minority opinion was in favour of cutting seals off documents and preserving them separately. Jenkinson agrees that "handling, even the most careful, must be dangerous" to seals,[22] but the Public Record Office has never favoured this drastic method, and certainly in a local record office there would be little justification for it on the grounds of excessive handling: medieval deeds are consulted relatively infrequently, and when they are the inquirer will probably want to see the deeds as well. The new type of seal bag gives very good protection from a hard table: the seal can be extracted and laid on the bag by lifting at the document and without touching the seal itself at all.

A broken seal without missing parts can be repaired by melting the wax at the back of the seal with a heated knife, so that the wax runs down into the crack between the pieces. Alternatively, the repairer can supply some new material, consisting of a mixture of two parts of pure beeswax and one part of powdered resin (the recipe of medieval seals) as an adhesive: the wax and the resin, melted and mixed together, are applied to the fractured surface a little at a time with a smooth blade, after being heated on the knife in the flame of a spirit lamp. Heated pins can be inserted to hold the fragments of the seal together.

A missing piece of seal is replaced by building up with repair wax, moulded to shape by the repairer's wet hands. Quite a lot of replacement—for instance in the case of a Great Seal—may be necessary: it is desirable to reproduce the original diameter, but, of course, the replaced wax will be flat, with the original fragment rising in relief from it.

Medieval seals are usually of one of three colours: natural (which may have darkened to yellow), red (which may be nearer brown) or green. *Local Records* suggest that seals, of whatever colour, should be repaired with natural wax,[23] but as long as there is no possibility of mistaking the new wax for the old there seems no reason why a green seal should not be repaired with green wax; the effect, important, for instance, in exhibitions, is much more appealing.

Neither Jenkinson in his *Manual* nor *Local Records* say anything about the repair of applied (*en placard*) seals. This seems to be a problem still troubling repairers and was raised at one of their meetings in 1961. It was then suggested that cracks might be repaired by inserting wax in them with a knife, or that the seal might be held together by a ring of wax round it. Covering the seal with lisse was not advocated.[24]

Design of the Repair Room

A repair room should be as generous in size as possible. Standards of provision vary: in one of the largest public libraries, containing a self-styled record office, repair work is conducted on a balcony. To some extent the effectiveness of the room will depend also on its shape, and the positioning of windows, doors, and heating equipment, but, as far as size is concerned, Mr. Collis, who has written more than anyone else about repair provision in local repositories, decides that "500 sq. ft is barely adequate and 600 sq. ft not too lavish".[25] A repair room should provide accommodation for traditional repair of paper and parchment, repair by lamination, repair of large maps, binding, and the storage of all supplies, including reserves. If a repair room is being designed on fairly ample lines—for example in a new record office—it is sensible to allow for the eventual appointment of a second repairer.

The room needs to be very light, particularly about the repair bench. The repair room of the Somerset Record Office, with an area of 520 ft², has nine 5-ft fluorescent tubes, positioned over the various working areas. It is also abundantly supplied with natural light, so much so that in summer the glare has to be counteracted by venetian blinds on the windows and roller blinds on the roof lights. There should be adequate ventilation, to the exclusion, however, of draughts, particularly at the working level of the benches: the Somerset Record Office achieves this with hopper windows. Also needed in abundance are power points, strategically sited at working places: for instance, for the stove, water heater, glue pot, kettle, repair bench illuminated inset, anglepoise lamp, and laminating press. To some extent, two repairers duplicate the need for power points, although the Somerset Record Office, with two repairers, has nine points, while Nottingham University Department of Manuscripts, with only one repairer, has eight points, and does not find them too many.

The most important working place in a repair room is the repair bench; its siting and its dimensions need careful consideration. It is usual for the repairer to work standing at the bench, so it needs to be about 3 ft high; but it is useful to provide knee-holes and foot rests under the glass inset where the repairer can work seated on a stool. The Staffordshire Record Office, however, has a quite different arrangement: instead of a repair bench running along one wall at standing height, there is a large repair table in the centre of the room, at which two repairers can sit. The fitting-out of the repair bench also needs thought so that equipment and materials are as near as possible to the repairer's hand. The Somerset Record Office repair bench, being designed for two repairers, is 18 ft 6 in. long; each repairer has a water-heater, a sink, a glass inset, and two power points. Between these two sets of equipment there is a 6-ft-wide drawer unit containing tools and working quantities of paper, parchment, silk gauze, etc. The working surface of the Somerset bench is Formica; at Nottingham University the bench is solid teak which has proved pleasing in appearance and satisfactory in performance.

At Somerset the glass insets, each 3 ft 9 in. × 2 ft 6 in. and fitted with obscured glass, are set flush in the bench. At Nottingham the light frame is separate from the bench and fixed at an angle. In both cases the lighting is by strip lights, Somerset's frame having two 3-ft strips arranged on a base which moves backwards and forwards on runners. Nottingham's "kitchen equipment" is sited on the repair bench itself, but at Somerset, where things are on a bigger scale, there is a separate kitchen unit with three power points, sink, water-heater, two free-standing industrial boiling plates, electric kettle, electric glue-pot, and with utensil cupboards underneath. This kitchen unit is positioned to serve both repair bench and binding bench.

Nottingham has a medium-size general-purpose press, with a platen area of 2 ft 6 in. × 2 ft 0 in., standing on the floor, and a small copying press, 1 ft 6 in. × 1 ft 0 in. Somerset, in addition to several small copying presses, has a large Interwood quick-acting veneer press (model F.S.I.) with withdrawable press-table of surface area 3 ft 7 in. × 3 ft. 3 in. and loading height of 2 ft 0 in., bolted into the concrete floor. The Warwickshire Record Office has the same model. This press is very desirable, but is rather expensive and takes up considerable space and height; in any case a record office will need a more general-purpose press as well. Presses should be positioned as near as possible to the bench top.

Of the remaining pieces of repair room equipment the map table and the wall board have already been discussed. The binding bench most generally used is probably the Queen's Bench made by Russell:

this is 4 ft 2 in. long × 2 ft 11 in. wide × 2 ft 9 in. high, and has a cupboard, a lying press, a ruler, and a plough with a 26-in. blade. An all-steel cupboard is desirable in which to store bottles, chemicals, etc. Repair rooms need plenty of table-working area: documents require support not only during repair but also while they are waiting for make-up or trimming. At Somerset this area is partly provided by a combined table and drawer unit; some of the drawers in this unit are large—3 ft 0 in. × 2 ft 9 in. × $3\frac{1}{4}$ in.—for the storage of paper, boards, etc.; the table top provides valuable working area—e.g. for collating sections of volumes and general make-up purposes—and resting surface for large documents awaiting trimming.

Final items needed are a laminating press, a drying (or size) rack, and a rack on which to store bookcloth, buckram, strawboard, millboard, etc. Somerset's storage rack, made of Dexion, is 3 ft 9 in. long × 1 ft 9 in. wide × 7 ft 6 in. high. The drying rack can be in the form of a clothes rack which lets down from the ceiling, but perhaps more convenient is a light rack which can be moved about the room: the one at Nottingham, made of wood, has plasticated curtain wires on which documents are unlikely to stick.

Two general principles govern the design of a manuscripts repair room: maximum safety for the documents and ease of movement for the repairer. The room should be located away from the rest of the department to avoid danger from draughts and from the dust that results from staff movement; the repair bench should be shielded from the door-opening. Kitchen equipment should preferably be separated from both the repair bench and the binding bench. A very desirable adjunct to a repair room, which has so far not been included in many record offices, is a repairer's strong room. In Mr. Collis's words, "it seems pointless to have a document repaired and then to subject it to the risk of damage simply because there is no place to keep it until it is ready for return to the strong room";[26] such a strong room would be equipped with a large table and a few racks, and would be served by a trolley. Minimum movement for the repairer involves, firstly, grouping stationary equipment conveniently together, and, secondly, allowing room for circulation of mobile equipment.

13. REPROGRAPHY

IN A selective "Bibliography of archive administration" (*Journal of the Society of Archivists*, October 1960, pp. 67–73) Mr. R. H. Ellis includes a short section on "Photography and reproduction", which contains fourteen references. In the introductory note to this section he says that "of the technical subjects with which the archivist needs to have some acquaintance, photography is the most voluminous in its literature". It is, therefore, interesting to notice that few articles on photography have appeared in either *Archives* or the *Journal of the Society of Archivists*, and that the index to *Local Records* fails to mention photography at all: a measure of the disinterest of English archivists in the subject. County record offices, even when exceptionally well endowed in other respects, have been particularly deficient in this service. Large public libraries are somewhat better equipped, but inadequately in proportion to their size. Great institutions like the Public Record Office and the British Museum have, of course, large photographic establishments, but delays in supplying reproductions have often been inordinate.

A well-equipped and efficient photographic service in a record office is eminently desirable to satisfy both internal and external needs. It can, moreover, be a lucrative source of income for the office. The organization of a photographic unit needs careful attention. Photographers in the past, though frequently skilled craftsmen, have sometimes developed a secluded mystique, readily conducive to semi-independence of the parent body, autonomously established rates of work, and accessibility to the influence of extraneous pressures. While acknowledging the photographer's skilled status it is essential to keep him within the mainstream of the institution's activities. He must be responsible for his productivity to a senior member of the office, through whom all orders for photographic work should go, while being available for consultation in case of technical difficulty. In return for

159

his co-operativeness in this way the photographer becomes an active part of the institution, sharing the satisfaction of increased production, improving his prospect of promotion, and enjoying the improved equipment which increased income enables the office to buy. It was reorganization along these lines which made it possible for the Nottingham University Department of Manuscripts to increase its production five-fold between 1963 and 1965, and vastly to improve its technical resources.

Record offices naturally vary in the photographic demands made on them. In general, there is a greater call for copies of manuscripts of national or international interest than of those of purely local importance. Yet it is probably safe to say that every repository has manuscript material of potential photographic interest to someone, and if its holdings are sufficiently publicized requests for copies will come in. Photography of manuscripts has both internal and external uses. Internally, it can enable a repository to fill gaps in its series with copies of manuscripts elsewhere; secondly, it can provide security copies, to be kept separately from the original manuscripts; thirdly, it allows a research worker to see a copy of a document which is too frail to be produced; and fourthly, it is very useful for exhibitions and other educational purposes. Externally, photography can produce certified copies for legal requirements; and it extends access to manuscripts to students working far away from the repository. It is this last function which is probably the most important of all, which takes up most of the photographic time of a repository, and which brings in most income.

A photographic unit needs to be both quick and versatile, and so the more equipment it has the better. Since photographic equipment is expensive, however, the unit will usually have to expand gradually. Probably the greatest photographic demand on local record offices today is for "eye-legible" copies, supplied as quickly as possible, and of adequate quality. Before the last war an eye-legible copy would have been either a photograph or a Photostat. During and shortly after the war it would have meant normally a contact copy, such as a "Copy-cat", with photograph and Photostat retained in special cases. Since the 1950s it has usually implied one of an increasingly large variety of processes, mainly employing a contact method, and marketed under a bewildering medley of trade names, with photograph and Photostat still maintaining their specialized uses. As far as eye-legible copies are concerned the discussion among archivists and customers revolves round the comparable quality, speed, convenience, and cost of the various processes and methods. Meanwhile, the demand for a second type of document-copy, the microcopy, and especially the microfilm, has steadily mounted, though it has affected record offices with documents of mainly local interest less than those with long runs of manuscripts of national importance.

There is a further aspect of photography which specially concerns record offices: the supply of copies of particularly large originals, especially maps. At present this difficulty has not been widely solved. Even university photographic departments are not as adequately equipped for the purpose as might have been expected; commercial photographers are often the only local bodies with suitable equipment, but archivists are naturally reluctant to deposit documents of importance and ungainliness outside their offices.

Reprography, a comprehensive term invented in recent years, which includes the narrower "photography", and covers the corpus of processes and methods used for both copying and duplicating documents, is a complex, technical subject in which archivists are only partially involved. An archivist who feels the need to appreciate the framework into which his miscellany of equipment, processes, and methods fits, can approach the subject as a whole through such works as H. R. Verry, *Document Copying and Reproduction Processes*, London, 1958, and W. R. Hawken, *Copying Methods Manual*, American Library Association, 1966. The present résumé, approaching the subject from an archivist's point-of-view, subdivides it as follows: firstly, processes which, though slow and costly, produce high-quality results or are required by particular circumstances; secondly, quick processes of numerous kinds, appropriate in various circumstances or for various purposes; thirdly, copies of particularly large items; and fourthly, microfilm.

(i) **Slow Processes**

(a) *Photograph*

The silver halide process of the photograph remains an essential element in reprography. Although photography is wet, slow, and expensive, no other copying process so far devised can reproduce its quality and versatility. Its methods are basic in the training of a skilled craftsman, and it continues to provide the standard by which to judge the results of other processes. The archivist needs photographs, for instance, in exhibitions and for publication; a record office, therefore, should have an adequate dark room, good cameras, and lighting, developing, and printing equipment.

(b) *Photostat*

Because of the slowness and expense of photography, the need was felt for a process which, while approaching the photograph in quality, would be quicker and cheaper. This was provided by the Photostat. The Photostat machine is essentially a large camera with a prismatic mirror attached to the lens. The mirror, by reversing the image, produces a readable copy in both the negative and the print, and also allows the copyholder to be used in a horizontal position, thus saving space and giving greater speed of operation. The Photostat camera is a very large machine, really needing a room of its own. It is the same as an ordinary camera, except that in place of the roll of film it has a roll of silver halide paper, onto which the copy is directly made. In an ordinary camera the negative film bears the image in reverse. The image on the paper in a Photostat camera is the right way round, achieved by the reversing prism in front of the lens.

The Photostat can copy documents up to 40×30 in., but the largest print it can produce is 24×18 in., because 18 in. is the width of the roll of sensitive paper (350 ft long) which the camera accommodates. A Photostat reproduces an original manuscript finely enough for close study of the writing, and, although it is somewhat disconcerting to have black and white reversed, a negative is adequate for most purposes. With the recent advent of quick copying devices the Photostat is probably less used than it was. However, institutions like the Public Record Office, the British Museum, and the Bodleian Library continue to use the Photostat on a large scale because of restrictions on copying manuscripts by contact methods; and smaller repositories, when they have one, find the Photostat useful for copying large (though not very large) items.

(ii) **Quick Processes**

The modern revolution in business document copying began in 1950, the year in which several radically new processes—including diffusion-transfer-reversal, Thermofix, and Xerography—became commercially available in the U.S.A. "Photocopying was suddenly taken out of the dark room and the hands of trained technicians and placed in well-lighted offices where clerical personnel without any knowledge of the photographic process were soon making reproductions of documents in seconds. . . . Whereas in 1950 there were only a handful of ways to reproduce a document, there are now more than two dozen."[1]

From a welter of competing processes, methods, and trade names catering primarily for commercial needs, academic institutions like libraries and record offices must painfully select the versions which seem most likely to meet their own rather specialized requirements. However, whatever advantages these quick processes may generally have, and whatever individual variation there may be in quality, they share a basic limitation: whereas the optical method of copying used in both photograph and Photostat can vary the size of reproduction, the contact method which the quick processes use can produce copies only the same size as the original.

The earliest contact method of copying dates from the beginnings of photography, and consisted of nothing more than a light source above a sheet of glass which held a piece of sensitized material in contact with the document. The next development was a box, deep enough to contain the light source, and covered with a sheet of glass and a cover plate; the document and the sensitized paper are placed in contact on the glass and held firmly together by means of the cover. Either direct or reflex contact can be used: direct if the light passes through the document, reflex if through the sensitized paper. For direct contact copying the original needs to be written on one side only. Because reflex contact is the version normally used (although there is some loss of resolution due to light scattering effects) the method in general is often referred to as reflex contact.

The contact method of making photocopies was extensively used during the last war for reproducing blueprints, and one specific trade name—Copycat—became, like Photostat, identified with the genus;

wartime Copycat machines have continued to give yeoman (if rather erratic) service until quite recent times. For copying small documents a small machine is used in which the cover is clipped into place by manual pressure. In a much bigger version, used for copying fairly large items such as maps, pressure is obtained by sucking air out from beneath a rubber apron, thus using atmospheric pressure. This large type of machine is the cheapest way of copying large items, and continues to be used, for instance, in the architecture and planning departments of local authorities, in university geography departments, and in the Public Record Office when documents are too big to be Photostated.

The advantages of the contact box, then, are that it can produce actual size copies in one piece of documents measuring up to 60 × 40 in., and that the apparatus is simpler and less expensive than a Photostat. However, it gets a lot of hard wear because of the pressure needed to bring paper and document close together, and with time the quality of reproduction can suffer. A further disadvantage is that, unlike the Photostat, the negative gives a reversed image which is unusable in itself; making a positive involves a second printing and a second sheet of paper; thus the process is rather slow and, in this respect, expensive.

So far we have been speaking of the contact method of copying in what might be called its primitive phase. Since 1950, however, the explosion in document copying for commercial purposes has led to important refinements in the method. In the original, e.g. Copycat, phase the negative and positive had to be processed away from the machine in wet chemicals. The office copying machines introduced a semi-wet method of processing, in which the chemicals are incorporated in the machine itself: after exposure negative and positive are fed between rollers and through a bath of chemical; the final copy emerges practically dry.

One of the processes introduced after 1950 was diffusion-transfer-reversal. This originated with Agfa and Gevaert, who supplied materials to numerous manufacturers of apparatus; the result has been to mask a common process with a wide variety of trade names. The process produces a reverse reading negative and a right reading positive in a single operation lasting less than a minute under the light conditions of an ordinary room. When they emerge from the machine the two sheets are rather damp but they become dry after a few minutes exposure to the air. No control over the quality of copies is possible during processing; if a copy has been incorrectly exposed, the entire copying procedure must be repeated at a different exposure.

Some machines incorporating the diffusion-transfer-reversal principle are designed to copy books as well as single documents. In this case their design is important, and particularly the book-angle, i.e. the angle which the page being copied subtends to the rest of the volume: for efficient copying of the inner margin of the page this angle should be less than 90°. The smaller the book-angle the better the contact with the exposing surface, and the less the danger of damaging the spine of the volume in trying to achieve contact. Secondly, the exposure surface of the printer should have no wooden or metal edging which will obscure text close to the inner margin. Little technique is needed in copying loose sheet originals, though fragile documents should only be copied on printers that have relatively low intensity light sources and generate no appreciable amount of heat. Much more technique is required with bound volumes, where the problems include getting complete coverage, and achieving uniform contact over the entire text area without applying excessive force.

A machine of the diffusion-transfer-reversal type used by the Nottingham University Department of Manuscripts is the Dalcopier, which has been found very satisfactory for copying both single documents and books. The model in this case is a "Consul", which combines exposing and developing equipment in one unit, protects the liquid chemicals when not in use, and needs servicing only infrequently. Dalcopies approach photographs in the quality of their tone-reproduction, are easier and cheaper to make, and can substitute for photographs on all but the most demanding occasions. Another machine, smaller than the Dalcopier, with a specialized use which can be very helpful to archivists, is the Contoura. Its exposing unit incorporates an air cushion which helps in getting evenness of pressure when making contact with the document. Secondly, because the exposing unit is held from above, it can be used to copy parts of large documents, such as maps, which are otherwise difficult to copy.

Most of the contact copying processes developed since 1950 have been silver halide processes. A radical departure from this conventional photocopying has been the development of electro-photographic methods for the formation of an image, based on physical and electrical, rather than chemical phenomena. The best known electrostatic process so far developed is Xerography, which consists of the electro-magnetic arrangement, and fusing, of carbon particles in facsimile of the original. Xerography is excellent at reproducing fine line detail, but poor in conveying "tonality", or the variations in shades of grey from white to black. Designed principally for the copying of office records, Xerography is, so far, unrivalled in ease, speed, and comparative cheapness, for the reproduction of print, typescript, and line drawings. Because, however, of its inability to reproduce tone, Xerography is not ideal for reproducing manuscripts. The writing of a document may certainly transfer adequately, but background tone is drained away and replaced by dots: the result is loss of feel of the original; a Dalcopy provides much more faithful reproduction. Nevertheless, when legibility is the main requisite, and relative cheapness a weighty consideration—for instance, for teaching purposes—Xerography is a very worth-while process for reproducing manuscripts. Moreover, a record office may have easier access to this process than to any other, so the archivist may need to accept Xerox copies and be thankful; in any case, because they are on ordinary paper, they are pleasant to the touch, compared with the rather clammy feel of some chemical papers. Finally, since Xerox copies are produced automatically, reproduction is consistent; and since there are no liquid chemicals, there is no danger of discoloration from bad washing.

Numerous types of Xerographic equipment have been developed for purposes (such as fast production of multiple copies, or making enlargements from microfilm copies of engineering drawings) which do not directly concern the archivist. He is most likely to be interested in the model most in use in local government offices and libraries—the 914 copier. This makes original-size copies of up to 9 × 14 in. from either loose sheets or bound volumes, at a maximum rate of seven copies a minute. Compared with other "quick" copying processes Xerox is fast and fairly simple to operate. However, some skill is required in copying bound volumes: the depth of field of the lens on the 914 copier is comparatively small and, as a result, the copying of tightly bound volumes with narrow inner margins may be difficult, if not impossible—some operators use a wooden roller to press down the inside of the spine of the volume.

It might be thought that, in an institution prepared (at any rate for internal purposes) to absorb labour costs, it would be possible to reduce the cost of Xerox copy to little more than the price of the paper. Unfortunately, however, Xerox machines cannot, at present, be bought outright, and the rent is such that the cost per copy to the operator is never lower than 2p, and the charge made by an institution to its external customers normally 4p to 5p.

(iii) **Copies of Large Items**

With the increasing availability to record offices of conventional quick copying equipment, the provision of copies of outsize items, particularly maps, is now, perhaps, their principal worry. As we have seen, the contact box can deal with documents up to 60×40 in. (which it reproduces original size) and the Photostat with ones up to 40×30 in. (which it reduces to 24×18 in.). But tithe maps, for instance, can reach 17 ft in length. The difficulty is not so much the provision of enormous prints (which will not often be required) as the sheer handling of the elephantine original. The solution must lie in the employment of optical means. One of the best known cameras for this work, and one often found in commercial photographers or specialist institutions, is the Statfile.

The Statfile consists of a large, horizontal camera, suspended on rails for ease of movement, and incorporating a copyholder and a light source. The size of film normally used is half-plate ($6\frac{1}{2} \times 4\frac{3}{4}$ in.), though larger film is possible. The finished print can be anything up to 60×40 in. The final quality is good because of the extra-large film that is used: in fact, besides being designed to cope with particularly large originals, the Statfile is intended for copying material which is not suitable for reduction to smaller negative sizes.

Such cameras would clearly involve a record office in expense which it might not be able immediately to face. May not a more realistic solution lie in relatively homely improvisation? One local history society, wanting a tithe map copy which the county record office was unable to provide, and which the Public Record Office was willing to supply for £64, simply hung the parish copy from a cupboard and photographed it in sections with a tripod camera. It should be within the capability of a fairly enterprising record office to emulate this example, even if it means devising a method of hanging which will meet its more exacting standards of preservation.

(iv) **Microfilm**

Until the recent outburst in quick-copying the greatest reprographic demand on manuscript repositories was probably for microfilm. The microfilm era really dates from the last war. Before then it was only just beginning: Jenkinson, in a footnote (p. 63) in the second edition (1937) of his *Manual of Archive Administration*, says "cheaper and much more rapid devices [than the photostat] using cinema film are now being perfected. A student working recently with one of these made easily in one day over 1000 tiny negatives to be used later with a projecting lantern." In Jenkinson's opinion, it was "probable that the extended use of photographic facilities, which make the production of photographic copies easy and inexpensive, will do much to help in the preservation of Archives".[2] This was borne out by subsequent experience: microfilm, because of its speed and smallness, was clearly the most valuable of these photographic aids, and during the war large quantities of archives were microfilmed.

Microfilming for preservation has continued since the war, if a little less dramatically. However, the bulk of microfilming has probably been in response to research workers' demands. Clearly, for a student working on a lengthy run of documents away from a repository, microfilm has great advantages—of convenience, compactness, speed of copying, but, above all, comparative cheapness: to buy a bromide reproduction of a manuscript volume of 300 pages he would have to pay about £40; for a Xerox copy about £15; but for a microfilm only about £5.

A microfilm is a miniature transparency, usually 35 mm wide, and one-twelfth to one-twenty-fourth of the size of the original: for manuscripts and documents the smallest possible degree of reduction should be used, preferably not more than one-eighteenth. Some microfilm is double-perforated; the best cameras, however, do not need any perforation, and this is an advantage since no film at the edge is then wasted. The area of one image is called a frame; if the size of the document allows it, two images can be included within the space of what would normally be one frame: this is called a double-frame. Laboriously, microfilm can be improvised with any 35-mm camera. It is better to use a large, automatic camera—one which holds 100 ft of film and moves the film on itself. 35-mm film gives eight frames to the foot; allowing for lead in, spacing, and tail, 100 ft of film should produce something over 700 frames. This 100 ft of film will fit into a box $3\frac{1}{2} \times 3\frac{1}{2} \times 1\frac{1}{4}$ in.

The microfilm camera incorporates a light meter which, on some models, has to be swung out over the item to be copied. The documents in a series to be microfilmed are often of a similar lightness or darkness, but if one occurs which is very different from the others the operator will need to take a new reading on his light meter. Since a microfilm camera has considerable focus tolerance, the writing in the various parts of even a wrinkled document will usually be in focus. Sometimes, however, it is difficult to obtain even focus with a thick book in which there is wide variation between the height near the inner margin of a page and the height at its outer edge. In this case a book-holder can be used: a box in which two balanced metal plates on which the book rests bring facing pages of the volume up to the same level; a glass top is then brought down and firmly clipped in position before each frame is taken. A book-holder is certainly useful, but limited by its size: sometimes it is almost impossible to microfilm an extra-fat volume; the only solution may be to use a heavy glass plate, but this is cumbersome, and the photographer needs an assistant and plenty of time.

Various sizes of microfilm camera are available. For microfilming big items like newspapers one of the larger models is needed. Some fairly slim volumes of newspapers can be microfilmed in bound form, but it may be necessary in other cases (and perhaps desirable in all) to take the volumes apart before microfilming.

If, as is usual, a lengthy run of documents is to be microfilmed, care should be taken with the preparation of the series before it is handed to the photographer; he has enough to worry about in getting the right exposure, and siting each document on the camera platform. One of the virtues of microfilming is the speed at which it can be done. If he is not impeded an operator can easily make a thousand or more frames a day. This means he must not be involved in, or held up by, the preparation of the material: the documents must be arranged beforehand in straightforward bundles, with clips removed, dog-ears flattened, pages unfolded and all the right way up, and each item clearly numbered and in order. The photographer must also be given precise instructions about what is and what is not to be microfilmed. All this can mean an hour's, perhaps several hours', preparatory work on the documents (perhaps by a junior, though certainly by a responsible junior): no labour is saved, but in this instance it is the microfilmer's time and the "turn-round" in the photographic unit which are important.

The roll of microfilm itself also needs careful documentation. Thus each roll should start with a title-page giving a brief description of the series and the main reference letters and numbers. The Public Record Office even inserts a slip at the bottom of every frame, giving the reference number of the document. At the end of the roll the title-page should appear again, and "END", or, if there is more than one reel, "TO BE CONTINUED", with "CONTINUED FROM . . ." on the title-page of the next reel. (It might be thought that the person who prepared the documents for microfilming would also write out the title-pages, but experience shows that photographers are artistic chaps who like to design them themselves in their own neat script.) Before a microfilm is sent to the customer it should be checked for legibility and completeness—in microfilming it is rather easy to miss a document or a page in a long series; it is possible to cut up a roll and splice in missing frames, but this can be tedious and time-consuming. The importance of clear ordering and numbering of the documents before microfilming is evident when it comes to checking.

Although a skilled photographer can extend the repertoire of a microfilm camera—for instance, by increasing its power of reduction—and although things go wrong which it needs a photographer to diagnose, if not repair, microfilming itself is a repetition, not a skilled, job. An unskilled junior can get through a large amount of microfilming, and it is, in fact, desirable for as many members of the record office staff as possible to understand the operation of the microfilm camera so that microfilming can go on in an emergency.

When the operator has finished exposing a roll of microfilm it can be sent off to the manufacturer for developing. However, if the repository does any quantity of microfilming it may find it advisable to do its own processing because of possible delays, mistakes, or technical inflexibility on the part of the firm. It is possible to have an intermediate position in which the repository develops short runs of microfilm (say up to 50 ft) and sends longer runs for commercial development, but, in the end, the repository will probably find it best to have the equipment necessary to process the full length of 100 ft.

It is also desirable for a repository to have a machine for making positive from negative microfilm. The process, in which the negative prints onto a positive roll by passing over a light source, is quick (about 15 minutes), automatic, and dry. Positive microfilm is pleasanter for the student to read because it shows up as black on white; secondly, it is a worth-while policy, particularly in the case of long, uninterrupted runs of documents, for a repository to supply positive microfilm to its customer, and keep the negative itself: when a second order is received for a microfilm of the same manuscripts it can then be made more quickly and more cheaply.

The virtues of microfilm—speed, compactness, relative cheapness— are clear. For the reduction of large masses of manuscripts to manageable bulk, either for supplementary preservation purposes or for remote research, microfilm is unrivalled by any other copying process. However, though microfilm is easy to make, it is tedious and inconvenient to use. It shares the awkwardness of the medieval roll, while adding a peculiarly modern impediment: the need to project the tiny transparencies on to a screen in order to read them at all. The transparencies can only be looked at one at a time, two cannot be put side by side for comparison, and easy reference from one part of the roll to another is impossible. All students who use microfilm complain about the tiringness as well as the tiresomeness of looking at it over long stretches in semi-darkness. All would prefer, if they could get them cheaply enough, eye-legible prints of their documents and manuscripts. It is in this direction that the most striking recent advances have been made; perhaps they will go even further.

14. THE EDUCATIONAL USE OF ARCHIVES

At a meeting of the British Records Association in 1961 one contributor to a discussion on the educational use of archives asked how archivists could still be debating the subject when the first record office was founded in 1925; what other use, he wondered, did records have?[1] Admittedly, the speaker was an education officer attached to a record office, but some archivists, also, have argued that the ultimate purpose of archive preservation is educational—"to make accessible the raw material of history to the enquirer . . . for some vaguely envisaged 'cultural end' ".[2] However, one of the charges levelled at public libraries is that they stress accessibility at the expense of "archival sanctity", and at least one archivist (the county archivist of Kent) is adamant that the preservation of his records is the archivist's first duty; their accessibility and educational use are secondary and peripheral.[3] Some archivists, in fact, appear to favour "some sort of archivistic ideal"[4]—the preservation of archives for their own sake, even if they are never used; while, for others, the ability promptly to produce their authorities' administrative records on request is more significant than the educational value of their archives to the outside public.

An individual archivist can feel in his own work the tension between these opposing views—constantly balancing the demands of publicity, accessibility, and educational activity against the basic needs of listing and cataloguing. Publicity can win him further facilities and staff but, on the other hand, the people who really know—scholars and discerning students—appreciate when a record office is catering for them efficiently. Mr. Hull, quoting Mr. Emmison, maintains that an office should engage in a wide educational service only when "the basic duties of cataloguing, etc." are accomplished,[5] and one fundamentalist (Mr. Steer of Sussex) goes so far as to plead for "another twenty-five years so that we can get our masses of documents in

172

good order".[6] Yet, even while an archivist is carefully avoiding the extremes of scholarly eremitism and reckless display, he may, in fact, be falling between two stools and getting the worst of both worlds.

Most archivists feel it worth while to hold fairly frequent exhibitions, even (or, perhaps, especially) in the early days of a record office's existence; a tradition has grown up that this is the way to attract notice and deposits. Yet many exhibitions of local records are amateurishly done, with inadequate exhibition room, makeshift equipment, and poor display technique. Although a number of established record offices have converted rooms, or parts of rooms, for temporary or even permanent exhibitions, no newly built record office has a purpose-built exhibition room. Public libraries and (especially) modern museums have developed greater expertise in display than record offices. Liverpool probably leads the field among public libraries for regular, large-scale exhibitions, meticulously prepared, and opened with panache. Pictorial and manuscript material which has perhaps not seen the light of day for decades, and which is certainly unknown to the general public, is attractively presented to inquisitive eyes.

Two aspects of such an ambitious policy of display may give an orthodox archivist pause: firstly, the sheer amount of physical handling which manuscripts receive during the preparation of an exhibition; and secondly, the vulgarization implied by this sort of treatment of this sort of material. While the first anxiety has considerable point, the second is, perhaps, a matter of degree: the *vulgarization* can, after all, be *haute*—exhibition of historical material not in a meretricious way, but with respect and understanding, and conveying to the uninitiated the archivist's own feeling of excited discovery. Flair for display combined with respect for history is very evident, for instance, in the exhibition hall of the Archives Départementales at Rouen: the wide stairs leading to the hall, and the hall itself, richly carpeted; the exhibition cases finely illuminated; the displayed manuscripts mingled with *objets d'art*—as in an exhibition devoted to Joan of Arc in which one of the cases contained simply two items: a large document concerned with the English occupation, and a contemporary sword suspended diagonally in mid-air. Two-dimensional manuscripts are greatly enhanced when exhibited with three-dimensional objects, even if these are merely seals, which, when cleaned and polished, can be very attractive, especially if they are green or red. Colour is another quality which should be generously introduced into displays of manuscripts: velvet or silk backgrounds of various colours—red or green or blue— are pleasant, but, failing that, coloured paper is better than nothing.

Every aspect of manuscript display needs to be carefully considered. The archivist must train his eye: it would be nice if he could take a course in shop-window display—the French gift in this field is striking even in small provincial towns. Exhibition notes, too, need a lot of thought: the archivist has to develop an interesting, succinct style, and he must also decide just how much information to give; this will depend partly on his clientele. Some archivists find it fatally easy to overload the slips; on the other hand, descriptions are sometimes ludicrously inadequate. To overcome what seems a natural reluctance in visitors to read exhibition notes, the archivist should make not only their matter but their presentation as attractive as possible: for instance, by typing the notes on pastel-shade, matt-finished slips, selected to tone with the backing cloth or paper. Above all, an electric typewriter is to be desired: typescript gives an amateur, makeshift look to a display; the nearer one can approximate to print the better.

The most suitable equipment for the display of manuscripts and archives has not yet been adequately investigated. No exhibition cases, purpose-designed for the display of manuscripts, are commercially available, but some have been specially constructed by the National Library of Scotland and by Leicester Museum. The Edinburgh case is large, upright, and rests against the wall; occupying the whole of its interior is a slightly inclined stand in grey wood, with narrow horizontal shelves: the case is clearly designed for the display of volumes, arranged in varying patterns. The other example, very ingenious, is in the archives department of Leicester Museum. Again, the case is upright, but this time is designed for showing documents, and that without any obvious means of support—the trick is to provide the support by sandwiching the document between the glass frontage and a backing of foam rubber; seals, too, can be supported in this way. The design is very attractive: the cases are tastefully constructed in wrought iron; but they are not easy to dismantle.

General feeling among archivists would probably be in favour of upright display of manuscripts. This goes against the library tradition of horizontal cases for books, but vertical display is more striking and allows more people to look at one time. The difficulty lies in combining the display of heavy volumes with single-sheet documents. Until a suitable display case for the vertical exhibition of volumes has been designed it is perhaps necessary to combine horizontal with vertical cases. Vertical cases are expensive, and when included in the furnishing of a new exhibition room tend to be heavy and immobile, and sometimes awkward to open and clean. A record office display case should aim at maximum mobility and flexibility: easily movable, certainly within the exhibition room; suitable for use either alone or in conjunction with horizontal cases and tables; and, perhaps, readily dismountable and transportable for assembly elsewhere, yet preserving the security of the exhibits in their new setting.

In a useful article in the *Journal of the Society of Archivists*, April 1962,[7] Mr. Lionel Bell gives specifications for a type of case which can be made to order "by a good furniture manufacturer in consultation with a lighting engineer". He deals with the sort of materials to use inside the case: "it has been known for the use of a cork composition to result in sulphur damage to the contents, and for oak to damage metal objects, such as lead bullae". One sometimes sees hygrometers inside display cases, but, in Bell's opinion, "it is not practicable to insulate the interior of a case against the atmosphere", and so the case itself "should only be placed in a room in which the temperature and humidity conditions are acceptable for documents. It should, however, be made largely dustproof." He says quite a lot, too, about lighting: for instance, the desirability of internal lighting to avoid reflections; certain types of fluorescent tube provide the most adequate lighting with the minimum of both heat and ultraviolet light. He has interesting proposals about methods of mounting documents: he believes in holding them in position with strips of cellulose acetate which are then attached to the back of the display board with sellotape. Finally, he gives a general warning that "risks may be involved if any document is left permanently on exhibition", and purists among archivists will be interested to hear that "to reduce the effect of ultraviolet light to an absolute minimum it is possible to have documents in sliding frames or drawers which can be pulled out by the visitor"; but, as Bell says, "a row of drawers makes for an uninteresting display which would be likely to daunt all but the most earnest visitor. This method is not, therefore, recommended except when the material to be displayed is exceptionally light-sensitive."

In default of ideal, or even elaborate, vertical display cases, very serviceable vertical display stands can be made from Sundaela board, which receives drawing pins more readily than ordinary hardboard, and on which documents can be arranged more easily than on peg-board. Nottingham University Department of Manuscripts has twelve of these, some 8 × 4 ft and some 4 ft square, which can be mounted either on to the walls of the exhibition room or on to lightweight steel legs.

Even quite small exhibitions take a long time to prepare. As soon as a repository engages intensively in exhibition work it becomes sensible to employ an exhibitions assistant, as at the Liverpool Record Office. The most attractive and extensive exhibition accommodation among county records offices is probably at Ingatestone, a Tudor mansion outside Chelmsford rented by the Essex County Council. In this case exhibitions are only part of an ample policy of publicity; Essex was the first county record office to launch an ambitious educational programme, and is widely known for a large number of varied publications concerned with archives: guides to records, introductions to palaeography, and catalogues of exhibitions among others. It has set out its stall for schoolchildren, for instance, by presenting each year a prize for the best essay based on original material in the office, but, particularly, by employing a full-time education officer, seconded from the education department, whose activities include taking selections of documents to schools, talking to classes in the lecture room at Ingatestone Hall, and publishing source books of Essex history. Other record offices have followed Essex's example. The arrangement takes a lot of the educational burden off an archivist's shoulders, and this, no doubt, will be welcomed by those purists among archivists who feel their main concern is archive preservation. On the other hand, for an archivist who is himself actively interested in education, a situation in which the teacher is not finally responsible to him, may prove a little awkward; it will call for understanding on both sides.

An important educational relationship of a record office is with neighbouring colleges of education; thus Worcestershire provides formal lectures for students at two colleges and this helps them "to use the record office intelligently and to exploit its resources in their teaching". The relationship has not always been smooth; archivists complain, for instance, that students arrive with impossible topics to investigate—say, the agricultural history of a whole county, or a subject which is inadequately documented: tutors, they feel, are to blame for insufficient knowledge of the resources of the record office or, worse, lack of understanding of the character of historical source material.

Both students and tutors in colleges of education thus need instruction in local archives in general, and in the facilities of the local record office in particular; this need has increased now that colleges mount three- and four-year courses. Desirable would be a regular visit by someone from the record office to the college to talk to the students of the whole history department. In default of this, contact on a narrower front can be useful. Thus at Nottingham fifteen to twenty students from the College of Education spend one day each year in the Department of Manuscripts. In the morning the staff speak about the Department's manuscripts in general, and about eight to ten selected groups of records in particular; in the afternoon the students, working in pairs, investigate these groups of records. The occasion is meant primarily to introduce students to archives, but they may also wish to select one or other of the groups of documents as the basis for a thesis.

Such an operation, elementary as it sounds, can have important educational results, not least for the archivist himself. Selecting suitable groups of records for students can be a hard and long job. The archivist is aiming at choosing a group of records which is not too big, not too small, but just right for an interesting, satisfying, rewarding topic. But, as archivists well know, records do not readily lend themselves to this. In themselves they are not really about a subject at all, and a researcher has to look through large quantities of documents for relevant information, perhaps even then not finding it. In a way, selection of groups of records for students is really only one stage beyond the common fallacy that archives are like books, equipped with lists of contents and indexes. Nevertheless the archivist can use the occasion to point this very moral: to indicate, for instance, that a study of the life of the third duke of Portland might require several years' work in examining thousands of documents not only in this record office but in numerous others up and down the country; might not a much less ambitious topic, say "Changes in garden design at Thoresby in the eighteenth century", be an acceptable alternative? Such a decision, confronting the student with the difficulties of research, is itself educational. The experience is also instructive for the archivist. In attempting to think up suitably tailored subjects, with limited time in which to investigate the extent of relevant information in the documents, he can make mistakes. What at first sight appears a promising group can easily turn out to be deficient in some way: they may be very useful sources of information on the topic but require very experienced research work to extract it.

Archivists of the purist school would consider such activities as outside the archivist's genuine orbit. Thus Mr. Hull, the county archivist of Kent, has warned that there should be "a limit to this educational work. Members were primarily archivists, not educationists."[8] At the other extreme Mr. Edwards, education officer of the Essex Record Office, urges "the actual handling of documents and objects by the younger children", and for another member of the Essex staff "the actual appearance of documents was stimulating for children".[9] The fact that, educationally, there is no adequate substitute for the original manuscript was appreciated many years ago when the Lancashire Record Office mounted small exhibitions (for example, nineteen documents on "Shakespeare's Lancashire") in glass-topped cases, fitted these into travelling boxes, and, accompanied by an archivist, transported them to schools where, along with explanatory pamphlets, they were available for a day or part of a day. There is no doubt about the enthusiasm of those archivists who are interested in education, and many are anxious to interest students of all ages; even the Bodleian shows colour slides of illuminated manuscripts to children before they visit the Library to see the manuscripts themselves on exhibition. On the other hand, the chairman of the British Records Association discussion which has already been quoted, Professor Hurstfield, a historian, while having "nothing but admiration for the proposal to bring adult students into contact with documents . . . felt a little reserve about the idea of bringing children into close contact with them"[10]—a sentiment which seemed to go against both the spirit and the letter of much that had previously been said.

One educational activity in which archivists are slowly becoming more interested is the production of "archive teaching units". Up till recently their development owed more to academic and commercial enterprise than to the concern of traditional record offices. Responsibility for the original idea and for the rather ungainly title is uncertain, but the credit for its early, enthusiastic development must go to Mr. G. Batho, lecturer in education at Sheffield University. In Mr. Batho's practice, a group of, perhaps, eight teachers (or students of education), having chosen a topic which has national significance as well as local historical interest—for instance, the imprisonment of Mary Queen of Scots at Sheffield—meets regularly to work over it: selecting relevant documents from local repositories, writing notes on the topic in general and the chosen items in particular, arranging for photocopies to be made of the documents, and, finally, constructing a "unit", consisting of sets of documents and notes—one set for each child in a class—accompanied by a number of carefully selected large wall illustrations. Mr. Batho aims his units at secondary school pupils, especially in the upper forms where the syllabus allows special study of short periods of history. He suggests lines of inquiry, sometimes includes questions for pupils to answer, but refrains from dictating any particular type of treatment to the teacher.

The exact lines of dissemination of the idea of archive teaching units are difficult to distinguish, but those who have been influenced by Mr. Batho include Newcastle City Record Office, Newcastle University Department of Education, the Worcestershire Record Office, and Nottingham University Department of Manuscripts. Mr. Batho produced about a dozen units, and his achievement was all the more creditable considering the circumstances: although he had a ready supply of students, his access to material (mainly in the Sheffield City Library) and to photographic equipment was only indirect. There therefore seemed much to recommend an attempt by a repository holding archives of national, political importance as well as local, economic interest, situated in an academic environment with a department and an institute of education a few yards away, and having the services of a fairly well-equipped photographic unit, to emulate Mr. Batho's pioneer work. In 1965 Nottingham University Department of Manuscripts recruited two groups, each of five teachers, to work on topics selected from ten suggested to them. Having chosen "The invasion of England in 1688" (based on the papers of William Bentinck, the intimate friend of William III) and "Working class unrest in Nottingham, 1800–1850", the groups met one evening a week and each produced, in two terms, a substantial archive teaching unit consisting of facsimiles of a dozen selected documents, ample introductory information, and several very large wall illustrations; each unit was made up in thirty sets, stoutly boxed, and ready for class use.

The two Nottingham units were experimental, and the Department of Manuscripts, certainly, learnt a great deal as the work went along. One basic difference from the Sheffield units was clear: these had been initiated by an educationalist, whereas at Nottingham the sponsors were archivists, dependent on teachers for advice about, for instance, the most suitable topics, the best method of presentation, the most telling selection of documents. The Nottingham organizers felt just that little bit too far away from practical teaching to be able to assess satisfactorily both the general value of archive teaching units, and the effectiveness of a particular unit. While it was hoped that the teachers who produced the units would profit from their research experience there was no doubt that the main benefit was to be looked for in the children. The crucial questions, therefore, were: do archive teaching units have educational value in schools, and, if so, how can they best achieve it?

Two conferences of teachers held to discuss the merits of archive teaching units (and attended by representatives of Messrs. Jonathan Cape, who obligingly referred to the Nottingham units as *Jumbo Jackdaws*) particularized these questions rather than provided answers to them. All were enthusiastic about the value of introducing archive material, even in facsimile, to schoolchildren, but there were no clear solutions to some of the problems involved: uncertainty seemed to arise both from teachers' inexperience in this field and from variety in teaching situations. Perhaps the results of the Nottingham exercise can best be summed up in a series of further pointed questions, whose answers may emerge from greater experience. How far can a unit be adapted to different ages and abilities, and still remain a unit? Does scaling down a unit mean, in fact, breaking it up and reducing it to simple illustrative material? How practicable is it to use one of these rather elaborate teaching aids, given curriculum restrictions? If there are certain ages in certain kinds of school when the curriculum is less confining should archive teaching units be aimed frankly and solely at them? Can units be used in primary schools? Are they more relevant to less academic teaching? How much are academic pupils interested in local history? Are teachers really asking for a richer supply of illustrative material, and, if so, would something less elaborate and less sophisticated than archive teaching units be more appropriate? Even in this fragmented field the need for close liaison between teachers and archivists remains.

The Nottingham units, because they remained at a photographic stage, proved to be rather cumbersome. They were also somewhat expensive to produce, partly because of the cost of the large wall illustrations (though this can be—and has been by Mr. Batho— dramatically reduced by the substitution of dye-line for bromide prints) but more because of irreducible charges for the paper used in making photocopies. Since then, however, admirable printed archive teaching units, modelled in their wallet format on *Jackdaws*, selling at about the same price, but containing more material, have been produced by Newcastle University Department of Education, Manchester branch of the Historical Association, and the Department of Education and Science. Record offices, too, are unwinding themselves—for instance, Essex, with two "teaching portfolios" on highways and towns in which many of the items have palaeographical usefulness as well as straightforward historical interest, Flint, with a less ambitious production on roads, and Warwick, with a unit on enclosure in which the large size of the maps is reminiscent of the style of the Nottingham units. It seems likely that the production of archive teaching units will continue to expand. It still remains to be seen, however, how economic and practical they prove in classroom use. Nevertheless, they are one of the most pleasing examples so far of the educational use of archives.

NOTES

Introduction

1. T. R. Schellenberg, *Modern Archives: Principles and Techniques*, Melbourne, 1956, p. 3.
2. E. W. Ivey, "The records to be kept for business purposes", *Aslib Proceedings*, vol. 10, no. 9, Sept. 1958, pp. 211–16. "The author believes that most business houses keep far too many routine records. He carried out a survey of the records of his own organization, and found that 4% only had some historical value: the rest were merely routine documents, and should be destroyed as soon as it was safe" (*Journal of Documentation*, vol. 15, no. 2, June 1959, p. 126).
3. Alan Everitt, *The Agricultural History Review*, vol. 18, part 1, 1970, pp. 77–78.
4. *Committee on Departmental Records: Report*, London, H.M.S.O., Cmd. 9163, 1954, p. 6.

1. The Nature of Archives

1. For discussion of the dictionary definition of archives see Sir Hilary Jenkinson, *A Manual of Archive Administration*, reissue of revised second edition, London, 1965, p. 3, and T. R. Schellenberg, *Modern Archives: Principles and Techniques*, Melbourne, 1956, p. 11.
2. *Manual*, 1965, p. 11. Jenkinson subsequently loosened the wording of his definition by omitting "legitimate" and by altering the opening to read "drawn up . . . during the conduct of Affairs of any kind" (*Guide to the Public Records, Part I: Introductory*, London, 1949, p. 2).
3. In his *Manual*, 1965 (p. 12) Jenkinson speaks simply of "two . . . features of extraordinary value and importance"—*impartiality* (derived from the first part of his definition) and *authenticity* (derived from the second part). But in *Guide to the Public Records*, 1949 (p. 2), he adds two other "elements" or "essential 'Archive' qualities" which he does not name but which are here called *naturalness* and *interrelationship*.
4. *Guide to the Public Records*, 1949, p. 2.
5. *Manual*, 1965, p. 12.
6. *Ibid.*
7. *Guide to the Public Records*, 1949, p. 2.
8. Mr. Raymond Irwin pursues the identity even further: "It is in fact impossible in practice . . . to draw a hard and fast line between manuscript documents and printed books, and most libraries, being interested in the matter rather than the form of their treasures, collect both" (*Librarianship: Essays on Applied Bibliography*, London, 1949, p. 68).
9. Schellenberg, *Modern Archives*, 1956, p. viii.
10. T. R. Schellenberg, *The Management of Archives*, New York and London, 1965, p. 66.
11. Philip Hepworth, *Archives and Manuscripts in Libraries*, Library Association pamphlet no. 18, 2nd ed., London, 1964, p. 11.

12. *Manual*, 1965, part II, 6, "Primary Duties of the Archivist: (ii) Moral Defence of Archives", pp. 83–123.

13. As a straight-faced example of authorized access, Jenkinson offers the case of wartime storage of public records at Belvoir Castle: since the Duke of Rutland wished to remain resident in the castle, "we solved the difficulty by appointing him temporarily a member of our Staff; and this was not a meaningless gesture on either side" (Hilary Jenkinson, *The English Archivist: a New Profession*, London, 1948, p. 26).

14. Schellenberg, *Management of Archives*, 1965, pp. ix–x.

15. Jenkinson, *Manual*, 1965, pp. 8–9.

16. *Ibid.*, p. 33.   17. *Ibid.*, p. 151.   18. *Ibid.*, p. 183.   19. *Ibid.*, p. 149.

20. *Ibid.*, p. 151.   21. *Ibid.*, p. 152.   22. *Ibid.*   23. *Ibid.*, p. 153.

24. Jenkinson, "Modern archives: some reflexions on T. R. Schellenberg: *Modern Archives—Principles and Techniques*", *Journal of the Society of Archivists*, vol. I, no. 5, April 1957, p. 149.

25. Jenkinson, *Manual*, 1965, pp. 149–50.

26. Schellenberg, *Modern Archives*, 1956, p. 16.

27. *Guide to the Contents of the Public Record Office*, London, H.M.S.O., vol. 1, 1963, p. 10.

28. Jenkinson, *Manual*, 1965, Appendix V, "Archive History: an Illustration", pp. 224–41.

29. *Guide to the Public Records*, 1949, pp. 7–8.

30. V. H. Galbraith, *An Introduction to the Use of the Public Records*, Oxford, 1935, p. 12.

31. *Guide to the Public Records*, 1949, p. 8.

32. Jenkinson, *Manual*, 1965, pp. 39–41.

33. Galbraith, *Introduction*, 1935, pp. 11–13.

34. I. P. Collis, review of Jenkinson's *Manual*, 1965, *Archives*, vol. VII, no. 36, Oct. 1966, pp. 248–50.

35. Schellenberg, *Modern Archives*, 1956, p. 14.

36. *JSA*, Apr. 1957, pp. 147–9.

37. Schellenberg, *Modern Archives*, 1956, p. 15.

38. *JSA*, Apr. 1957, p. 149.

39. Collis, *Archives*, Oct. 1966, p. 249.

40. Jenkinson, *Manual*, 1965, p. 41.

2. Archives in England

1. Jenkinson, *The English Archivist: a New Profession*, 1948, p. 11.

2. Galbraith, *An Introduction to the Use of the Public Records*, 1935, pp. 1–2.

3. See *Guide to the Public Records*, 1949, pp. 9–10, and, for the Record Commission, Peter Walne, "The Record Commissions, 1800–1837", *Journal of the Society of Archivists*, vol. II, no. 1, Apr. 1960, pp. 8–16.

4. Jenkinson, *Manual*, 1965, p. 109.

5. Galbraith, *Introduction*, 1935, p. 2.

6. *D.K. Rep. XIII*, p. 30, quoted in *Guide to the Contents of the Public Record Office*, vol. I, 1963, p. 2.

7. *Guide to the Public Records*, 1949, p. 10.

8. *Committee on Departmental Records: Report*, 1954, pp. 48–49.

9. Galbraith, *Introduction*, 1935, pp. 4–5.

10. *Guide to the Public Records*, 1949, p. 10.

11. *Ibid.*, p. 11.   12. *Ibid.*

13. See *Guide to the Contents of the Public Record Office*, vol. I, 1963, pp. 1–2, and *Committee on Departmental Records: Report*, 1954, p. 10.
14. *Guide to the Public Records*, 1949, p. 1.
15. Sir Edward Coke's definition of a record, quoted in *Guide to the Contents of the Public Record Office*, vol. I, 1963, p. 2.
16. *Guide to the Public Records*, 1949, p. 15.
17. *Ibid.,* p. 28.
18. For details of the agreement of 1845–6 and the order in council of 1852 see *Guide to the Public Records*, 1949, pp. 13–15, and *Committee on Departmental Records: Report*, 1954, pp. 12–15.
19. Report of address by Mr. H. C. Johnson on 125 years of record keeping at the Public Record Office, *Archives*, vol. IV, no. 21, Lady Day 1959, p. 17.
20. H. C. Johnson, "The Public Record Office and its problems," *Bulletin of the Institute of Historical Research*, vol. 42, no. 105, May 1969, pp. 86–95.
21. Jenkinson, *The English Archivist*, 1948, p. 11.
22. R. H. Ellis, "The Historical Manuscripts Commission, 1869–1969", *JSA*, vol. II, no. 6, Oct. 1962, p. 233. Mr. Ellis has examined the important contribution of one of these "thoughtful people"—George Harris (1809–90)—to the establishment of the HMC in "The centenary of the Royal Commission on Historical Manuscripts: origins and transformations", *JSA*, vol. III, no. 9, April 1969, pp. 441–52.
23. Ellis, *JSA*, Oct. 1962, p. 233.
24. *Ibid.*, p. 234.   25. *Ibid.*   26. *Ibid.*
27. Ellis, *JSA*, Oct. 1962, p. 235.
28. G. D. Ramsay, "The publication of English records: some reflections on Mr. Mullins's *Texts and Calendars*", *Archives*, vol. IV, no. 23, Lady Day 1960, p. 142.
29. Jenkinson, *The English Archivist*, 1948, pp. 11–12.
30. *Ibid.*, pp. 12–13.
31. *Local Records: their Nature and Care*, ed. L. J. Redstone and F. W. Steer, London, 1953, p. 221.
32. Advertisement of the British Records Association appearing on the back of each issue of *Archives*.
33. British Records Association, *Work in Archives, 1948–55* (reprinted from *Five Years' Work in Librarianship*, 1958), p. 15.
34. *Work in Archives, 1948–55*, pp. 2–3.
35. British Records Association, *Thirty-third Report of Council . . . for the year 1964–1965*, 1965, p. 18.
36. *Local Records*, 1953, p. 223.
37. Felicity Ranger, "The National Register of Archives, 1945–1969", *JSA*, vol. III, no. 9, Apr. 1969, p. 452.
38. Ellis, *JSA*, Oct. 1962, p. 235.
39. Ranger, *JSA*, Apr. 1969, p. 454.
40. Ellis, *JSA*, Oct. 1962, p. 235.
41. Ranger, *JSA*, Apr. 1969, pp. 454–5, 459.
42. Historical Manuscripts Commission, *The National Register of Archives*, H.M.S.O., 1945 (publicity pamphlet), p. 6.
43. See Felicity Ranger, "The common pursuit", *Archives*, vol. IX, no. 43, Apr. 1970, pp. 121–9, for a defence of English guides to manuscripts against Philip Hepworth's adverse comparison with the American *National Union Catalog of Manuscript*

Collections in "Manuscripts and non-book materials in libraries", *Archives*, vol. IX, no. 42, Oct. 1969. Miss Ranger says, "The National Register of Archives was started in 1945. Had it been started fifteen to twenty years later, it might well have taken the form of a union catalogue."

44. *Local Records*, p. 223.
45. Ranger, *JSA*, Apr. 1969, p. 459.
46. Ellis, *JSA*, Apr. 1969, p. 449.
47. Ranger, *JSA*, Apr. 1969, p. 462.
48. Ranger, *JSA*, Apr. 1969, p. 460.
49. Ellis, *JSA*, Apr. 1969, p. 449.
50. Ranger, *JSA*, Apr. 1969, p. 453.
51. Ellis, *JSA*, Oct. 1962, p. 235.
52. Ellis, *JSA*, Apr. 1969, p. 449.
53. Ranger, *JSA*, Apr. 1969, p. 462.
54. Ellis, *JSA*, Apr. 1969, p. 449.
55. Ranger, *JSA*, Apr. 1969. p. 461.
56. Ranger, *JSA*, Apr. 1969, pp. 461–2.
57. Ellis, *JSA*, Oct. 1962, p. 235.
58. *Ibid.*, p. 236.   59. *Ibid.*, p. 237.
60. British Records Association, *Work in Archives, 1956–60*, p. 446.
61. Ellis, *JSA*, Oct. 1962, p. 242.
62. *Ibid.*, p. 236.   63. *Ibid.*, pp. 237–8.   64. *Ibid.*, p. 238.   65. *Ibid.*, p. 240.
66. *Ibid.*
67. Ranger, *JSA*, Apr. 1969, p. 454.
68. Ellis, *JSA*, Apr. 1969, p. 451.
69. *Archives*, vol. V, no. 28, Mich. 1962, p. 234.

3. The Archives Scene

1. Historical Manuscripts Commission, *Record Repositories in Great Britain. A list prepared by a joint committee of the Historical Manuscripts Commission and the British Records Association*, H.M.S.O., London, 1st ed. 1964, 2nd ed. 1966, 3rd ed. 1968.
2. *List of Record Repositories in Great Britain. Reports from Committees, no. 5*, British Records Association. London, 1956.
3. *Archives*, vol. VII, no. 35, Apr. 1966, p. 133.
4. G. R. C. Davis, "Some home thoughts for the English archivist from abroad?", *Archives*, vol. IV, no. 23, Lady Day 1960, p. 176.
5. *Archives*, Apr. 1966, p. 134.
6. *Ibid.*
7. Edwin Welch, letter to the editor, *Archives*, vol. VII, no. 36, Oct. 1966, p. 235.
8. Michael Cook, "Regional archives offices: some reflections", *Journal of the Society of Archivists*, vol. III, no. 6, Oct. 1967, pp. 271–2.
9. Above, p. 30.
10. G. R. C. Davis, *Archives*, Lady Day 1960, pp. 176–7.
11. Edwin Welch, *Archives*, Oct. 1966, p. 235.
12. Ida Darlington, "Record offices in Greater London", *Journal of the Society of Archivists,* vol. III, no. 5, Apr. 1967, pp. 248–50.
13. Edwin Welch, *Archives*, Oct. 1966, p. 235.
14. Maurice Bond, "Archives services and smaller repositories. VI. English archives: an integrated service", *Archives*, vol. IV, no. 24, Mich. 1960, pp. 199–203.

15. Maurice Bond, *Archives*, Mich. 1960, p. 201.
16. *Ibid.*, pp. 200–1.
17. *Archives for All*, prepared by F. G. Emmison, Essex Record Office, Chelmsford, 1956.
18. Maurice Bond, *Archives*, Mich. 1960, p. 201.
19. Michael Cook, *JSA*, Oct. 1967, pp. 271–2.
20. Kenneth Garside, Librarian, King's College London, letter to the editor of *Archives*, vol. VII, no. 36, Oct. 1966, p. 236.
21. Kenneth Garside, *Archives*, Oct. 1966, p. 237.

4. The Archives Profession

1. Hilary Jenkinson, *The English Archivist: a New Profession*, London, 1948.
2. Jenkinson, *The English Archivist*, 1948, pp. 11–13.
3. *Ibid.*, pp. 14–15.   4. *Ibid.*, pp. 16–23.   5. *Ibid.*, p. 23.   6. *Ibid.*, pp. 23–24.
7. *Ibid.*, p. 25.   8. *Ibid.*, p. 27.   9. *Ibid.*, p. 13.   10. *Ibid.*, pp. 30–31.
11. *Journal of the Society of Archivists*, vol. III, no. 6, Oct. 1967, pp. 265–71.
12. *Business Archives*, no. 32, June 1970, p. 6.
13. Society of Archivists, *Annual Report of the Council, 1968–1969* (typescript), pp. 7–8.
14. Felix Hull, "Limits", *JSA*, vol. II, no. 4, Oct. 1961, pp. 138–40.
15. E. Kenneth Timings, "The archivist and the public", *JSA*, vol. II, no. 5, Apr. 1962, pp. 179–83.
16. Schellenberg, *Modern Archives*, 1956, pp. 235–6.
17. Jenkinson, *The English Archivist*, 1948, p. 30.

5. Modern Archives and Business Archives

1. Edwin Welch, "Records management", *Journal of the Society of Archivists*, vol. III, no. 4, Oct. 1966, p. 198.
2. "The image of the archivist", editorial note, *Archives*, vol. VII, no. 36, Oct. 1966, p. 189.
3. Schellenberg, *Modern Archives*, 1956, pp. viii, 26–28.
4. Ida Darlington, "Methods adopted by the London County Council for the preservation or disposal of modern records", *JSA*, vol. I, no. 5, Apr. 1957, p. 141.
5. *Committee on Departmental Records. Report*, Cmd. 9163, H.M.S.O., 1954.
6. *Guide to the Public Records*, 1949, section 12, "Elimination", pp. 26–30, from which the following quotations are taken.
7. J. H. Collingridge, "Implementing the Grigg report", *JSA*, vol. I, no. 7, Apr. 1958, p. 179.
8. *Guide to the Public Records*, 1949, p. 30.
9. Collingridge, *JSA*, vol. I, no. 7, Apr. 1958, p. 179.
10. *JSA*, Apr. 1958, p. 180.
11. *Ibid.*, p. 179.   12. *Ibid.*, p. 184.
13. Even so, "some establishments flatly refused to hand them [i.e. their records] over to the Public Record Office even when this was required by Act of Parliament" (D. B. Wardle, *Archives*, vol. VIII, no. 37, Apr. 1967, p. 31).
14. *JSA*, Apr. 1958, p. 184.
15. Ida Darlington, *JSA*, Apr. 1957, pp. 140–6.
16. *JSA*, Apr. 1957, p. 141.
17. In an appendix Miss Darlington gives two examples of schemes of records disposal —for the Children's Officer and the Welfare Department. Each scheme illustrates

the detail into which the archivist must go: detail of the administration of the department, the precise records which result, the regulations concerning records, and the attitude towards records which is likely to arise in a particular department.
18. *JSA*, Apr. 1957, p. 143.
19. For a rather disjointed report of the symposium, in the form of "a connected series of notes" from the amalgamated contributions of various members, see *JSA*, vol. III, no. 8, Oct. 1968, pp. 417–23.
20. Edwin Welch, "Records management", *JSA*, Oct. 1966, pp. 198–9.
21. *JSA*, Oct. 1966, p. 199.
22. Michael Cook, "Regional archives offices: some reflections", *JSA*, vol. III, no. 6, Oct. 1967, pp. 271–5.
23. *JSA*, Oct. 1967, pp. 271–2.
24. *Ibid.*, p. 273.   25. *Ibid.*, p. 274.   26. *Ibid.*
27. *JSA*, Oct. 1966, pp. 199.
28. *Ibid.*, p. 199.   29. *Ibid.*, p. 198.
30. J. H. Collingridge, "Records management in England since the Grigg report", *JSA*, vol. II, no. 6, Oct. 1962, pp. 242–7.
31. *JSA*, Oct. 1968, p. 417.
32. Schellenberg, *Modern Archives*, 1956, p. 26.
33. *JSA*, vol. I, no. 2, Oct. 1955, pp. 47–49.
34. *JSA*, Oct. 1968, p. 417.
35. *Ibid.*, p. 419.   36. *Ibid.*
37. Discussion, "Automation and archives", Society of Archivists annual general meeting, 1964, *JSA*, vol. III, no. 1, Apr. 1965, p. 41.
38. *JSA*, Apr. 1965, p. 41.
39. *Ibid.*, p. 41.
40. "Archives in the computer age", editorial note, *Archives*, vol. VII, no. 34, Oct. 1965, p. 73.
41. *Archives*, Oct. 1965, p. 73.
42. *Ibid.*, p. 73.
43. *JSA*, Apr. 1965, p. 41.
44. *Archives*, Oct. 1965, p. 74.
45. *JSA*, Oct. 1967, p. 271.

6. Archives in Libraries

1. Quoted, *Archives*, vol. I, no. 4, Mich. 1950, p. 1.
2. *Liverpool Prints and Documents Catalogue*, Liverpool Library, Museum and Arts Committee, Liverpool, 1908.
3. John L. Hobbs, *Libraries and the Materials of Local History*, London, 1948, p. 14.
4. Hobbs, *Libraries and the Materials of Local History*, 1948, p. 15.
5. *Ibid.*, p. 17.
6. "Archives in libraries", *Library Association Record*, 1951, pp. 263–4.
7. *Local Records*, 1953, p. 53. See also Philip Hepworth, *Archives and Manuscripts in Libraries*, Library Association pamphlet no. 18, London, 1958, p. 15.
8. P. Hepworth, "Archives and manuscripts in libraries—1961", *Library Association Record*, vol. 64, 1962, pp. 269–83. See also Philip Hepworth, *Archives and Manuscripts in Libraries*, Library Association pamphlet no. 18, 2nd ed., London, 1964, pp. 15–17.
9. Hepworth, *Archives and Manuscripts in Libraries*, 1964, p. 17.

10. Hepworth, *Archives and Manuscripts in Libraries*, 1964, p. 17.
11. *Guide to the Manuscript Collections in the Sheffield City Libraries*, Libraries, Art Galleries and Museums Committee, Sheffield, 1956, p. v.
12. *Guide to the Manuscript Collections in the Sheffield City Libraries, Supplement I, 1956–62* (typescript), n.d., pp. 3–5.
13. Hepworth, *Archives and Manuscripts in Libraries*, 1958, p. 29.
14. *Ibid.*, pp. 13–14.
15. J. L. Kirby, *Archives*, vol. III, no. 20, Mich. 1958, p. 253.
16. Ida Darlington, "Record offices in Greater London", *Journal of the Society of Archivists*, vol. III, no. 5, Apr. 1967, pp. 248–50.
17. *Library Association Record*, vol. 64, 1962, p. 283.
18. See J. H. Hodson, "A university archive repository: the University of Nottingham Department of Manuscripts", *Archives*, vol. V, no. 27, Lady Day 1962, pp. 145–50.
19. *Archives*, vol. III, no. 20, Mich. 1958, p. 253.
20. *Local Records*, 1953, p. 28.
21. Schellenberg, *The Management of Archives*, 1965, p. 67.
22. *Ibid.*, p. 69.

7. Bringing in the Archives

1. *Local Records*, 1953, p. 68.
2. *Ibid.*, p. 68.
3. Francis W. Steer, "Obiter dicta et scripta", *Journal of the Society of Archivists*, vol. III, no. 5, Apr. 1967, pp. 241–5. See also his article "The archivist, the public and the stately home", *JSA*, vol. II, no. 7, Apr. 1963, pp. 316–18.
4. See "Owner and custodian: relations between owners of deposited records and repositories", a discussion at the annual general meeting of the Records Preservation Section of the British Records Association, 1965, *Archives*, vol. VII, no. 35, Apr. 1966, pp. 153–6.
5. *Archives*, April, 1966, p. 154.
6. *Ibid.*, p. 155.   7. *Ibid.*

9. The Enemies of Archives

1. For deep storage in Finland, Sweden, and the U.S.A., proof at least against conventional bombing, see *Archivum*, vol. VI, 1956, pp. 83–84, and Ida Darlington, " 'In the rock': a brief account of the National Archives of Finland", *Journal of the Society of Archivists*, vol. II, no. 1, Apr. 1960, pp. 34–36.
2. *Archivum*, vol. VI, 1956, p. 16.
3. A. E. A. Werner, "The preservation of archives", *JSA*, vol. I, no. 10, Oct. 1959, p. 283.
4. Werner, *JSA*, Oct. 1959, p. 283.
5. *Ibid.*, p. 283.   6. *Ibid.*, p. 284.
7. Ivor P. Collis, "The use of thymol for document fumigation", *JSA*, vol. 4, no. 1, Apr. 1970, pp. 53–54.
8. Maurice F. Bond and A. D. Baynes-Cope, "Fungicides", *JSA*, vol. 4, no. 1, Apr. 1970, p. 52.
9. *The Use of Santobrite*, House of Lords Record Office memorandum, 1960.
10. Bond and Baynes-Cope, *JSA*, Apr. 1970, p. 51.
11. Werner, *JSA*, Oct. 1959, p. 284.

12. *Archives*, vol. VI, no. 29, Lady Day 1963, p. 17.
13. W. H. Langwell, "The protection of paper and parchment against dampness in storage", *JSA*, vol. III, no. 2, Oct. 1965, pp. 82–85.
14. F. D. Armitage, review of W. H. Langwell's *The Conservation of Books and Documents* (1957), *JSA*, vol. I, no. 7, Apr. 1958, pp. 203–4.
15. *Archives*, vol. VI, no. 29, Lady Day 1963, p. 18.
16. *Ibid.*   17. *Ibid.*
18. *Archives*, vol. IV, no. 24, Mich. 1960, p. 208.
19. K. C. Newton, "The Essex Record Office in new surroundings", *JSA*, vol. III, no. 1, Apr. 1965, p. 29.
20. Werner, *JSA*, Oct. 1959, p. 285.
21. *Ibid.*
22. "Sulphur dioxide pollution of the atmosphere", *JSA*, vol. I, no. 10, Oct. 1959, pp. 291–3.
23. "Sulphur dioxide pollution of the atmosphere: a further report", *JSA*, vol. II, no. 5, Apr. 1962, pp. 221–2.
24. "Atmospheric sulphur and the durability of paper", *JSA*, vol. II, no. 4, Oct. 1961, pp. 166–7.
25. Werner, *JSA*, Oct. 1959, p. 285.
26. *Ibid.*   27. *Ibid.*, p. 286.
28. D. B. Wardle, "A note on document repair at the Public Record Office", *JSA*, vol. II, no. 4, Oct. 1961, p. 164.
29. "An archivist's note on the conservation of documents", *JSA*, vol. I, no. 9, Apr. 1959, p. 254.
30. *JSA*, Oct. 1961, pp. 164–5.
31. "Lamination for all?", *JSA*, vol. II, no. 6, Oct. 1962, p. 272.
32. *JSA*, Apr. 1959, p. 253.
33. *JSA*, Oct. 1959, p. 288.
34. A. W. M. Hughes, "Insect pests of books and paper", *Archives*, no. 7, Lady Day 1952, p. 19.
35. H. J. Plenderleith, "Insects among archives", British Records Association Technical Section, *Bulletin no. 18*, 1945, pp. 2–6.
36. *Archives*, Lady Day 1952, p. 19.
37. Plenderleith, B.R.A., *Bulletin no. 18*, 1945, p. 4.
38. *Ibid.*, p. 5.   39. *Ibid.*

10. Shelves and Boxes

1. J. R. Ede, "Steel shelving for record storage", *Journal of the Society of Archivists*, vol. II, no. 3, Apr. 1961, p. 114.
2. Ede, *JSA*, Apr. 1961, p. 114.
3. *Ibid.*, p. 115.
4. "Report and comment: mobile shelving", *Archives*, vol. VII, no. 33, Apr. 1965, p. 53.
5. Ede, *JSA*, Apr. 1961, p. 119.
6. I am grateful to Mr. D. B. Wardle for permission to reproduce the following diagrams and calculations of strong-room storage provision, obtained from lectures on archive administration given by him in the School of Librarianship and Archives, University College London, 1949–50. Mr. Wardle mentions an interesting proposal which he made in the 1930s for the improvement of the inconveniently

high strong rooms in the P.R.O. basement. Since, owing to the ceiling construction, the effective height of the rooms was somewhat less than 12 ft, a conventional mezzanine floor was not possible, Mr. Wardle suggested "vertical staggering" of gangways and racks on the upper and lower floors respectively, so that headroom, at the cost of a little shelf space, was never less than 6 ft. For economic reasons this plan could not be adopted and, instead, the shelves above the 8 ft level were regarded as a "notional" upper floor for storing less frequently used records.

11. The Arrangement and Description of Archives

1. T. R. Schellenberg, *The Management of Archives*, 1965, p. 32.
2. *Ibid.*, p. 200.
3. *Local Records*, 1953, p. 73.
4. *Ibid.*
5. F. W. Steer. "Obiter dicta et scripta", *JSA*, vol. III, no. 5, Apr. 1967, p. 243.
6. Steer, *JSA*, vol. III, no. 5, Apr. 1967, p. 243.
7. Schellenberg, *The Management of Archives*, 1965, pp. 106–7.
8. *Ibid.*, pp. 107–8. 9. *Ibid.*, p. 220. 10. *Ibid.*, pp. 224–33.
11. Jenkinson, *A Manual of Archive Administration*, 1965, p. 115.
12. Somerset County Council, County Records Committee, *Interim Handlist of Somerset Quarter Sessions Documents and other Official Records*, 1947, p. 24.
13. Jenkinson, *Manual*, 1965, p. 115.
14. *Local Records*, 1953, p. 80.
15. *Guide to the Manuscript Collections in the Sheffield City Libraries*, 1956, p. x.
16. Schellenberg, *The Management of Archives*, 1965, p. 222.
17. *Ibid.*, p. 57.
18. Jenkinson, *Manual*, 1965, p. 125.
19. *Ibid.*, p. 131.
20. *Local Records*, 1953, p. 79.
21. Schellenberg, *The Management of Archives*, 1965, p. 51.
22. *Ibid.*, pp. 297–8. 23. *Ibid.*, p. 298.
24. F. G. Emmison, "Needle-searching or spoon-feeding", *JSA*, vol. I, no. 3, Apr. 1956, pp. 75–79.

12. Repair

1. G. H. Fowler, *The Care of County Monuments*, 1st ed. 1923.
2. *JSA*, vol. II, no. 2, Oct. 1960, p. 71.
3. D. B. Wardle, "A note on document repair at the Public Record Office", *JSA*, vol. II, no. 4, Oct. 1961, p. 164.
4. Wardle, *JSA*, Oct. 1961, p. 164.
5. Roger H. Ellis, "An archivist's note on the conservation of documents", *JSA*, vol. I, no. 9, Apr. 1959, p. 253.
6. Harold J. Plenderleith and Anthony Werner, "Technical notes on the conservation of documents", *JSA*, vol. I, no. 7, Apr. 1958, pp. 195–201.
7. Ellis, *JSA*, Apr. 1959, pp. 252–4.
8. A. E. A. Werner, "The preservation of archives", *JSA*, vol. I, no. 10, Oct. 1959, p. 288.
9. Wardle, *JSA*, Oct. 1961, p. 164.

10. D. B. Wardle, "Lamination for all?", *JSA*, vol. II, no. 6, Oct. 1962, p. 272.
11. W. H. Langwell, "The Postlip duplex lamination processes", *JSA*, vol. II, no. 10, Oct. 1964, p. 472.
12. *Local Records*, 1953, p. 95.
13. *Archives*, Apr. 1966, p. 153.
14. Jenkinson, *Manual*, 1965, p. 68.
15. *Local Records*, 1953, p. 95.
16. Jenkinson, *Manual*, 1965, pp. 75–78.
17. Jenkinson, *Manual*, 1965, pp. 215–18.
18. *Local Records*, 1953, p. 96.
19. *Map Repair: wall-board equipment and process* (typescript), Somerset Record Office, July 1963.
20. Hilary Jenkinson, *A Manual of Archive Administration including the Problems of War Archives and Archive Making*, Oxford, 1922, p. 63.
21. *JSA*, Oct. 1961, pp. 164–5.
22. Jenkinson, *Manual*, 1922, p. 64.
23. *Local Records*, 1953, pp. 96–97.
24. Report of meeting of document repairers, *JSA*, vol. II, no. 5, Apr. 1962, p. 231.
25. I. P. Collis, *Somerset Record Office: the repair block* (typescript), June 1963.
26. *Ibid.*, p. 6.

13. Reprography

1. W. R. Hawken, *Copying Methods Manual*, 1966, p. 85.
2. Jenkinson, *Manual*, 1965, p. 63.

14. The Educational Use of Archives

1. A. C. Edwards (Essex Record Office), *Archives*, vol. V, no. 25, Lady Day 1961, p. 15.
2. E. Kenneth Timings, "The archivist and the public", *JSA*, vol. II, no. 5, Apr. 1962, p. 182.
3. Felix Hull, "Limits", *JSA*, vol. II, no. 4, Oct. 1961, pp. 138–40.
4. Timings, *JSA*, Apr. 1962, p. 182.
5. Hull, *JSA*, Oct. 1961, p. 138.
6. Francis W. Steer, "The archivist, the public and the stately home", *JSA*, vol. II, no. 7, Apr. 1963, p. 318.
7. *JSA*, vol. II, no. 5, Apr. 1962, pp. 216–19.
8. *Archives*, Lady Day 1961, p. 14.
9. *Ibid.*, p. 15.   10. *Ibid.*, p. 16.

SELECT BIBLIOGRAPHY

THE following list consists of those books and articles which have been used in the preparation of this book. It should be supplemented by reference to the bibliographies contained in: R. H. Ellis (ed.), "Select bibliography of archive administration", *Journal of the Society of Archivists*, vol. II, no. 2, Oct. 1960, pp. 67–73; *Guide to the Public Records, Part I: Introductory*, 1949, pp. 69–70; Sir H. Jenkinson, *A Manual of Archive Administration*, 1965, pp. 242–6; *Local Records*, ed. L. J. Redstone and F. W. Steer, 1953, pp. 229–40; and T. R. Schellenberg, *The Management of Archives*, 1965, pp. 373–6. Current bibliographies of archive administration appear in successive volumes of *Archivum*, Congrès International des Archives, Paris, 1951– .

The list is arranged:

GENERAL

SETTING

      The archives scene
      The archives profession
      Archives bodies

CUSTODY

      Record office principles and practices
      Public records and the Public Record Office
      Archives in libraries
      Modern archives
      Business archives

TREATMENT

      Buildings
      Equipment
      Damage, protection, and repair
      Reprography
      The educational use of archives

GENERAL

BRITISH RECORDS ASSOCIATION, *Work in Archives, 1948–55* (reprinted from The Library Association, *Five Years' Work in Librarianship, 1951–1955*, 1958).

BRITISH RECORDS ASSOCIATION, *Work in Archives, 1956–60* (reprinted from The Library Association, *Five Years' Work in Librarianship, 1956–1960*, 1963).

BRITISH RECORDS ASSOCIATION, "Work in archives, 1961–1965", *Archives*, vol. VIII, no. 40, Oct. 1968, pp. 193–203 (reprinted from The Library Association, *Five Years' Work in Librarianship, 1961–1965*, 1968).

COLLIS, I. P., review of Sir H. Jenkinson, *A Manual of Archive Administration*, 1965, *Archives*, vol. VII, no. 36, Oct. 1966, pp. 248–50.

DARLINGTON, I., "Archives and archivists, 1964", *Progress in Library Science*, ed. R. L. Collison, 1965, pp. 57–79.

EDE, J., "Archives in the tropics", review of *A Manual of Tropical Archivology*, ed. Yves Pérotin, 1966, *JSA*, vol. III, no. 7, Apr. 1968, pp. 364–7.

ELLIS, R. H., review of T. R. Schellenberg, *The Management of Archives*, 1965, *Archives* vol. VIII, no. 37, Apr. 1967, pp. 55–56.

FOWLER, G. H., *The Care of County Muniments*. London, County Councils Association, 1st ed. 1923, 2nd ed. 1928, 3rd ed. 1939.

JARVIS, R. C., "Jenkinson re-issued", review of Sir H. Jenkinson, *A Manual of Archive Administration*, 1965, *JSA*, vol. III, no. 5, Apr. 1967, pp. 254–6.

JENKINSON, H., *A Manual of Archive Administration, including the Problems of War Archives and Archive Making*, Oxford, Clarendon Press, 1922.

JENKINSON, H., *A Manual of Archive Administration*, new and revised edition, London, Percy Lund, Humphries & Co., 1937.

JENKINSON, Sir H., *A Manual of Archive Administration*, a reissue of the revised second edition with an introduction and bibliography by Roger H. Ellis, London, Percy Lund, Humphries & Co., 1965.

KATHPALIA, Y. P., "Comments on Mr. Jeffrey Ede's review article on *Manual of Tropical Archivology*", *JSA*, vol. III, no. 9, Apr. 1969, pp. 494–6.

PÉROTIN, Y. (ed.), *A Manual of Tropical Archivology*, Paris, Mouton & Co. and École Pratique des Hautes Études, 1966.

REDSTONE, L. J. and F. W. STEER, *Local Records: Their Nature and Care*, London, G. Bell & Sons, 1953.

SCHELLENBERG, T. R., *The Management of Archives*, New York and London, Columbia University Press, 1965.

SETTING

The archives scene

BOND, M. F., "Archives services and smaller repositories. VI: English archives: an integrated service", *Archives*, vol. IV, no. 24, Mich. 1960, pp. 199–203.

BRITISH RECORDS ASSOCIATION, *British Records after the War, being a summary of the reports and memoranda prepared by a special committee of the council of the British Records Association*, Nov. 1943, 6 pp.

BRITISH RECORDS ASSOCIATION, *List of Record Repositories in Great Britain*, Reports from committees, no. 5, 1956.

BRITISH RECORDS ASSOCIATION, "Specialized repositories and archive principles", *Archives*, vol. VIII, no. 37, Apr. 1967, pp. 33–37.

CHARMAN, D., "On the need for a new local archives service for England", *JSA*, vol. III, no. 7, Apr. 1968, pp. 341–7.

COLLINGRIDGE, J. H., "Liaison between local record offices and the Public Record Office in the light of the Public Records Act 1958", *JSA*, vol. II, no. 10, Oct. 1964, pp. 451–7.

DARLINGTON, I., "Record offices in Greater London", *JSA*, vol. III, no. 5, Apr. 1967, pp. 248–50.

DAVIS, G. R. C., "Some home thoughts for the English archivist from abroad?", *Archives*, vol. IV, no. 23, Lady Day 1960, pp.176–7.

DOUGLAS, D. C., "Local archives and national history", *Society of Local Archivists Bulletin no. 14*, Oct. 1954, pp. 20–28.

GARSIDE, K. [letter to the editor about the Centre for Military Archives at King's College London], *Archives*, vol. VII, no. 36, Oct. 1966, pp. 236–7.

HISTORICAL MANUSCRIPTS COMMISSION, *Record Repositories in Great Britain: a list prepared by a joint committee of the Historical Manuscripts Commission and the British Records Association*, London, H.M.S.O., 1st ed. 1964, 2nd ed. 1966, 3rd ed. 1968.

HULL, F., "The local authority record office—whither?", *JSA*, vol. III, no. 7, Apr. 1968, pp. 357–8.

McCALL, R. H. and others, "Archives services and smaller repositories", *Archives*, vol. IV, no. 24, Mich. 1960, pp. 189–203.

MASTER OF THE ROLLS' ARCHIVES COMMITTEE, *Proposals for the Control of English Archives, being a memorandum submitted to the Master of the Rolls in October 1946*, 6 pp.

OWEN, A. E. B., "Too many repositories?": editorial, *Archives*, vol. VII, no. 35, Apr. 1966, pp. 133–4.

RALPH, E. and HULL, F. "The development of local archive service in England", *Essays in Memory of Sir Hilary Jenkinson*, edited for the Society of Archivists by A. E. J. Hollaender, 1962.

RAMSAY, G. D., "The publication of English records: some reflections on Mr. Mullins's *Texts and calendars*", *Archives*, vol. IV, no. 23, Lady Day 1960, pp. 138–48.

RIDLEY, N. "The Local Government (Records) Act, 1962: its passage to the statute book", *JSA*, vol. II, no. 7, Apr. 1963, pp. 288–92.

WELCH, E. [letter to the editor about the number and quality of repositories], *Archives*, vol. VII, no. 36, Oct. 1966, p. 235.

The archives profession

BUSINESS ARCHIVES COUNCIL [note of changes in syllabus of archives diploma course at University College London to take effect 1970–71], *Business Archives*, no. 32, June 1970, p. 6.

ELLIS, R. H., "The British archivist and his Society", *JSA*, vol. III, no. 2, Oct. 1965, pp. 43–48.

ELLIS, R. H., "The British archivist and history", *JSA*, vol. III, no. 4, Oct. 1966, pp. 155–60.

ELLIS, R. H., "The British archivist and his training", *JSA*, vol. III, no. 6, Oct. 1967, pp. 265–71.

IRWIN, R., "The education of an archivist", *Essays in memory of Sir Hilary Jenkinson*, edited for the Society of Archivists by A. E. J. Hollaender, 1962, pp. 178–89.

JENKINSON, H., *The English Archivist: a New Profession*, London, H. K. Lewis & Co., 1948.

JENKINSON, Sir H., "Roots", *JSA*, vol. II no. 4, Oct. 1961, pp. 131–8.

OWEN, A. E. B., "The image of the archivist", editorial, *Archives*, vol. VII, no. 36, Oct. 1966, pp. 189–90.

SOCIETY OF ARCHIVISTS, "The training of archivists", discussion at annual general meeting 1962, *JSA*, vol. II, no. 7, Apr. 1963, pp. 330–1.

Archives bodies

(i) *Business Archives Council*

BRITISH RECORDS ASSOCIATION [note on training courses in care of business archives], *Archives*, vol. V, no. 28, Mich. 1962, p. 235.

BRITISH RECORDS ASSOCIATION [report of discussion of scheme for cooperation between B.R.A. and B.A.C.], *Archives*, vol. IV, no. 21, Lady Day 1959, pp. 13–15.

BRITISH RECORDS ASSOCIATION, *Work in Archives, 1956–60*, pp. 443–4.

BUSINESS ARCHIVES COUNCIL, *Business Archives*, 1958– .

BUSINESS ARCHIVES COUNCIL, *Methods of Listing, Indexing and Reporting on Business Archives*, 1959.
BUSINESS ARCHIVES COUNCIL, *Quarterly Newsletter*, 1958– .

(ii) *British Records Association*

BOND, M. F., "The British Records Association and the modern archive movement," *Essays in Memory of Sir Hilary Jenkinson*, edited for the Society of Archivists by A. E. J. Hollaender, 1962, pp. 71–90.
BRITISH RECORDS ASSOCIATION, *Archives*, twice yearly, 1949– .
BRITISH RECORDS ASSOCIATION, *British Records Association, 1932 to 1947, being a report from the joint secretaries on their retirement*, 1948, 25 pp.
BRITISH RECORDS ASSOCIATION, *Proceedings*, 1933–48.
BRITISH RECORDS ASSOCIATION, *Report of council, annual report of the Records Preservation Section, accounts, and changes in the list of members*, 1933– .
BRITISH RECORDS ASSOCIATION, *Work in Archives, 1948–55*, pp. 2–4.
BRITISH RECORDS ASSOCIATION, *Work in Archives, 1956–60*, pp. 440–2.
SOCIETY OF LOCAL ARCHIVISTS, "The local record office and the British Records Association", *Local Records*, 1953, pp. 221–2.

(iii) *Historical Manuscripts Commission*

BAILLIE, H. M. G., "The use of the resources of the Historical Manuscripts Commission", *JSA*, vol. III, no. 9, Apr. 1969, pp. 462–6.
BRITISH RECORDS ASSOCIATION, *Work in Archives, 1948–55*, pp. 7–11.
BRITISH RECORDS ASSOCIATION, *Work in Archives, 1956–60*, pp. 446–8.
ELLIS, R. H., "The centenary of the Royal Commission on Historical Manuscripts: origins and transformations", *JSA*, vol. III, no. 9, Apr. 1969, pp. 441–52.
ELLIS, R. H., "The Historical Manuscripts Commission, 1869–1969", *JSA*, vol. II, no. 6, Oct. 1962, pp. 233–42.
ELLIS, R. H., "The publication of English records: II. The Historical Manuscripts Commission", *Archives*, vol. IV, no. 24, Mich. 1960, pp. 218–19.
HISTORICAL MANUSCRIPTS COMMISSION, *Reports to the Crown*, 1870– .
OWEN, A. E. B., "The Historical Manuscripts Commission, 1869–1969", editorial, *Archives*, vol. IX, no. 41, Apr. 1969, p. 1.
RAMSAY, G. D., "The publication of English records", *Archives,* vol. IV, no. 23, Lady Day 1960, pp. 138–48.

(iv) *International Congress on Archives*

BRITISH RECORDS ASSOCIATION, reports on Congresses:
    1st (Paris, 1950), *Archives*, vol. I, no. 4, Mich. 1950, pp. 13–15.
    2nd (The Hague, 1953), *Archives*, vol. II, Mich. 1953, pp. 94–95.
    3rd (Florence, 1956), *Archives*, vol. II, no. 16, Mich. 1956, pp. 497–8.
    4th (Stockholm, 1960), *Archives*, vol. V, no. 25, Lady Day 1961, pp. 17–20.
    5th (Brussels, 1964), *Archives*, vol. VII, no. 33, Apr. 1965, pp. 23–24.
    6th (Madrid, 1968), *Archives*, vol. IX, no. 41, Apr. 1969, pp. 42–43.
CONGRÈS INTERNATIONAL DES ARCHIVES, volumes of *Archivum* devoted to Congress papers and proceedings: I, 1951; III, 1953; VI, 1956; X, 1960; XIV, 1964.

(v) *National Register of Archives*

ATKINSON, R. L., 'Lt.-Col. G. E. G. Malet, O.B.E.', obituary, *Archives*, vol. I, no. 8, Mich. 1952, pp. 3–6.

BRITISH RECORDS ASSOCIATION, *Work in Archives, 1948–55*, pp. 11–14.

BRITISH RECORDS ASSOCIATION, *Work in Archives, 1956–60*, pp. 448–50.

EVERSHED, LORD, *The Times*, 31 Oct. and 1 Nov. 1955.

HISTORICAL MANUSCRIPTS COMMISSION, *Bulletin of the National Register of Archives*, no. 1, 1948–no. 14, 1967.

HISTORICAL MANUSCRIPTS COMMISSION, *The National Register of Archives*, H.M.S.O., 1945, 7 pp.

OWEN, A. E. B., "Twenty years on: the National Register of Archives", editorial, *Archives*, vol. VII, no. 33, Apr. 1965, p. 1.

RANGER, F., "The National Register of Archives, 1945–1969", *JSA*, vol. III, no. 9, Apr. 1969, pp. 452–62.

SOCIETY OF LOCAL ARCHIVISTS, "The local record office and the National Register of Archives", *Local Records*, 1953, pp. 223–7.

(vi) *Society of Archivists*

BRITISH RECORDS ASSOCIATION, *Work in Archives, 1948–55*, pp. 14–16.

BRITISH RECORDS ASSOCIATION, *Work in Archives, 1956–60*, pp. 442–3.

RALPH, E. and HULL, F. "The development of local archive service in England", *Essays in memory of Sir Hilary Jenkinson*, 1962, pp. 57–70.

SOCIETY OF ARCHIVISTS, *Journal*, twice yearly, 1955– .

SOCIETY OF LOCAL ARCHIVISTS, *Bulletin*, nos. 1–14, 1947–1954.

CUSTODY

Record office principles and practices

BARNES, T. G., "The local record office and the historian's apprenticeship", *JSA*, vol. II, no. 1, Apr. 1960, pp. 25–33.

BRITISH RECORDS ASSOCIATION, "Conflict between custody and use of records", discussion, *Archives*, vol. VIII, no. 37, pp. 37–39.

BRITISH RECORDS ASSOCIATION, "Facilities for access", discussion, *Archives*, vol. I, no. 3, Lady Day 1950, pp. 36–39.

BRITISH RECORDS ASSOCIATION, "Owner and custodian: relations between owners of deposited records and repositories", discussion, *Archives*, vol. VII, no. 35, Apr. 1966, pp. 153–6.

BRITISH RECORDS ASSOCIATION, "The preparation of lists, indexes and inventories", discussion, *Archives*, vol. I, no. 5, Lady Day 1951, pp. 37–39.

BRITISH RECORDS ASSOCIATION, "Publicity for records", discussion, *Archives*, vol. VIII, no. 39, Apr. 1968.

BRITISH RECORDS ASSOCIATION, "Record offices and the senior researcher", discussion, *Archives*, vol. IX, no. 41, Apr. 1969, pp. 34–36.

BRITISH RECORDS ASSOCIATION, *Rules for dealing with accumulation of documents*, memorandum no. 11, Jan. 1949, 6 pp.

COLLIS, I. P., "The arrangement and listing of private and estate muniments: some considerations", *Society of Local Archivists Bulletin no. 10*, Oct. 1952, pp. 10–16.

EMMISON, F. G., "Lists, indexes and inventories", *Archives*, vol. I, no. 5, Lady Day 1951, pp. 24–27.

EMMISON, F. G., "Needle-searching or spoon-feeding", *JSA*, vol. I, no. 3, Apr. 1956, pp. 75–79.

EMMISON, F. G., " 'Repatriation' of 'foreign' estate and family archives", *Archives* vol. II, no. 16, Mich. 1956, pp. 467–76.

HULL, F., "Facilities for access", *Archives*, vol. I, no. 3, Lady Day 1950, pp. 20–23.

HULL, F., "Limits", *JSA*, vol. II, no. 4, Oct. 1961, pp. 138–40.

LAMB, W. K., "Keeping the past up to date" *JSA*, vol. II, no. 7, Apr. 1963, pp.285–8.

LANCASTER, J. C. and others, "Some views on 'sanctity' ", *Archives*, vol. III, no. 19, Lady Day 1958, pp. 159–71.

LECONFIELD, LORD, and others, "The care of records by the private owner", *Archives*, vol. II, no. 10, Mich. 1953, pp. 74–85.

OWEN, A. E. B., "Historians and records", editorial, *Archives*, vol. VI, no. 32, Oct. 1964, pp. 199–201.

OWEN, A. E. B., review of *Lexicon of Archive Terminology*, International Council of Archives, 1964, *Archives*, vol. VII, no. 33, Apr. 1965, pp. 57–58.

PUBLIC RECORD OFFICE, *Principles governing the elimination of ephemeral or unimportant documents in public or private archives*, n.d., post-1943, 4 pp.

RANGER, F., "The common pursuit", *Archives*, vol. IX, no. 43, April 1970, pp. 121–9.

SOCIETY OF ARCHIVISTS, "Problems involved in answering postal enquiries", discussion, *JSA*, vol. II, no. 3, Apr. 1961, pp. 128–9.

SOCIETY OF ARCHIVISTS, report by index working party, *JSA*, vol. III, no. 9, Apr. 1969, p. 510.

SOMERVILLE, SIR ROBERT, "Archives or records", letter, *Archives*, vol. VII, no. 34, Oct. 1965, pp. 93–94.

STEER, F. W., "The archivist, the public and the stately home", *JSA*, vol. II, no. 7, Apr. 1963, pp. 316–18.

STEER, F. W., "The historian and local record repositories", *Archives*, vol. II, no. 15, Lady Day 1956, pp. 382–6, 402–4.

STEER, F. W., "Obiter dicta et scripta", *JSA*, vol. III, no. 5, April 1967, pp. 241–5.

TIMINGS, E. K., "The archivist and the public", *JSA*, vol. II, no. 5, Apr. 1962, pp. 179–83.

TIMINGS, E. K., "The archivist and the public: a postscript", *JSA*, vol. II, no. 8, Oct. 1963, pp. 366–7.

WALNE, P., "Lexicon of archive terminology", letter, *Archives*, vol. VII, no. 35, Apr. 1966, pp. 163–6.

Public records and the Public Record Office

BRITISH RECORDS ASSOCIATION, "The Public Record Office—needs of the next decade", discussion, *Archives*, vol. V, no. 27, Lady Day 1962, pp. 131–6.

BROWN, R. A., "The public records and the historian", *JSA*, vol. II, no. 1, Apr. 1960, pp. 1–8.

EDE, J. R., "The Public Record Office and its users", *Archives*, vol. VIII, no. 40, Oct. 1968, pp. 185–92.

GALBRAITH, V. H., *An Introduction to the Use of the Public Records*, Oxford, Clarendon Press, 1934.

JOHNSON, C., "The Public Record Office", *Studies presented to Sir Hilary Jenkinson*, ed. J. Conway Davies, London, O.U.P., 1957, pp. 178–95.

JOHNSON, H. C., "The publication of English records: I. The Public Record Office", *Archives*, vol. IV, no. 24, Mich. 1960, pp. 214–18.

JOHNSON, H. C., "The Public Record Office", report of address on one hundred years of record keeping at the Public Record Office, *Archives*, vol. IV, no. 21, Lady Day 1959, pp. 15–17.

JOHNSON, H. C., "The Public Record Office and its problems", *Bulletin of the Institute of Historical Research*, vol. 42, no. 105, May 1969, pp. 86–95.

MABBS, A. W., "The Public Record Office and the second review", *Archives*, vol. VIII, no. 40, Oct. 1968, pp. 180–4.

NICHOLAS, H. G., "The public records: the historian, the national interest and official policy", *JSA*, vol. III, no. 1 Apr. 1965, pp. 1–6.

OWEN, A. E. B., "Congestion in the Public Record Office: facts and figures", editorial note, *Archives*, vol. VIII, no. 38, Oct. 1967, pp. 61–62.

PUBLIC RECORD OFFICE, *Guide to the Contents of the Public Record Office*, London, H.M.S.O., vols. I, II, 1963; vol. III, 1968.

PUBLIC RECORD OFFICE, *Guide to the Public Records, Part I: Introductory*, London, H.M.S.O., 1949.

PUGH, R. B., "Publishing the public records: a replication", *Archives*, vol. V, no. 26, Mich. 1961, pp. 78–83.

WALNE, P., "The Record Commissions, 1800–1837", *JSA*, vol. II, no. 1, Apr. 1960, pp. 8–16.

Archives in libraries

BRITISH RECORDS ASSOCIATION, "The work of libraries in archive administration", discussion, *Archives*, vol. II, no. 9, Lady Day 1953, pp. 33–38.

ELLIS, R. H., "Local history, archives and libraries", *Library Association Scarborough Conference Papers and Discussion*, 1960, pp. 9–16.

HEPWORTH, P., *Archives and Manuscripts in Libraries*, Library Association pamphlet no. 18, London, The Library Association, 1st ed. 1958, 2nd ed. 1964.

HEPWORTH, P., "Archives and manuscripts in libraries—1961", *Library Association Record*, vol. 64, 1962, pp. 269–83.

HEPWORTH, P., "Manuscripts and non-book materials in libraries", *Archives*, vol. IX, no. 42, Oct. 1969, pp. 90–97.

HOBBS, J. L., *Libraries and the Materials of Local History*, London, Grafton, 1948.

HOBBS, J. L., *Local History and the Library*, London, Andre Deutsch, 1962.

HOBBS, J. L., "Local records and the library", *Library Association Record*, vol. 51, 1949, pp. 177–9.

HODSON, J. H., "Archivist in bookland", *North Western Newsletter*, Library Association North West Branch, no. 15, May 1952, pp. 1–2.

HODSON, J. H., "The Liverpool Record Office", *Society of Local Archivists Bulletin no. 13*, Apr. 1954, pp. 39–41.

HODSON, J. H., "A university archive repository: the University of Nottingham Department of Manuscripts", *Archives*, vol. V, no. 27, Lady Day 1962, pp. 145–50.

IRWIN, R., *Librarianship: Essays on Applied Bibliography*, London, Grafton, 1949.

IVEY, E. W., "The records to be kept for business purposes", *Aslib Proceedings*, vol. 10, no. 9, Sept. 1958, pp. 211–16.

JENKINSON, SIR H., *The Liverpool Record Office: an address at the opening of the Liverpool Record Office, 26 November 1953*, Liverpool Public Libraries.

KIRBY, J. L., review of P. Hepworth, *Archives and Manuscripts in Libraries*, 1958, *Archives*, vol. III, no. 20, Mich. 1958, pp. 253–4.

LIBRARY ASSOCIATION, "The place of archives and manuscripts in the field of librarianship: a statement of policy approved by the Library Association Council, November 1968", *JSA*, vol. III, no. 10, Oct. 1969, pp. 582–3.

LIVERPOOL, CORPORATION OF, Free Public Libraries, *Catalogue of Liverpool prints and documents*, Library, Museum and Arts Committee, Liverpool, 1908.

RENSHAW, M. A., "A university repository", *Library Association Record*, vol. 56, 1954, pp. 75–80.

SHEFFIELD CITY LIBRARIES, *Guide to the Manuscript Collections in the Sheffield City Libraries*, Libraries, Art Galleries and Museums Committee, Sheffield, 1956, *Supplement I, 1956–62* (typescript), n.d.

STEPHENS, G. B., "Archives in libraries", *Library Association Record*, vol. 53, 1951, pp. 263–4.

Modern archives

BRITISH RECORDS ASSOCIATION, *Modern Records: preservation and salvage*, memorandum no. 10, July 1948, 2 pp.

BRITISH RECORDS ASSOCIATION, *The Preservation of Modern Records: general advice*, memorandum no. 18, May 1964, 4 pp.

BRITISH RECORDS ASSOCIATION, "The records of science and technology, with thoughts on their disposal", discussion, *Archives*, vol. VIII, no. 37, Apr. 1967, pp. 28–32.

BARRATT, C. and THOMPSON, C. H., "The preservation and classification of modern local government archives: two views: I. The town clerk, by C. Barratt, II. The county archivist, by C. H. Thompson", *Archives*, vol. I, no. 7, Lady Day 1952, pp. 1–12.

BURKE, E. E., "Records management in the Central African Archives", *JSA*, vol. I, no. 3, Apr. 1956, pp. 62–66.

CHARMAN, D., "The archivist and modern local government records", *Society of Local Archivists Bulletin no. 14*, Oct. 1954, pp. 2–9.

CHARMAN, D. and COOK, M. "The archive services of East Africa", *Archives*, vol. VIII, no. 38, Oct. 1967, pp. 70–80.

COLLINGRIDGE, J. H., "Implementing the Grigg report", *JSA*, vol. I, no. 7, Apr. 1958, pp. 179–84.

COLLINGRIDGE, J. H., "Records management in England since the Grigg report", *JSA*, vol. II, no. 6, Oct. 1962, pp. 242–7.

COLLINGRIDGE, J. H., review of T. R. Schellenberg, *Modern Archives: Principles and Techniques*, 1955, and T. R. Schellenberg, *The Appraisal of Modern Public Records*, 1956, *Archives*, vol. III, no. 17, Lady Day 1957, pp. 52–56.

COMMITTEE ON DEPARTMENTAL RECORDS [Grigg Committee], *Report*, Cmd. 9163, H.M.S.O., 1954.

COOK, M., "Regional archives offices: some reflections", *JSA*, vol. III, no. 6, Oct. 1967, pp. 271–5.

COOK, M. and others, "The management of records: report of the symposium held in Cambridge, 11–13 January 1968", *JSA*, vol. III, no. 8, Oct. 1968, pp. 417–23.

DARLINGTON, I., "The London Government Act 1963 and its effect on local records in the Greater London area", *JSA*, vol. III, no. 6, Oct. 1967, pp. 291–6.

DARLINGTON, I., "Methods adopted by the London County Council for the preservation or disposal of modern records", *JSA*, vol. I, no. 5, April 1957, pp. 140–6.

DARLINGTON, I., "The weeding and disposal of files", *JSA*, vol. I, no. 2, Oct. 1955, pp. 47–49.

HULL, F., "County of Kent working party on county records: report and recommendations", *JSA*, vol. III, no. 10, Oct. 1969, pp. 572–5.

HULL, F., "The destruction of administrative records: the county repository and the Grigg report", *JSA*, vol. I, no. 2, Oct. 1955, pp. 41–43.

HULL, F., "The management of modern records", *JSA*, vol. 4, no. 1, Apr. 1970, pp. 45–50.

JARVIS, R. C., "The Grigg report: II, The Public Record Office", *JSA*, vol. I, 1955, pp. 10–13.

JEFFREYS, A., "Manuscript sources for the history of science", *Archives*, vol. VII, no. 34, Oct. 1965, pp. 75–79.

JENKINSON, Sir H., "The future of archives in England", *JSA*, vol. I, no. 3, Apr. 1956, pp. 57–61.

JENKINSON, Sir H., "Modern archives: some reflexions on T. R. Schellenberg: *Modern archives: principles and techniques*", *JSA*, vol. I, no. 5, Apr. 1957, pp. 147–9.

JENKINSON, Sir H., "Roots", *JSA*, vol. II, no. 4, Oct. 1961, pp. 131–8.

JONES, P. E., "The Grigg report: I. Departmental records", *JSA*, vol. I, 1955, pp. 7–9.

KULA, S., "The storage of archive film", *JSA*, vol. II, no. 6, Oct. 1962, pp. 270–2.

LAMB, W. K., "The fine art of destruction", *Essays in Memory of Sir Hilary Jenkinson*, ed. A. E. J. Hollaender, 1962, pp. 50–56.

MABBS, A. W., "The Public Record Office and the second review", *Archives*, vol. VIII, no. 40, Oct. 1968, pp. 180–4.

OWEN, A. E. B., "Archives in the computer age", editorial, *Archives*, vol. VII, no. 34, Oct. 1965, pp. 73–74.

OWEN, A. E. B., "The image of the archivist", editorial, *Archives*, vol. VII, no. 36, Oct. 1966, pp. 189–90.

PUBLIC RECORD OFFICE, *Guide to the Public Records, Part I: Introductory*, "Elimination", pp. 26–30, "Limbo", pp. 30–32, London, H.M.S.O., 1949.

ROADS, C. H., "Film as historical evidence", *JSA*, vol. III, no. 4, Oct. 1966, pp. 183–91.

SCHELLENBERG, T. R., *Modern Archives: Principles and Techniques*, Melbourne, F. W. Cheshire, 1956.

SHADD, D., "Some problems in providing reference service at a records centre", *JSA*, vol. II, no. 2, Oct. 1960, pp. 61–67.

SLOCOMBE, M., "Storage of tape recordings", *JSA*, vol. I, no. 8, Oct. 1958, pp. 226–8.

SMITH, C. R., "The preservation of the present", *JSA*, vol. III, no. 3, Apr. 1966, pp. 133–5.

SMITH, W., "Archival selection: a Canadian view", *JSA*, vol. III, no. 6, Oct. 1967, pp. 275–80.

SOCIETY OF ARCHIVISTS, "Automation and archives", discussion, *JSA*, vol. III, no. 1, Apr. 1965, p. 41.

WALTON, H. M., "Destruction schedules: quarter sessions', magistrates courts' and coroners' records", *JSA*, vol. III, no. 2, Oct. 1965, pp. 61–75.

WELCH, E., "Records management", *JSA*, vol. III, no. 4, Oct. 1966, pp. 198–9.

Business archives

BARKER, T. C. and others, *Business History*, Historical Association, Helps for Students of History no. 59, 1960.

BRITISH RECORDS ASSOCIATION, "Practical co-operation in the field of business archives", discussion, *Archives*, vol. IV, no. 21, Lady Day 1959, pp. 13–15.

BRITISH RECORDS ASSOCIATION, "The publication of business records", report by working party, *Archives*, no. 6, Mich. 1951, pp. 17–30.

BUSINESS ARCHIVES COUNCIL, *Business Archives* (formerly *Quarterly Newsletter*), 1958– .

CHALONER, W. H., "Business records and local history", *Society of Local Archivists Bulletin no. 12*, Oct. 1953, pp. 21–25.

CHINNERY, G. A., "Commercial practice in the 18th century as a guide to repositorial classification of business records", *Society of Local Archivists Bulletin no. 10*, Oct. 1952, pp. 22–26.

JAMES, R. L. M., "Brewing records: an inquiry and its lessons", *Archives*, vol. VII, no. 36, Oct. 1966, pp. 215–20.

MACMILLAN, D. S., "Australian business archives; problems and solutions", *Archives*, vol. III, no. 20, Mich. 1958, pp. 238–45.

MACMILLAN, D. S., "Business archives—a survey of developments in Great Britain, the United States of America and in Australia", *Essays in memory of Sir Hilary Jenkinson*, ed. A. E. J. Hollaender, 1962.

MATHIAS, P., "Historical records of the brewing industry", *Archives*, vol. VII, no. 33, Apr. 1965, pp. 2–10.

NATIONAL REGISTER OF ARCHIVES, *Sources of Business History in Reports of the National Register of Archives* (typescript), 1965– .

PAYNE, P. L., "Business archives and economic history: the case for regional studies", *Archives*, vol. VI, no. 29, Lady Day 1963, pp. 21–29.

TREATMENT

Buildings

[Information about the buildings of particular British record offices will be found in the series, "Local archives of Great Britain", which has appeared regularly in *Archives* since 1949.]

ANDERSSON, I., "New installations of archives", *Archivum*, vol. VI, 1956, pp. 11–18.

BOND, M. F., "The new record repository at the Houses of Parliament", *Archives*, vol. VI, no. 30, Mich. 1963, pp. 85–94.

BOND, M. F., review of M. Duchein, *Les Bâtiments et équipements d'archives*, Paris, International Council of Archives, 1966, *Archives*, vol. VIII, no. 39, Apr. 1968.

BRITISH RECORDS ASSOCIATION, "Strong-room construction: the architects' point of view" [by E. Carter], *British Records Association Technical Section Bulletin no. 16*, 1946, pp. 9–14.

BRITISH RECORDS ASSOCIATION, "Strong-room construction: the archivist's point of view", *British Records Association Technical Section Bulletin no. 16*, 1946, pp. 1–8.

COLLIS, I. P., "The ideal layout of a local record repository", *Archives*, vol. I, no. 6, Mich. 1951, pp. 31–35; vol. I, no. 7, Lady Day 1952, pp. 52–59.

COLLIS, I. P., "Notes on modern archive buildings in England, Wales and Northern Ireland", *Archivum*, vol. VI, 1956, pp. 100–5.

DARLINGTON, I., " 'In the rock': a brief account of the National Archives of Finland", *JSA*, vol. II, no. 1, Apr. 1960, pp. 34–36.

DUCHEIN, M., "Les bâtiments d'archives départementales en France", *Archivum*, vol. VI, 1956, pp. 108–76.

DUCHEIN, M., *Les Bâtiments et équipements d'archives*, Conseil international des archives, Paris, 1966.

ELLIS, R. H. and ELLIS, J., "Archivist and architect: an ideal design for a limbo record repository", *Archives*, vol. I, no. 8, 1952, pp. 20–29.

HEDAR, S. "On building archives", *Archivum*, vol. VI, 1956, pp. 83–87.

SCHELLENBERG, T. R., "Modern archival building", *Archivum*, vol. VI, 1956, pp. 88–92.

Equipment

ATKINSON, R. L., "Notes on showcases", *British Records Association Technical Section Bulletin no. 16*, 1946, pp. 20-23.

BELL, L., "Showcases", *JSA*, vol. II, no. 5, Apr. 1962, pp. 216–19.

BRITISH RECORDS ASSOCIATION, "Report and comment: mobile shelving", *Archives*, vol. VII, no. 33, Apr. 1965, pp. 52–53.

EDE, J. R., "Steel shelving for record storage", *JSA*, vol. II, no. 3, Apr. 1961, pp. 114–19.

EMMISON, F. G., "Shelves and boxes", *British Records Association Technical Section Bulletin no. 16*, 1946, pp. 14–18.

WILLIAMS, W. O., "Shelving of an aluminium alloy", *Archives*, vol. I, no. 2, Mich. 1949, pp. 30–32.

Damage, protection, and repair

ARMITAGE, F. D., review of W. H. Langwell, *The Conservation of Books and Documents*, 1957, *JSA*, vol. I, no. 7, Apr. 1958, pp. 203–4.

BOND, M. F. and BAYNES-COPE, A. D., "Fungicides", *JSA*, vol. 4, no. 1, Apr. 1970, pp. 51–52.

BRITISH RECORDS ASSOCIATION, *The Care of Records: notes for the owner or custodian*, memorandum no. 19, Oct. 1965, 6 pp.

BRITISH RECORDS ASSOCIATION, "Exhibition of document repairs", report, *Archives*, vol. II, no. 11, Lady Day 1954, pp. 145–50.

BRITISH RECORDS ASSOCIATION, "Faded writing", *Technical Section Bulletin no. 16*, 1946, pp. 42–43.

BRITISH RECORDS ASSOCIATION, *First aid for damaged manuscripts*, memorandum no. 6, 1942, 2 pp.

BRITISH RECORDS ASSOCIATION, "First-aid for Florence", *Archives*, vol. VIII, no. 37, April 1967, pp. 24–25.

BRITISH RECORDS ASSOCIATION, "Insects and moulds: prevention and cure", discussion, *Archives*, vol. I, no. 7, Lady Day 1952, pp. 34–35.

BRITISH RECORDS ASSOCIATION, "Lamination and related questions", discussion, *Archives*, vol. I, no. 3, Lady Day 1950, pp. 29–32.

BRITISH RECORDS ASSOCIATION, "Materials for repair and packing", discussion, *Archives*, vol. I, no. 5, Lady Day 1951, pp. 28–34.

BRITISH RECORDS ASSOCIATION, "Stored documents and damp: a few reminders", *Technical Section Bulletin no. 18*, 1945, pp. 6–7.

BRITISH RECORDS ASSOCIATION, "Strong-room climate", discussion, *Archives*, vol. II, no. 15, Lady Day 1956, pp. 399–402.

BRITISH RECORDS ASSOCIATION, "The technical care of records: latest information for the private owner and smaller repository", discussion, *Archives*, vol. VI, no. 29, Lady Day 1963, pp. 16–18.

CHURCH, R. W., "U.S. investigation into lamination", *JSA*, vol. I, no. 7, Apr. 1958, pp. 202–3.

CLAY, C., "Notes on treatments for library bindings", British Records Association Technical Section, *Bulletin* no. 16, 1946, pp. 35–37.

COLLIS, I. P., *Map Repair: wall-board equipment and process* (typescript), Somerset Record Office, July 1963.

COLLIS, I. P., *Somerset Record Office: the repair block* (typescript), Somerset Record Office, June 1963.

COLLIS, I. P., "The technical care of records: document conservation in the local repository", *Archives*, vol. VI, no. 29, Lady Day 1963, pp. 4–7.

COLLIS, I. P., "The use of thymol for document fumigation", *JSA*, vol. 4, no. 1, Apr. 1970, pp. 53–54.

CUNNINGHAM, J. K. H., "The protection of records and documents against fire", *JSA*, vol. III, no. 8, Oct. 1968, pp. 411–17.

DARLINGTON, I., "The lamination of paper documents", *JSA*, vol. I, no. 4, Oct. 1956, pp. 108–10.

ELLIS, R. H., "The archivist as a technician," *JSA*, vol. I, no. 5, Apr. 1957, pp. 146–7.

ELLIS, R. H., "An archivist's note on the conservation of documents", *JSA*, vol. I, no. 9, Apr. 1959, pp. 252–4.

ELLIS, R. H., "The technical care of records: latest information for the private owner and smaller repository", *Archives*, vol. VI, no. 29, Lady Day 1963, pp. 1–3.

EVANS, D. L., review of Adelaide E. Minogue, *The Repair and Preservation of Records* 1943, British Records Association Technical Section, *Bulletin* no. 18, 1945, pp. 8–14.

FOWLER, G. H., "Maps", British Records Association Technical Section, *Bulletin* no. 16, 1946, pp. 23–27.

FOWLER, G. H., "Paste", British Records Association Technical Section, *Bulletin* no. 16, 1946, pp. 18–19.

HOUSE OF LORDS RECORD OFFICE, *The Use of Santobrite*, memorandum, 1960.

HUDSON, F. L. and MILNER, W. D., "Atmospheric sulphur and the durability of paper", *JSA*, vol. II, no. 4, Oct. 1961, pp. 166–7.

HUGHES, A. W. M., "Insect pests of books and paper", *Archives*, vol. I, no. 7, Lady Day 1952, pp. 19–22.

JENKINSON, SIR H., "Effects of surrounding conflagration on the contents of a city strong room", British Records Association Technical Section, *Bulletin* no. 16, 1946, pp. 40–42.

JENKINSON, SIR H., "Paste: the use of alum", British Records Association Technical Section, *Bulletin* no. 16, 1946, p. 19.

LANGWELL, W. H., "Accelerated ageing tests for paper", *JSA*, vol. III, no. 5, Apr. 1967, pp. 245–8.

LANGWELL, W. H., *The Conservation of Books and Documents*, London, Pitman, 1957.

LANGWELL, W. H., "The deterioration of newsprint in impure atmospheres", *JSA*, vol. I, no. 6, Oct. 1957, pp. 173–4.

LANGWELL, W. H., "Lamination of documents", *JSA*, vol. II, no. 2, Oct. 1960, pp. 73–74.

LANGWELL, W. H., "Methods of deacidifying paper", *JSA*, vol. III, no. 9, Apr. 1969, pp. 491–4.

LANGWELL, W. H., "Observations on paper embrittlement", *JSA*, vol. I, no. 6, Oct. 1957, pp. 172–3.

LANGWELL, W. H., "The Postlip Duplex lamination processes", *JSA*, vol. II, no. 10, Oct. 1964, p. 472.

LANGWELL, W. H., "The preservation of paper records", *Archives*, vol. II, no. 11, Lady Day 1954, pp. 136–7.

LANGWELL, W. H., "The preservation of unstable papers", *Archives*, no. 4, Mich. 1950, pp. 40–43.

LANGWELL, W. H., "The protection of paper and parchment against dampness in storage", *JSA*, vol. III, no. 2, Oct. 1965, pp. 82–85.

LANGWELL, W. H., "Recent developments in Postlip lamination processes", *JSA*, vol. III, no. 7, Apr. 1968, pp. 360–1.

LANGWELL, W. H., "The vapour phase deacidification of books and documents", *JSA*, vol. III, no. 3, Apr. 1966, pp. 137–8.

MURRAY, H. D., "Examination of burnt documents", British Records Association Technical Section, *Bulletin* no. 16, 1946, pp. 44–46.

NIXON, H. M., "Lamination of paper documents with cellulose acetate foil", *Archives*, vol. I, no. 2, Mich. 1949, pp. 32–36.

NIXON, H. M., review of S. M. Cockerell, *The Repairing of Books*, 1958, *Archives*, vol. IV, no. 22, Mich. 1959, pp. 113–14.

PLENDERLEITH, H. J., *The Conservation of Prints, Drawings, and Manuscripts*, London, Museums Association, 1937.

PLENDERLEITH, H. J., "Decipherment of charred documents", British Records Association Technical Section, *Bulletin* no. 16, 1946, pp. 43–44.

PLENDERLEITH, H. J. "Insects among archives", British Records Association Technical Section, *Bulletin* no. 18, 1945, pp. 2–6.

PLENDERLEITH, H. J., "Mould in the muniment room", *Archives*, vol. I, no. 7, Lady Day 1952, pp. 13–18.

PLENDERLEITH, H. J., "A note on dust problems in repositories", British Records Association Technical Section, *Bulletin* no. 19, July 1948, pp. 4–5.

PLENDERLEITH, H. J. and HOLNESS, R. F. G. "Protection of records against bookworm: fumigation of archives", British Records Association Technical Section, *Bulletin* no. 16, 1946, p. 35.

PLENDERLEITH, H. J. and WERNER, A. E. A., "Technical notes on the conservation of documents", *JSA*, vol. I, no. 7, Apr. 1958, pp. 195–201.

RIDGE, A. D., "On the use of thymol", *JSA*, vol. II, no. 1, Apr. 1960, pp. 38–39.

RYDER, M. L., "Parchment—its history, manufacture and composition", *JSA*, vol. II, no. 9, Apr. 1964, pp. 391–9.

SKELTON, R. A., "The conservation of maps", Society of Local Archivists, *Bulletin* no. 14, Oct. 1954, pp. 13–19.

SOCIETY OF ARCHIVISTS, "Educational meeting of repairers [1959]", *JSA*, vol. II, no. 1, Apr. 1960, p. 36.

SOCIETY OF ARCHIVISTS, "Meeting of document repairers [1961]", *JSA*, vol. II, no. 5, Apr. 1962, pp. 230–1.

SOCIETY OF ARCHIVISTS, "The repairers' meeting at Southampton, 28th–29th June 1965", *JSA*, vol. III, no. 3, Apr. 1966, pp. 153–4.

SOCIETY OF ARCHIVISTS, "Sulphur dioxide pollution of the atmosphere", report, *JSA*, vol. I, no. 10, Oct. 1959, pp. 291–3.

SOCIETY OF ARCHIVISTS, "Sulphur dioxide pollution of the atmosphere: a further report", *JSA*, vol. II, no. 5, Apr. 1962, pp. 221–2.

Society of Archivists, "Sulphur dioxide test papers", *JSA*, vol. 4, no. 1, Apr. 1970, pp. 64–65.

Tottle, H. F., "Strong-room climate", *Archives*, vol. II, no. 15, Lady Day 1956, pp. 387–97.

Wardle, D. B., "Lamination for all?", *JSA*, vol. II, no. 6, Oct. 1962, p. 272.

Wardle, D. B., "A note on document repair at the Public Record Office", *JSA*, vol. II, no. 4, Oct. 1961, pp. 164–5.

Wells, P. J., "Extending available repair space", *JSA*, vol. II, no. 8, Oct. 1963, pp. 374–5.

Werner, A. E. A., "Lamination with Genotherm plastic film", *JSA*, vol. II, no. 1, Apr. 1960, p. 38.

Werner, A. E. A., "The preservation of archives", *JSA*, vol. I, no. 10, Oct. 1959, pp. 282–8.

Reprography

British Records Association, "Infra-red photography in record work", Technical Section *Bulletin* no. 16, 1946, pp. 28–29.

British Records Association, "Microphotography: some technical notes", Technical Section *Bulletin* no. 17, 1943, pp. 3–8.

British Records Association, "The uses and problems of photography in the study of manuscripts", discussion, *Archives*, vol. VI, no. 31, Apr. 1964, pp. 154–7.

Hawken, W. R., *Copying Methods Manual*, American Library Association, 1966.

Jenkinson, Sir H. and Sayce, L. A., "Some notes on the application of microphotography to archives", British Records Association Technical Section, *Bulletin* no. 16, 1946, pp. 30–35.

Masters, B. R., "The microfilming of records with special reference to work recently carried out at Exeter", Society of Local Archivists, *Bulletin* no. 11, Apr. 1953, pp. 22–26.

Owen, A. E. B., "Photographic services", editorial, *Archives*, vol. VIII, no. 40, Oct. 1968, p. 206.

Owen, A. E. B., "Problems of photocopying", editorial, *Archives*, vol. VIII, no. 37, Apr. 1967, p. 1.

Sixth International Congress on Archives, Madrid, September 3 to 6, 1968, *Report of the Microfilming Committee*, presented on its behalf by Albert H. Leisinger, Jr., Secretary, Washington, 1968.

Verry, H. R., *Document Copying and Reproduction Processes*, London, Fountain Press, 1958.

The educational use of archives

British Records Association, "The use of archives in education", discussion, *Archives*, vol. V, no. 25, Lady Day 1961, pp. 14–16.

Department of Education and Science, *Archives and Education*, education pamphlet no. 54, London, H.M.S.O., 1968.

Emmison, F. G., *Archives for All*, Essex Record Office, 1956.

Emmison, F. G., letter replying to R. B. Pugh, "Guides or exhibitions" (*Archives*, 1956, pp. 494–6), *Archives*, vol. III, no. 17, Lady Day 1957. p. 43.

Fines J. and Steel, D. J., "College of education students in the archives office" *Archives*, vol. IX, no. 41, Apr. 1969, pp. 22–28.

HUMPHREYS, D. W. and EMMISON, F. G., *Local History for Students*, National Council of Social Service, n.d., *ca.* 1966, 24 pp.

OWEN, A. E. B., "Archives and the user", editorial, *Archives*, vol. IX, no. 42, Oct. 1969, p. 63.

OWEN, D. M., "Beginning local history", *Archives*, vol. VIII, no. 39, Apr. 1968, pp. 155–8.

PUGH, R. B., "Guides or exhibitions", *Archives*, vol. II, no. 16, Mich. 1956, pp. 494–6.

SOCIETY OF ARCHIVISTS, review of *The Great Famine, 1845–52*, first of a series of "Education facsimiles" produced by the Public Record Office of Northern Ireland, *JSA*, vol. 4, no. 1, Apr. 1970, pp. 66–67.

SOCIETY OF ARCHIVISTS, review of three archive teaching units (*Coals from Newcastle*, 1968, *Travel in the Turnpike Age*, 1968, and *Railways in the Making*, 1969) produced by the Department of Education, University of Newcastle upon Tyne, *JSA*, vol. 4, no. 1, Apr. 1970, pp. 83–84.

WILDE, S. M., review of University of Newcastle upon Tyne archive teaching units, *Archives*, vol. IX, no. 42, Oct. 1969, p. 112.

INDEX

209

DATE DUE